Welcome to Kaua~~i~~

Hawaii's ultimate tropical paradise, Kauai has amazing natural wonders to explore, from the velvety green, accordion-folded cliffs of Napali Coast to the multicolor vistas of Waimea Canyon. Sunseekers choose favorites from more than 50 miles of beaches, while hikers and kayakers have abundant options in unspoiled beauty. Best of all, laidback Kauai is one of the state's least-crowded islands, with low-key resorts and mellow former plantation villages. As you plan your upcoming travels to Kauai, please reconfirm that places are still open and let us know when we need to make updates by writing to us at editors@fodors.com.

TOP REASONS TO GO

- **Beaches:** Pristine strips of sand and palm-fringed shores make vacation dreams real.

- **Napali Coast:** Its towering cliffs astonish all who see them from land, sea, or air.

- **Outdoor fun:** Kauai offers great surfing and snorkeling, plus top-notch golf and hiking.

- **Charming towns:** Artsy Hanapepe, colorful Hanalei, historic Koloa, and more invite lingering.

- **Kayaking:** Paddling on a river is a tranquil way to discover the island's allure.

- **Scenic drives:** Cruise the North Shore's Route 560 or the West Side's Waimea Canyon Drive.

Contents

Fodor's Features

MAPS

Chapter 1

EXPERIENCE KAUAI

24 ULTIMATE EXPERIENCES

Kauai offers terrific experiences that should be on every traveler's list. Here are Fodor's top picks for a memorable trip.

1 Hike the Kalalau Trail

Winding 11 taxing miles along rugged Napali Coast, this is one of the world's most outrageous hikes. The first 2 miles to Hanakapiai Beach are fairly moderate; the two- to three-day round-trip hike includes camping along the way (permit required). *(Ch. 7)*

2 Coastal Sunset Sail

Kauai sunsets are sublime, and perhaps the best way to experience that magical hour of the day is by boat, facing the stunning Napali Coast. *(Ch. 7)*

3 Relax on Poipu Beach

Popular with tourists and locals, Poipu Beach has calm waters ideal for snorkeling, and you might just spot an endangered Hawaiian monk seal. *(Ch. 5)*

4 Mountain Tubing

A century ago, Lihue Plantation dug waterways to irrigate its fields. Now you can take a tubing tour via the waterways for a glimpse of Kauai's hidden interior. *(Ch. 7)*

5 Sunrise on the Royal Coconut Coast

Kauai's Royal Coconut Coast—Lydgate State Park and the Ke Ala Hele Makalae biking/walking path are great vantage points—is the perfect place to watch the sunrise. *(Ch. 4, 7)*

6 Seek Out the Menehune

The mythical Menehune are said to be descendants of the island's first settlers. Their "work" is found throughout Kauai, including Alekoko Fishpond near Lihue. *(Ch. 4)*

7 Learn Island History

The island's most important receptacle of island culture and history, the Kauai Museum covers topics like geological formation and Hawaiian kings. *(Ch. 4)*

8 Admire Spouting Horn

Shooting water as high as 50 feet, Kauai's version of Old Faithful was once guarded by a lizard. Today, you can still hear her roar. *(Ch. 5)*

9 Go Deep-Sea Fishing

The deep Pacific waters surrounding Kauai are teeming with fish. Charters, which depart from Lihue or Port Allen, visit the best spots and provide all the gear. *(Ch. 7)*

10 Hanalei Valley Views

In a land of stellar vistas, the North Shore's Hanalei Valley stands out; head to the viewpoint on Route 56 just outside the town of Hanalei. *(Ch. 3)*

11 Helicopter Vistas

Kauai's interior is best seen via helicopter. Tours give access to breathtaking scenery like Napali Coast and Waimea Canyon. *(Ch. 7)*

12 Visit Sacred Heiau

Remains of sacred structures of the Kauai kingdom are found in Wailua along Route 580 between the mouth of the Wailua River and Mt. Waialeale. *(Ch. 4)*

13 Kapaa Town

Meander through Kapaa Town the first Saturday evening of each month as merchants show off their wares, food trucks sizzle, bands play, and locals "talk story." *(Ch. 4)*

14 Eat Shave Ice

The Hawaiian version of a snow cone—shave (never "shaved") ice topped with a sugary syrup and condensed milk—is found throughout Kauai.

15 Sun-Kissed Farmers' Markets

Known as the Garden Isle, Kauai boasts numerous farmers' markets with the freshest fruits.

16 Cocktails Overlooking Bali Hai

Order a tropical cocktail at the Happy Talk Lounge and enjoy an enchanting sunset over Hanalei Bay. *(Ch. 3)*

17 Bird- and Whale-Watching

The northernmost point of the inhabited Hawaiian Isles, Kilauea Point has stunning ocean and coast views and amazing opportunities for bird- and whale-watching. *(Ch. 3, 7)*

18 Waimea Canyon

A vast canyon on the island's West Side, this geologic wonder measures a mile wide, more than 14 miles long and 3,600 feet deep. *(Ch. 6, 7)*

19 Attend a Luau

At a traditional luau guests are treated to Hawaiian-style storytelling, complete with hula, traditional knife dancing, and poi fire ball throwing. *(Ch. 4, 5)*

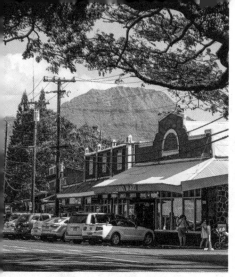

20 Old Koloa Town

In 1835, Koloa's first sugar mill ushered in Hawaii's era of sugar production. Today, many of the historic buildings are shops and restaurants. (Ch. 5)

21 Art in Hanapepe

Established over a century ago, Hanapepe is filled with bougainvillea-draped, plantation-style buildings that house cafés, boutiques, and art and crafts galleries. (Ch. 6)

22 World-Class Golf

Breathtaking beauty, quality, and a vast number of thrilling, heart-stopping holes help Kauai remain one of Hawaii's top golf destinations. (Ch. 7)

23 Kayaking to Secret Falls

Only Kauai has navigable rivers. Kayaking up the Wailua River leads you into a mystical realm of lush rain forests, velvety green mountains, and secret, crystal-clear waterfalls. (Ch. 4, 7)

24 Snorkel at Kee Beach

Kauai has many snorkeling beaches, but Kee (reservation needed) is one of the best, especially for beginners and kids. Spot parrotfish and green sea turtles. *(Ch. 3, 7)*

WHAT'S WHERE

1 North Shore.
Dreamy beaches, verdant mountains, breathtaking scenery, and abundant rain, waterfalls, and rainbows characterize the North Shore, which includes Kilauea, Princeville, Hanalei, and Haena.

2 East Side. This is Kauai's commercial and residential hub, dominated by the island's largest town, Kapaa. The airport, main harbor, and government offices are found in the county seat of Lihue. It can be a convenient base for travelers, too.

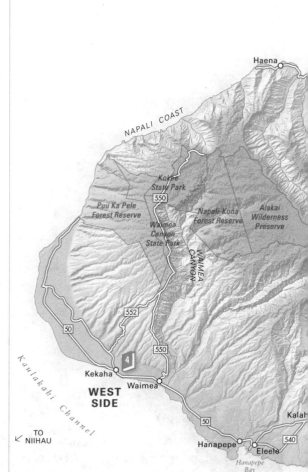

NORTH SHORE

Princeville
Hanalei Bay
560
Hanalei
Kilauea
1
56

Anáhola
56

Mamalahoa
Halelea
Forest Reserve

MAKALEHA MTS

Lihue-Koloa
Forest Reserve

581

Kapaa

Waialeale
5,148 ft

580
Wailua
Wailua Bay

2
EAST SIDE
56

Kilohana Crater
1,138 ft
583
Hanamaulu

Kahili
3,089 ft

Lihue
Lihue Airport

50
58

Lihue-Koloa
Forest Reserve

Nawiliwili Bay

50
alaheo
Lawai
520
0
530
Koloa

3
Poipu
SOUTH SHORE

Kauai Channel

0   5 mi
0   5 km

3 South Shore. Peaceful landscapes, sunny weather, and beaches that rank among the best in the world make the South Shore the resort capital of Kauai. The Poipu resort area is here, along with the main towns of Koloa and Lawai.

4 West Side. Dry, sunny, and sleepy, the West Side includes the historic towns of Hanapepe, Waimea, and Kekaha. The area is ideal for outdoor adventurers because it's both the entryway to Waimea Canyon and Kokee State Park and the departure point for most Napali Coast boat trips.

Kauai Today

Hawaii's worldwide fame came with a price. Kauai has never quite been prepared for what's happened to it—from early Polynesian voyagers bringing new plants and animals, to Europeans introducing livestock or diseases, to missionaries changing traditional ways, to barons of agriculture altering the land. Population growth and tourism have burdened the limited infrastructure and resources.

Hawaiian culture and tradition are resilient, however, and have experienced a renaissance over the past half century. There's a real effort to revive traditions and to respect history as the Islands go through major changes. New developments often have a Hawaiian cultural expert on staff to ensure cultural sensitivity and educate newcomers. Kauai's schools and community college offer courses in the Hawaiian language.

Nonetheless, development remains a huge issue for all Islanders—land prices still skyrocket, putting most areas out of reach for locals. Approximately 45% of recent new housing on Kauai is bought by off-island purchasers, often as second homes. Traffic is also a major problem on aging Kauai roads.

SUSTAINABILITY

Although sustainability is an effective buzzword and an authentic direction for the Islands' dining establishments, the reality is that 90% of Hawaii's food and energy is imported. However, solar power is making a major inroad in power production: on some sunny days, for a few hours, the Kauai electric grid is 100% powered by alternative energy sources. In fact, Kauai leads the state in alternative energy solutions, including hydro.

For many years, most of Kauai's land was used for monocropping of pineapple or sugarcane. Sugarcane is now a memory, and pineapple production has dropped precipitously. Dole, once the largest pineapple company in Hawaii, closed its plants in 1991, and after 90 years, Del Monte stopped pineapple production in 2008. But the Islands have perfected a sugar pineapple that is far less acidic, and market share is expanding.

BACK-TO-BASICS AGRICULTURE

Emulating the way Hawaiian ancestors lived and returning to their ways of growing and sharing a wide variety of foods have become statewide initiatives. Many Kauai locals buy all their fruit and produce from the numerous farmers' markets, which often feature in-season crops at reasonable prices. From home-cooked meals and casual plate lunches to fine-dining cuisine and new food trucks, sustainability trailblazers in Kauai's kitchens are enriching the island's culinary scene.

TOURISM AND THE ECONOMY

By 2019, the almost $18 billion tourism industry represented more than a third of Hawaii's state income. Naturally, this dependency caused economic hardship following the coronavirus outbreak in spring of 2020. When tourism reopened, albeit with strict testing protocols, hotel rates skyrocketed and a rental car shortage ensued. Some restaurants, hotels, shops, and even cultural institutions were forced to close. Change has been ongoing, and it's still a good idea to call ahead to verify that a property is in operation.

Kauaians enjoyed the calm during the travel bans and resolved to revive tourism in a more thoughtful, sustainable, and sensitive way. Beaches, parks, and scenic lookouts increasingly charge nonresidents admission or parking fees to manage impact. Companies employ cultural advisers and airlines show videos about nature protocols, with the hope of educating visitors that Hawaii is more than just a pretty picture. The focus now is on natural resource conservation, Hawaiian culture, community enrichment, and teaching residents and visitors alike to care for the land and respect each other—to always be *pono* (proper, righteous) and to "malama Kauai," or take care of Kauai.

The concept of *kuleana*, a word denoting both privilege and responsibility, is a traditional Hawaiian value. The privilege of visiting or living in such a sublime place comes with the responsibility to protect it.

SOVEREIGNTY

Political issues of sovereignty continue to divide Native Hawaiians, who have formed myriad organizations around the issue, each operating with a separate agenda and lacking one collectively defined plan. Ranging from achieving complete independence to solidifying a nation within a nation, existing sovereignty models remain fractured and their future unresolved.

The introduction of the Native Hawaiian Government Reorganization Act of 2009 attempts to set up a legal framework in which Native Hawaiians can attain federal recognition and coexist as a self-governed entity, similar to Native American status. Also known as the Akaka Bill, after former senator Daniel Akaka of Hawaii, this bill progressed in Congress but is still pending.

RISE OF HAWAIIAN PRIDE

After the overthrow of the monarchy in 1893, a process of Americanization began. Traditions were silenced in the name of citizenship. Teaching the Hawaiian language was banned from schools, and children were distanced from traditional customs. With the rise of the civil rights movement in the 1960s, though, Hawaiians began to reflect on their own national identity, bringing an astonishing

renaissance of the Hawaiian culture. The people of Hawaii—Hawaiian blood or not—have rediscovered language, hula, chanting, and even the traditional Polynesian arts of canoe building and wayfinding (navigation by the stars without use of instruments). This cultural resurrection is now firmly established in today's Hawaiian culture, with a palpable pride that exudes from residents young and old.

CHANGES ON THE NORTH SHORE

Kauai's North Shore experienced epic rainfall in 2018, with Hanalei receiving 50 inches of rain in one 24-hour period. The flooding cut off the only road beyond Princeville for long periods, and residents were forced to make many daily adjustments. The silver lining? With many areas forced to close, there was time to make improvements to parks, roads, and other infrastructure. Haena State Park, Kee Beach, and the Kalalau Trail are now cleaner and calmer, in part due to new park fees and permit requirements.

THE ARTS

The Hawaiian Islands have inspired artistic expression from the time they were first inhabited. From traditional *kapa*-cloth–making and ancient hula to digital filmmaking, the arts are alive and well. On Kauai, the community college's Performing Arts Center and the state-run War Memorial Convention Hall hold stage performances, and there are also a handful of community theater groups around the island. Live music abounds and can be heard at hotels, eateries, and beach parks where locals gather. Hanapepe and Kapaa are hubs of visual art galleries, and Kauai Society of Artists (KSA) runs an exhibit space in Kukui Grove Center in Lihue.

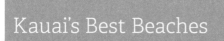

Kauai's Best Beaches

HANALEI PAVILION BEACH PARK
One of the most legendary beaches on Kauai, amid the largest bay on the island's North Shore, this 2-mile, family-friendly beach (actually several beaches) features a long pier with exceptional views. It's great for water activities, such as stand-up paddling, snorkeling, and swimming. *(Ch. 3)*

MAHAULEPU BEACH
This isolated beach is pristine and wild, from its windswept cliffs to the waves crashing on the shore. There are no lifeguards and the surf can be dangerous, so trek along the Mahaulepu Heritage Trail instead, spotting blowholes, lava tubes, and tide pools along the rocky coastline. *(Ch. 5)*

KEALIA BEACH PARK
East-facing Kealia is the spot to catch a sunrise on Kauai and a good lookout point for spotting whales during the winter. With strong waves, wind swell, and rough currents during most of the year, it's ideal for surfing and bodyboarding, or for biking along the coastal path. *(Ch. 4)*

ANINI BEACH PARK
Situated on Kauai's eastern shore, this sugar-white beach is a hot spot for the local crowd on weekends and offers plenty of shade as well as gorgeous mountain views of Kalalea. Although it's slightly off the beaten track, Anahola is a family-friendly, guarded beach, but it's important to note that swimming is protected in specific areas only. This destination is a draw for those who enjoy camping and picnics. *(Ch. 4)*

POLIHALE STATE PARK
Hawaii's longest stretch of sandy beach is situated on the westernmost point of the island and is well known for its spectacular sunset views. If you're seeking privacy, this 2-mile white-sand beach has high dunes and plenty of shade, an ideal getaway for the afternoon. Keep in mind this remote area is for the adventurous only: it has a bumpy access road that's a dusty 5 miles long and best navigated with a four-wheel drive vehicle. *(Ch. 6)*

LYDGATE BEACH PARK
This laid-back, family-friendly East Side beach is popular and offers an easy and relaxing beach experience. It's especially fun for children because it features amazing play equipment and an adjacent pool area that's protected from the larger waves by a rock wall. Lifeguards watch over the snorkelers who flock to this top spot to view tropical fish and other marine life. *(Ch. 4)*

TUNNELS BEACH (MAKUA)

Earning its nickname from the underwater lava tunnels offshore, this beach with calm, turquoise waters has ideal conditions for snorkeling and is teeming with marine life. Just around the bend is a scenic yet lively stretch of pale yellow sand. *(Ch. 3)*

ANAHOLA BEACH PARK

Although there are no lifeguards on this golden-sand, 3-mile beach, Anini is considered one of the safest places to swim on the island's North Shore during summer. Naturally protected by an expansive coral reef—the largest in all of Hawaii—it offers exceptional snorkeling, too. Windsurfers and campers also love this beach. *(Ch. 3)*

KALAPAKI BEACH

This lively, beautiful beach in Lihue, in front of a sprawling resort, provides protected swimming with an abundance of options and plenty of convenient amenities. Featuring smaller, forgiving waves and a sandy ocean floor, the area is ideal for most water activities, including beginner surfing and stand-up paddleboarding lessons. There's beach volleyball, too. Steps away from the sand, a number of shops sell standard beach supplies and local products, and there are cafés to grab lunch or a quick snack. *(Ch. 4)*

POIPU BEACH PARK

Popular Poipu is situated on the South Shore with a prime location in front of several major hotels. The wide, often noisy beach is optimal for snorkeling and swimming. It's also a fun spot for beginner surf lessons. *(Ch. 5)*

Kauai's Natural Wonders

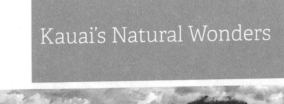

HANALEI VALLEY
With cascading waterfalls, gleaming taro patches, and the island's famous Hanalei River, the valley's beauty stretches for nearly 1,000 acres. Get a panoramic view from the Hanalei Valley Lookout or a close-up by kayak. *(Ch. 3)*

SPOUTING HORN
A popular island landmark near Poipu Beach on Kauai's South Shore, Spouting Horn is a blowhole that shoots ocean water into the air (often to an impressive 50 feet high) à la Old Faithful. This natural wonder is created from the pressure of ocean water being forced into an undersea lava tube. If you're lucky, you might spot a sea turtle or a whale during winter. *(Ch. 5)*

KALALAU TRAIL
This rugged hike (permit required) winds about 11 miles through the magnificent Napali Coast State Wilderness Park, offering stunning views of the Pacific Ocean. Suited for experienced hikers only, the challenging path traverses rocky mountain streams, crosses five valleys, and passes majestic waterfalls. Twisting along the high cliffs, the trail ends at Kalalau Beach. *(Ch. 3, 7)*

TREE TUNNEL
This dramatic, arching canopy along Maluhia Road began with a rancher's gift of 500 eucalyptus trees in 1911. The towering trees have survived two hurricanes and are nature's grand entry to the resort area of Poipu. *(Ch. 5)*

KILAUEA POINT NATIONAL WILDLIFE REFUGE
Bird-watchers adore this scenic reserve (reservations required) on a dormant volcano as it's home to diverse waterfowl and plenty of other wildlife. Visitors can tour the nearby lighthouse and spot turtles, whales, and monk seals. *(Ch. 3)*

WAILUA RIVER AND FALLS
Flowing past ancient temples, this meandering, 20-mile-long river ends in two spectacular and awe-inspiring waterfalls: Opaekaa Falls and Wailua Falls. Hiking here will require hours (or perhaps days), or you can drive to the Wailua Falls and Opaekaa Falls overlooks. (Ch. 4, 7)

WAIMEA CANYON STATE PARK
Considered the "Grand Canyon of the Pacific," this spectacular natural wonder is over 3,600 feet deep and stretches for 14 miles. Take in its brilliant dark pink, rust, and emerald hues at lookout points offering the ultimate backdrops for vacation selfies. (Ch. 6)

NAPALI COAST
This iconic stretch of Kauai's dramatic coastline features cliffs that soar nearly 4,000 feet above the Pacific Ocean. The breathtaking natural wonder is best admired at a distance, either from the water (ideally by catamaran or sailboat) or from the air by helicopter. (Ch. 3, 7)

KOKEE STATE PARK
Located north of Waimea Canyon, Kokee State Park offers breathtaking views along verdant pathways that ascend over 4,000 feet. With 45 miles of hiking trails and diverse terrain, this peaceful area is popular with campers. The park offers something for everyone, so day-trippers can choose an easy trail, visit the museum, or get a picnic from the lodge. (Ch. 6)

SLEEPING GIANT (NOUNOU MOUNTAIN)
Resembling a man resting on his back, this magnificent mountain range has several trails to choose from, but the East Trail is considered the most moderate, with parking close by. You can hike the 2-mile ascent to the top (across the giant's body to the area that would be his "forehead") and soak up some unobstructed island vistas. (Ch. 4, 7)

Flora and Fauna in Hawaii

KUKUI

The kukui, or candlenut, is Hawaii's state tree, and Hawaiians have had many uses for it. Oil was extracted from its nuts and burned as a light source and also rubbed on fishing nets to preserve them. The juice from the husk's fruit was used as a dye. The small kukui blossoms and nuts also have medicinal purposes.

PLUMERIA

Also known as frangipani, this fragrant flower is named after Charles Plumier, the noted French botanist who discovered it in Central America in the late 1600s. Plumeria come in shades of white, yellow, pink, red, and orange. The hearty, plentiful blossoms are frequently used in lei.

GARDENIA

The gardenia is a favorite for lei makers because of its sweet smell. The plant is native to tropical regions throughout China and Africa, but there are also endemic gardenias in Hawaii. The nanu gardenia is found only in the Islands and has petite white blossoms.

HONU

The *honu*, or Hawaiian green sea turtle, is a magical sight. The graceful reptile is an endangered and protected species in Hawaii. It's easier to encounter *honu* during a snorkeling or scuba-diving excursion, but they occasionally can be spotted basking on beaches.

HUMPBACK WHALES

Each year, North Pacific humpback whales make the long journey to Hawaii from Alaska. With its warm, protected waters, Hawaii provides the ideal place for the marine mammals to mate and to birth, and to nurse their young. They arrive between November and May, and their presence is an anticipated event. You can see them up close during whale-watching boat tours.

MONK SEAL

Known as the *ilio holo i ka uaua*, meaning "dog that runs in rough water," monk seals are endemic to Hawaii and critically endangered. The majority of these mammals, which can grow to more than seven feet long, live in the remote, uninhabited Northwestern Hawaiian Islands.

HIBISCUS

In 1923, the Territory of Hawaii passed a law designating hibiscus as Hawaii's official flower. While there are more than 30 introduced species of the large, colorful flowers throughout the Islands, there are five endemic types. The endemic hibiscus has yellow blossoms and is known in Hawaiian as *mao hau hele*, which means the "traveling green tree."

TROPICAL FISH

Approximately 25% of the fish species in the Islands are endemic. Snorkeling in Hawaii is a unique, fun opportunity to see colorful fish found nowhere else on Earth. Interestingly, Hawaii's state fish, the *humuhumunukunukuapuaa*, or reef trigger, is not endemic to the state.

PIKAKE

These small, delicate blossoms are known for their hypnotic, sweet scent. The jasmine flower was introduced from India and was a favorite of Princess Kaiulani. *Pikake*, which is the Hawaiian word for the blossom as well as for a peacock—another favorite of the princess—is the subject of many *mele*, or Hawaiian songs.

NENE GOOSE

Pronounced *nay-nay*, the endemic nene goose (Hawaii's state bird) is one of the world's rarest. A descendant of the Canada goose, it has been bred back from the edge of extinction and reintroduced into the wild. Use caution driving in national and state parks, which they frequent.

What to Eat and Drink in Hawaii

HAWAIIAN PLATE

The Hawaiian plate comprises the delicious, traditional foods of Hawaii, all on one heaping plate. You can find these combo meals anywhere, from roadside lunch wagons to five-star restaurants. Get yours with the melt-in-your-mouth shredded kalua pig, pork, or chicken *laulau* (cooked in ti leaves) with *lomi* salmon (diced salmon with tomatoes and onions) on the side and the coconut-milk *haupia* for dessert. Most Hawaiian plates come with the requisite two scoops of white rice. Don't forget to try *poi*, or pounded and cooked taro.

POKE

In Hawaiian, *poke* is a verb that means to slice and cut into pieces. It perfectly describes the technique Hawaiians have used for centuries to prepare poke the dish. The cubed raw fish, most commonly *ahi* (yellowfin tuna), is traditionally tossed with Hawaiian sea salt, *limu kohu* (red seaweed), or *inamona* (crushed kukui nuts). Today, countless varieties of this must-try dish are served in all kinds of restaurants across the Islands. Poke shacks offer no-frills, made-to-order poke.

SHAVE ICE

Shave ice is simple in its composition—fluffy ice drizzled in Technicolor syrups. Shave ice traces its roots to Hawaii's plantation past. Japanese laborers would use the machetes from their field work to finely shave ice from large frozen blocks and then pour fruit juice over it.

MUSUBI

Musubi are Hawaii's answer to the perfect snack. Portable, handheld, and salty, *musubi* are a great go-to any time of day. The local comfort food is a slice of fried Spam encased in packed white rice and snugly wrapped with nori, or dried seaweed. Available everywhere, *musubi* are usually just a few dollars.

MAI TAI

When people think of a Hawaiian cocktail, the colorful mai tai often comes to mind. It's the unofficial drink to imbibe at a luau and refreshingly tropical. This potent concoction has a rum base and is traditionally made with orange curaçao, orgeat, fresh-squeezed lime juice, and simple syrup.

SAIMIN

This only-in-Hawaii noodle dish is the culinary innovation of Hawaii plantation workers in the late 1800s who created a new comfort food with ingredients and traditions from their home countries.

Poke

MANAPUA

When *kamaaina*, or Hawaii residents, are invited to a potluck, business meeting, or even an impromptu party, you'll inevitably see a box filled with *manapua*. Inside these airy white buns are pockets of sweet *char siu* pork. Head to cities and towns around the Islands, and you'll find restaurants with manapua on their menus, as well as manapua takeout places serving a variety of fillings. There's sweet potato, curry chicken, *lap cheong* (or Chinese sausage)—and even sweet flavors, such as custard and *ube*, a purple yam popular in Filipino desserts.

LOCO MOCO

The traditional version of one of Hawaii's classic comfort-food dishes consists of white rice topped with a hamburger patty and fried eggs and generously blanketed in rich, brown gravy. Cafe 100 in Hilo on the Big Island is renowned as the home of the *loco moco*, but you'll find this popular staple everywhere. It can be eaten any time of day.

KONA COFFEE

In Kona, on the Big Island, coffee reigns supreme. There are roughly 600 coffee farms dotting the west side of the island, each producing flavorful (and quite expensive) coffee grown in the rich, volcanic soil. Kona coffee is typically hand-harvested from August through December.

MALASADA

Malasadas are a beloved treat in Hawaii. The Portuguese pastries are about the size of a baseball and are airy, deep-fried, and dusted with sugar. They are best enjoyed hot and filled with custard; fillings are a Hawaiian variation on the original.

What to Buy in Hawaii

LEI

As a visitor to Hawaii, you may well receive a lei, either a shell, kukui nut, or fragrant flower variety, as a welcome to the Islands. *Kamaaina* (Hawaii residents) mark special occasions by gifting lei.

MACADAMIA NUT CANDY

Macadamia nuts are native to Australia, but the gumball-sized nut remains an important crop in Hawaii. It was first introduced in the late 1880s as a windbreak for sugarcane crops. Today, mac nuts are a popular local snack and are especially good baked in cookies or other desserts.

LAUHALA

The hala tree is most known for its long, thin leaves and the masterful crafts that are created from them. Lauhala weavers make baskets, hats, mats, jewelry, and more, using intricate traditional patterns and techniques.

JEWELRY

Island-inspired jewelry comes in many styles. Tahitian pearl pendants and earrings are a local favorite, as are delicate, inexpensive shell pieces. The most coveted are Hawaiian heirloom bracelets in gold or silver with one's name enameled in Old English script.

ALOHA WEAR

Aloha wear in Hawaii has come a long way from the polyester fabrics with too-bright, kitschy patterns (although those still exist). Local designers have been creating dressy, modern aloha attire with softer prints that evoke Island botanicals, heritage, and traditional patterns. Hawaii residents don aloha wear for everything from work to weddings.

HAWAIIAN COFFEE

Reminisce about your Hawaii getaway each time you brew a cup of aromatic, full-bodied coffee, whether it's from Kona or Kauai. All the main islands grow distinctive coffee. Stores and cafés sell bags of varying sizes, and in some places you can buy direct from a farmer.

HAWAIIAN HONEY

With its temperate climate and bountiful foliage, Hawaii is ideal for honeybees. The Islands' ecosystem contributes to honeys with robust flavors and textures, including elixirs extracted from the blossoms of the macadamia nut tree, the lehua flower, and the invasive Christmasberry shrub.

KOA WOOD

If you're looking for an heirloom keepsake from the Islands, consider a koa wood product. Grown only in Hawaii, the valuable koa is some of the world's rarest and hardest wood. Hawaiians traditionally made surfboards and canoes from these trees, which today grow only in upland forests.

HAWAIIAN SEA SALT

A long tradition of harvesting salt beds by hand continues today on all the Islands. The salt comes in various colors, including inky black and brick red—the result of the salt reacting and mixing with activated charcoal and *alaea* (volcanic clay). It is renowned by chefs around the state.

UKULELE

In Hawaiian, *ukulele* means "the jumping flea." The small instrument made its way to the Islands in the 1880s via Portuguese immigrants who brought with them the four-string, guitar-like *machete de braga*. It is famous as a solo instrument today, with virtuoso artists like Jake Shimabukuro and Taimane Gardner popularizing the ukulele's versatile sound.

What to Read and Watch

HAWAIIAN MYTHOLOGY
BY MARTHA BECKWITH
This exhaustive work of ethnology and folklore was researched and collected by Martha Beckwith over decades and published when she was 69. *Hawaiian Mythology* is a comprehensive look at the Hawaiian ancestral deities and their importance throughout history.

HAWAII'S STORY BY HAWAII'S QUEEN, BY LILIUOKALANI
This poignant book by Queen Liliuokalani chronicles the 1893 overthrow of the Hawaiian monarchy and her plea for her people. It's an essential read to understand the political undercurrent and the push for sovereignty that exists in the Islands more than 125 years later.

LETTERS FROM HAWAII
BY MARK TWAIN
In 1866, when Samuel Clemens was 31, he sailed from California and spent four months in Hawaii. He eventually mailed 25 letters to the *Sacramento Union* newspaper about his experiences. Along the way, Twain sheds some cultural biases as he visits Kilauea Volcano, meets with Hawaii's newly formed legislators, and examines the sugar trade.

SHOAL OF TIME: A HISTORY OF THE HAWAIIAN ISLANDS BY GAVAN DAWS
Perhaps the most popular book by this best-selling Honolulu author is *Shoal of Time*. Published in 1974, the account of modern Hawaiian history details the colonization of Hawaii and everything that was lost in the process.

MOLOKAI BY ALAN BRENNERT
The writer's debut novel, set in the 1890s, follows a Hawaiian woman who contracts leprosy as a child and is sent to the remote, quarantined community of Kalaupapa on the island of Molokai, where she then lives. The Southern California–based author was inspired to write the book during his visits to Hawaii.

HAWAII SAYS "ALOHA" BY DON BLANDING
First published in 1928, this volume of enchanting, rhyming verse about Hawaii evokes the rich details about the Islands that mesmerized the author in the 1920s and for the rest of his life. Blanding also illustrated this and many other books and was later named Hawaii's poet laureate.

THE DESCENDANTS
Based on the book by local author Kaui Hart Hemmings, the film adaptation starring George Clooney and directed by Alexander Payne was filmed on Oahu and Kauai. It spotlights a contemporary, upper-class family in Hawaii as they deal with family grief and landholdings in flux.

BLUE HAWAII
The 1961 musical features the hip-shaking songs and moves of Elvis Presley, who plays tour guide Chadwick Gates. Elvis famously sings "Ke Kali Nei Au," or "The Hawaiian Wedding Song," at the iconic and now-shuttered Coco Palms Resort on Kauai. (The resort has remained closed since 1992 following Hurricane Iniki.)

MOANA
The release of *Moana* in 2016 was celebrated by many in Hawaii and the Pacific for showcasing Polynesian culture. The now-beloved animated movie, which tells the story of the demigod Maui, features the voice talents of Aulii Cravalho and Dwayne Johnson. In 2018, *Moana* was re-recorded and distributed in Olelo Hawaii, or the Hawaiian language, with Cravalho reprising her role. It marked the first time a Disney movie was available in Hawaiian.

Kids and Families

CHOOSING A PLACE TO STAY

Resorts: The Royal Sonesta Kauai Resort is a good choice in Lihue, and on the South Shore both the Grand Hyatt Kauai and Sheraton Kauai Resort have kids' activities. North Shore hotel guests can take their *keiki* (children) to the Anaina Hou Community Park playground, located behind the minigolf course on the main highway just outside Kilauea.

Condos: These rentals are a fantastic value for families. On the North Shore, there are numerous condo resort choices in Princeville, including Hanalei Bay Resort, with eight tennis courts and two pools. On the South Shore, Kiahuna Plantation Resort Kauai by Outrigger is a family favorite, with an excellent location that includes a swimmable beach adjacent to a grassy field great for picnics.

Transient Vacation Rentals (TVRs): These new kids on the block are rentals in homelike dwellings licensed for tourism. These rentals have in essence created another resort area along the North Shore—think private home with beach access. Make sure your renter is operating legally before paying.

OCEAN ACTIVITIES

On the beach: There are several beaches in Kauai that are nearly as safe as a pool— Anini Beach Park near the boat ramp and Hanalei Pavilion Beach Park on the North Shore, Lydgate Beach and Kalapaki Beach on the East Side, Poipu Beach Park on the South Shore, and Salt Pond Beach Park on the West Side.

On the waves: Surfing or stand-up paddling lessons are a great idea for kids, especially if the grownups want a little quiet time. Blue Seas Surfing School/Surf Kauai with Charlie is best for beginners, and you can book you or your kids a 1½-hour lesson with a champion.

The underwater world: If your kids are ready to try snorkeling, Kauai is a great place to introduce them to the underwater world. Get them comfortable with the basics at Lydgate Beach on the East Side, where there's no threat of a current. On its guided snorkel tours, SeaFun Kauai will show kids of all ages how to identify marine life and gives great beginner instruction (check availability in advance).

LAND ACTIVITIES

On the North Shore, kids will love Na Aina Kai, a botanical garden with a 16-foot-tall Jack and the Beanstalk bronze sculpture, gecko maze, tree house, kid-size train, and tropical jungle. On the East Side is Smith's Tropical Paradise, a 30-acre botanical garden.

Horseback riding is a popular family activity, and most of the tours on Kauai move slowly, so no riding experience is required. CJM Country Stables in Poipu also has a farm-animal petting zoo.

ATV tours are the activity of choice when it rains. Try Kauai ATV Tours, which has vehicles to accommodate families with kids ages five and older.

AFTER DARK

At night, younger kids get a kick out of a luau, as many shows incorporate young audience members. Older kids might find it all a bit lame, but there are a handful of new shows in the Islands that are more modern, incorporating acrobats, lively music, and fire dancers. If you have a teen in tow, we highly recommend going the modern route—try Luau Kalamaku in Lihue. The best luau for both *keiki* and *kupuna* (kids and seniors) is at Smith's Tropical Paradise, in Wailua. The setting is lovely, and there's kalua pig roasted in an earthen oven; hula, drum dances, and a fire knife dance are just part of the experience.

Weddings and Honeymoons

Hawaii is one of the country's foremost honeymoon destinations. Romance is in the air here, and the white, sandy beaches, turquoise water, swaying palm trees, balmy tropical breezes, and brilliant sunshine put people in the mood for love. So it goes without saying that Hawaii has also become a popular wedding destination, especially as new resorts and hotels entice visitors and with same-sex marriage legal. Once the knot is tied, why not stay for the honeymoon?

THE BIG DAY

Choosing the perfect place: You really have two choices to make: the ceremony location and where to hold a reception. For the former, Hawaii boasts stunning beaches, sea-hugging bluffs, gardens, private residences, resort lawns, and, of course, places of worship. As for the reception, there are these same choices, as well as restaurants and even a luau. If you decide to go outdoors, make sure to have a backup plan for inclement weather. If you're taking the plunge on a public beach, a state permit is required.

Finding a wedding planner: If you're planning to invite more than an officiant and your loved one to your ceremony, consider a Hawaii-based wedding planner who can help select a location, design the floral scheme, and recommend a photographer. They can also plan the menu and choose a restaurant, caterer, or resort, and suggest Hawaiian traditions to incorporate into your vows. If it's a resort wedding, most have on-site wedding coordinators; however, there are many independent planners around Kauai who specialize in certain types of ceremonies—by locale, size, religious affiliation, and so on. Share your budget. Get a proposal—in writing. Request a detailed list of the exact services they'll provide. If possible, meet the planner in person.

Getting your license: There's no waiting period in Hawaii, no residency or citizenship requirements, and no required blood test or shots. You can apply and pay the fee online; however, both partners must appear together in person before a marriage-license agent to receive the marriage license (the permit to get married) at the State Department of Health, The Wine Shop in Koloa, or an independent agent. You'll need proof of age—the legal age to marry is 18. Upon approval, a marriage license is immediately issued and costs $60. After the ceremony, your officiant will mail the marriage certificate to the state. Approximately four months later, you will receive a copy in the mail. The person performing your wedding must be licensed by the Hawaii Department of Health, even if he or she is a licensed officiant. Be sure to ask.

Wedding attire: In Hawaii, anything goes, from long, formal dresses with trains to bikinis. For men, a pair of solid-color slacks with a nice aloha shirt is appropriate. If you're getting hitched on the beach, why not go barefoot?

Local customs: The most obvious traditional Hawaiian wedding custom is the lei exchange, in which the bride and groom take turns placing a lei around the neck of the other—with a kiss. Bridal lei are usually floral, whereas the groom's is typically made of twisted ti or *maile,* a green leafy garland. Brides often also wear a *lei poo,* a circular floral headpiece.

THE HONEYMOON

Do you want champagne and strawberries delivered to your room? A breathtaking swimming pool? A five-star restaurant? Then a resort is the way to go. A small inn is also good if you're on a tight budget or don't plan to spend much time in your room. The lodging choices are almost as plentiful as the beaches here.

HAWAIIAN CULTURAL
TRADITIONS HULA, LEI, AND LUAU

HULA: MORE THAN A FOLK DANCE

Hula has been called "the heartbeat of the Hawaiian people" and also "the world's best-known, most misunderstood dance." Both are true. Hula isn't just dance. It is storytelling.

Chanter Edith McKinzie calls it "an extension of a piece of poetry." In its adornments, implements, and customs, hula integrates every important Hawaiian cultural practice: poetry, history, genealogy, craft, plant cultivation, martial arts, religion, protocol. So when 19th-century Christian missionaries sought to eradicate a practice they considered depraved, they threatened more than just a folk dance.

With public performance outlawed and private hula practice discouraged, hula went underground for a generation. The fragile verbal link by which culture was transmitted from teacher to student hung by a thread. Even increasing literacy did not help because hula's practitioners were a secretive and protected circle.

As if that weren't bad enough, vaudeville, Broadway, and Hollywood got hold of the hula, giving it the glitz treatment in an unbroken line from "Oh, How She Could Wicky Wacky Woo" to "Rock-A-Hula Baby." Hula became shorthand for paradise: fragrant flowers, lazy hours. Ironically, this development assured that hundreds of Hawaiians could make a living performing and teaching hula. Many danced 'auana (modern form) in performance; but taught kahiko (traditional), quietly, at home or in hula schools.

Today, decades after the cultural revival known as the Hawaiian Renaissance, language immersion programs have assured a new generation of proficient chanters, songwriters, and translators. Visitors can see more—and more authentic—traditional hula now than at any other time in the last 200 years.

Like the culture of which it is the beating heart, hula has survived.

Lei poo. Head lei. In *kahiko,* greenery only. In auana, flowers.

Face emotes appropriate expression. Dancer should not be a smiling automaton.

Shoulders remain relaxed and still, never hunched, even with arms raised. No bouncing.

Eyes always follow leading hand.

Lei. Hula is rarely performed without a shoulder lei.

Traditional hula skirt is loose fabric, smocked and gathered at the waist.

Arms and hands remain loose, relaxed, below shoulder level— except as required by interpretive movements.

Hip is canted over weight-bearing foot.

Knees are always slightly bent, accentuating hip sway.

Kupee. Ankle bracelet of flowers, shells, or foliage.

In kahiko, feet are flat. In auana, they may be more arched, but not tiptoes or bouncing.

BASIC MOTIONS

Speak or sing

Moon or sun

Grass shack or house

Mountains or heights

Love or caress

At backyard parties, hula is performed in bare feet and street clothes, but in performance, adornments play a key role, as do rhythm-keeping implements such as the *pahu* drum and the *ipu* (gourd).

In hula *kahiko* (traditional style), the usual dress is multiple layers of stiff fabric (often with a pellom lining, which most closely resembles *kapa*, the paperlike bark cloth of the Hawaiians). These wrap tightly around the bosom but flare below the waist to form a skirt. In pre-contact times, dancers wore only kapa skirts. Men traditionally wear loincloths.

Monarchy-period hula is performed in voluminous muumuu or high-necked muslin blouses and gathered skirts. Men wear white or gingham shirts and black pants.

In hula *auana* (modern), dress for women can range from grass skirts and strapless tops to contemporary tea-length dresses. Men generally wear aloha shirts, but sometimes grass skirts over pants or even everyday gear.

SURPRISING HULA FACTS

■ Grass skirts are not traditional; workers from Kiribati (the Gilbert Islands) brought this custom to Hawaii.

■ In olden-day Hawaii, *mele* (songs) for hula were composed for every occasion—name songs for babies, dirges for funerals, welcome songs for visitors, celebrations of favorite pursuits.

■ Hula *mai* is a traditional hula form in praise of a noble's genitals; the power of the *alii* (royalty) to procreate gave mana (spiritual power) to the entire culture.

■ Hula students in old Hawaii adhered to high standards: scrupulous cleanliness, no sex, daily cleansing rituals, certain food prohibitions, and no contact with the dead. They were fined if they broke the rules.

WHERE TO WATCH

If you're interested in "the real thing," there are annual hula festivals on each island. Check the individual island visitors' bureaus websites at ⊕ *www.gohawaii.com*.

If you can't make it to a festival, there are plenty of other hula shows—at most resorts, many lounges, and even at certain shopping centers. Ask your hotel concierge for performance information.

ALL ABOUT LEI

Lei brighten every occasion in Hawaii, from birthdays to bar mitzvahs to baptisms. Creative artisans weave nature's bounty—flowers, ferns, vines, and seeds—into gorgeous creations that convey an array of heartfelt messages: "Welcome," "Congratulations," "Good luck," "Farewell," "Thank you," "I love you." When it's difficult to find the right words, a lei expresses exactly the right sentiment.

WHERE TO BUY THE BEST LEI

Most airports in Hawaii have lei stands where you can buy a fragrant garland upon arrival. Every florist shop in the Islands sells lei; you can also treat yourself to a lei while shopping for provisions at any supermarket or box store. And you'll always find lei sellers at crafts fairs and outdoor festivals.

LEI ETIQUETTE

■ To wear a closed lei, drape it over your shoulders, half in front and half in back. Open lei are worn around the neck, with the ends draped over the front in equal lengths.

■ Pikake, ginger, and other sweet, delicate blossoms are "feminine" lei. Men opt for cigar, crown flower, and ti leaf lei, which are sturdier and don't emit as much fragrance.

■ Lei are always presented with a kiss, a custom that supposedly dates back to World War II when a hula dancer fancied an officer at a U.S.O. show. Taking a dare from members of her troupe, she took off her lei, placed it around his neck, and kissed him on the cheek.

■ You shouldn't wear a lei before you give it to someone else. Hawaiians believe the lei absorbs your mana (spirit); if you give your lei away, you'll be giving away part of your essence.

ORCHID

Growing wild on every continent except Antarctica, orchids—which range in color from yellow to green to purple—comprise the largest family of plants in the world. There are more than 20,000 species of orchids, but only three are native to Hawaii—and they are very rare. The pretty lavender vanda you see hanging by the dozens at local lei stands has probably been imported from Thailand.

MAILE

Maile, an endemic twining vine with a heady aroma, is sacred to Laka, goddess of the hula. In ancient times, dancers wore maile and decorated hula altars with it to honor Laka. Today, "open" maile lei usually are given to men. Instead of ribbon, interwoven lengths of maile are used at dedications of new businesses. The maile is untied, never snipped, for doing so would symbolically "cut" the company's success.

ILIMA

Designated by Hawaii's Territorial Legislature in 1923 as the official flower of the island of Oahu, the golden ilima is so delicate it lasts for just a day. Five to seven hundred blossoms are needed to make one garland. Queen Emma, wife of King Kamehameha IV, preferred ilima over all other lei, which may have led to the incorrect belief that they were reserved only for royalty.

PLUMERIA

This ubiquitous flower is named after Charles Plumier, the noted French botanist who discovered it in Central America in the late 1600s. Plumeria ranks among the most popular lei in Hawaii because it's fragrant, hardy, plentiful, inexpensive, and requires very little care. Although yellow is the most common color, you'll also find plumeria lei in shades of pink, red, orange, and "rainbow" blends.

PIKAKE

Favored for its fragile beauty and sweet scent, pikake was introduced from India. In lieu of pearls, many brides in Hawaii adorn themselves with long, multiple strands of white pikake. Princess Kaiulani enjoyed showing guests her beloved pikake and peacocks at Ainahau, her Waikiki home. Interestingly, pikake is the Hawaiian word for both the bird and the blossom.

KUKUI

The kukui (candlenut) is Hawaii's state tree. Early Hawaiians strung kukui nuts (which are quite oily) together and burned them for light; mixed burned nuts with oil to make an indelible dye; and mashed roasted nuts to consume as a laxative. Kukui nut lei may not have been made until after Western contact, when the Hawaiians saw black beads from Europe and wanted to imitate them.

LUAU: A TASTE OF HAWAII

The best place to sample Hawaiian food is at a backyard luau. Aunts and uncles are cooking, the pig is from a cousin's farm, and the fish is from a brother's boat.

But even locals have to angle for invitations to those rare occasions. So your choice is most likely between a commercial luau and a Hawaiian restaurant.

Some commercial luau are less authentic; they offer little of the traditional diet and are more about umbrella drinks, spectacle, and fun.

For greater culinary authenticity, folksy experiences, and rock-bottom prices, visit a Hawaiian restaurant (most are in anonymous storefronts in residential neighborhoods). Expect rough edges and some effort negotiating the menu.

In either case, much of what is known today as Hawaiian food would be as foreign to a 16th-century Hawaiian as risotto or chow mien. The pre-contact diet was simple and healthy—mainly raw and steamed seafood and vegetables. Early Hawaiians used earth ovens and heated stones to cook seafood, taro, sweet potatoes, and breadfruit and seasoned their food with sea salt and ground kukui nuts. Seaweed, fern shoots, sweet potato vines, coconut, banana, sugarcane, and select greens and roots rounded out the diet.

Successive waves of immigrants added their favorites to the ti leaf–lined table. So it is that foods as disparate as salt salmon and chicken long rice are now Hawaiian—even though there is no salmon in Hawaiian waters and long rice (cellophane noodles) is Chinese.

AT THE LUAU: KALUA PORK

The heart of any luau is the *imu*, the earth oven in which a whole pig is roasted. The preparation of an imu is an arduous affair for most families, who tackle it only once a year or so, for a baby's first birthday or at Thanksgiving, when many Islanders prefer to imu their turkeys. Commercial luau operations have it down to a science, however.

THE ART OF THE STONE

The key to a proper imu is the *pohaku*, the stones. Imu cook by means of long, slow, moist heat released by special stones that can withstand a hot fire without exploding. Many Hawaiian families treasure their imu stones, keeping them in a pile in the backyard and passing them on through generations.

PIT COOKING

The imu makers first dig a pit about the size of a refrigerator, then lay down *kiawe* (mesquite) wood and stones, and build a white-hot fire that is allowed to burn itself out. The ashes are raked away, and the hot stones covered with banana and ti leaves. Well-wrapped in ti or banana leaves and a net of chicken wire, the pig is lowered onto the leaf-covered stones. *Laulau* (leaf-wrapped bundles of meats, fish, and taro leaves) may also be placed inside. Leaves—ti, banana, even ginger—cover the pig followed by wet burlap sacks (to create steam). The whole is topped with a canvas tarp and left to steam for the better part of a day.

OPENING THE IMU

This is the moment everyone waits for: The imu is unwrapped like a giant present and the imu keepers gingerly wrestle out the steaming pig. When it's unwrapped, the meat falls moist and smoky-flavored from the bone, looking just like Southern-style pulled pork, but without the barbecue sauce.

WHICH LUAU?

Most resort hotels have luau on their grounds that include hula, music, and, of course, lots of food and drink. Each island also has at least one "authentic" luau. For lists of the best luau on each island, visit the Hawaii Visitors and Convention Bureau website at ⊕ *www. gohawaii.com.*

MEA AI ONO: GOOD THINGS TO EAT.

LAULAU
Steamed meats, fish, and taro leaf in ti-leaf bundles: fork-tender, a medley of flavors; the taro resembles spinach.

LOMI LOMI SALMON
Salt salmon in a piquant salad or relish with onions and tomatoes.

POI
Poi, a paste made of pounded taro root, may be an acquired taste, but it's a must-try during your visit.

Consider: The Hawaiian Adam is descended from *kalo* (taro). Young taro plants are called "keiki" (children). Poi is the first food after mother's milk for many Islanders. Ai, the word for food, is synonymous with poi in many contexts.

Not only that, locals love it. "There is no meat that doesn't taste good with poi," the old Hawaiians said.

But you have to know how to eat it: with something rich or powerfully flavored. "It is salt that makes the poi go in," is another adage. When you're served poi, try it with a mouthful of smoky kalua pork or salty lomi lomi salmon. Its slightly sour blandness cleanses the palate. And if you don't like it, smile and say something polite. (And slide that bowl over to a local.)

Laulau

Lomi lomi salmon

Poi

E HELE MAI AI! COME AND EAT!

Local-style Hawaiian restaurants tend to be inconveniently located in well-worn storefronts with little or no parking, outfitted with battered tables and clattering Melmac dishes, but they personify aloha, invariably run by local families who welcome tourists who take the trouble to find them.

Many are cash-only operations and combination plates, known as "plate lunch," are a standard feature: one or two entrées, two scoops of steamed rice, one scoop of macaroni salad, and—if the place is really old-style—a tiny portion of coarse Hawaiian salt and some raw onions for relish.

Most serve some foods that aren't, strictly speaking, Hawaiian, but are beloved of ka-maaina, such as salt meat with watercress (preserved meat in a tasty broth), or *akubone* (skipjack tuna fried in a tangy vinegar sauce).

The History of Hawaii

Hawaiian history is long and complex; a brief survey can put into context the ongoing renaissance of native arts and culture.

THE POLYNESIANS

Long before both Christopher Columbus and the Vikings, Polynesian seafarers set out to explore vast stretches of open ocean in double-hulled sailing canoes. From western Polynesia, they ventured back and forth between Samoa, Fiji, Tahiti, the Marquesas, and the Society Isles, settling on the outer reaches of the Pacific, Hawaii, and Easter Island as early as AD 300. The golden era of Polynesian voyaging peaked around AD 1200, after which the distant Hawaiian Islands were left to develop their own unique cultural practices and subsistence in relative isolation.

The Islands' symbiotic society was deeply intertwined with religion, mythology, science, and artistry. Ruled by an *alii*, or chief, each settlement was nestled in an *ahupuaa*, a pie-shape land division from the uplands where the *alii* lived through the valleys and down to the shores where the commoners resided. Everyone contributed, whether it was by building canoes, catching fish, making tools, or farming land.

A UNITED KINGDOM

When the British explorer Captain James Cook arrived in 1778, he was at first revered as a god. With guns and ammunition purchased from Cook, the chief of Hawaii Island, Kamehameha the Great, gained a significant advantage over the other *alii*. He united Hawaii into one kingdom in 1810, bringing an end to the frequent interisland battles that dominated Hawaiian life.

Tragically, the new kingdom was beset with troubles. Native religion was abandoned, and *kapu* (laws and regulations) eventually were abolished. The Europeans brought foreign diseases with them, and within a short few decades, the Native Hawaiian population was decimated.

New laws regarding land ownership and religious practices eroded the underpinnings of precontact Hawaii. Each successor to the Hawaiian throne sacrificed more control over the island kingdom. As Westerners permeated Hawaiian culture, Hawaii became more riddled with layers of racial issues, injustice, and social unrest.

MODERN HAWAII

In 1893, the last Hawaiian monarch, Queen Liliuokalani, was overthrown by a group of American and European businessmen and government officials, aided by an armed militia. This led to the creation of the Republic of Hawaii, which became a U.S. territory for the next 60 years. The loss of Hawaiian sovereignty and the conditions of annexation have haunted the Hawaiian people since the monarchy was deposed.

Pearl Harbor was attacked in 1941, which pulled the United States immediately into World War II. Tourism, from its beginnings in the early 1900s, flourished after the war and naturally inspired rapid real-estate development in Waikiki and around the Islands. In 1959, Hawaii became the 50th state. Statehood paved the way for Hawaiians to participate in the American democratic process, which was not universally embraced.

In the 1960s, Native Hawaiians began to reclaim their identity, from language to hula as a cultural practice to music, giving all Hawaii residents a renewed sense of unique place and pride in the world. This movement, called the Hawaiian Renaissance, has influenced life in the Islands ever since.

Chapter 2

TRAVEL SMART

2

Updated by
Mary F. Williamson

★ **MAJOR CITIES:**
Kapaa; Lihue (Kauai
county seat)

POPULATION:
73,298 (Kauai); 1.46 million
(Hawaii)

LANGUAGE:
English, Hawaiian

$ CURRENCY:
U.S. dollar

AREA CODE:
808

△ **EMERGENCIES:**
911

DRIVING:
On the right

⚡ **ELECTRICITY:**
120–220 v/60 cycles;
plugs have two or three
rectangular prongs

TIME:
Five hours behind New York;
six during daylight savings
time

WEB RESOURCES:
gohawaii.com/islands/kauai
dlnr.hawaii.gov
kauai.com

✈ **AIRPORT:**
Lihue Airport (LIH)

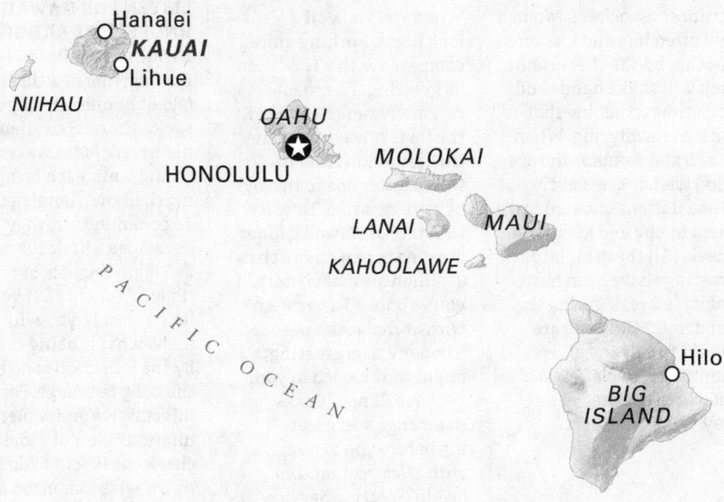

Hanalei
KAUAI
Lihue

NIIHAU

OAHU
★
HONOLULU

MOLOKAI

LANAI   *MAUI*

KAHOOLAWE

PACIFIC OCEAN

Hilo
BIG ISLAND

Know Before You Go

Do they really hand you a lei when you arrive? What are some common Hawaiian phrases? Is swimming at the beaches safe? How about the water quality? Traveling to Kauai is an easy adventure, but we've got tips to make your trip seamless and more meaningful. Below are all the answers to FAQs about Kauai and Hawaii.

DON'T CALL IT "THE STATES"

Hawaii was admitted to the Union in 1959, so residents can be somewhat sensitive when visitors refer to their own hometowns as "back in the States." Instead, share which state or region you call home. When you do, you won't appear to be such a *malihini* (newcomer).

WELCOME ISLAND-STYLE GREETINGS

Hawaii is a friendly place, and this is reflected in the day-to-day encounters with friends, family, and even business associates. Women will often hug and kiss one another on the cheek, and men will shake hands and sometimes combine that with a friendly hug. When a man and woman who are good friends greet each other, it is not unusual for them to hug and kiss on the cheek. (All these high-touch greetings have been hard habits to break during the pandemic.) Children are taught to call any elders "auntie" or "uncle," even if they aren't related; it's a way to show respect.

LOOK, BUT DON'T TOUCH

Help protect Hawaii's wildlife by loving it from a distance. Stay at least 10 feet away from turtles and 100 feet from monk seals, wherever you encounter them. Though they may not look it, coral are alive and fragile; harming them also harms the habitat for reef fish and other marine life. Avoid touching or stepping on coral, and take extra care when entering and exiting the water.

ENJOY A FRESH FLOWER LEI

When you walk off a long flight, nothing quite compares with a Hawaiian lei greeting. The casual ceremony ranks as one of the fastest ways to make the transition from the worries of home to the joys of your vacation. However, the state of Hawaii cannot greet each of its more than 8 million annual visitors. If you've booked a vacation with a wholesaler or tour company, a lei greeting might be included in your package. If not, it's easy to arrange a lei greeting before you arrive with ⊕ *leigreeting.com* or Alii Greeting Service

(⊕ *aliigreetingservice.com*). An orchid lei is standard and costs about $30 per person. You also can tuck a single flower behind your ear; a flower behind the left ear means you are in a relationship or unavailable, while the right ear indicates you are looking for love.

APPRECIATE THE HAWAIIAN LANGUAGE

While Hawaiian and English are both official state languages, the latter is used widely. Making the effort to learn some Hawaiian words can be rewarding, however. Hawaiian words you are most likely to encounter during your visit to the Islands are *aloha* (hello and goodbye), *mahalo* (thank you), *keiki* (child), *haole* (Caucasian or foreigner), *mauka* (toward the mountains), *makai* (toward the ocean), and *pau* (finished, all done). If you'd like to learn more Hawaiian words, check out ⊕ *wehewehe.org*.

LISTEN FOR HAWAII'S UNOFFICIAL LANGUAGE

Besides Hawaiian and English, there's a third (albeit unofficial) language spoken here. Hawaiian history includes waves of immigrants, each bringing their own language. To communicate, they developed a dialect known as Pidgin English, or "Pidgin" for short. If you listen closely, you will know what is being said by the inflections and by the body language. For an informative and sometimes hilarious view of Pidgin, check out *Pidgin to da Max* by Douglas Simonson and *Fax to da Max* by Jerry

Hopkins. Both are available at most local bookstores in the Hawaiiana sections and at variety stores. While it's nice to appreciate this unique Creole language, it's not wise to emulate it, as it can be considered disrespectful.

BE MINDFUL OF LOCAL CUSTOMS

If you've been invited to the home of friends living in Hawaii (an ultimate compliment), bring a small gift and take off your shoes when you enter their house. Take part in a cultural festival during your stay—a summer Bon Dance, for example—as there's no better way to get a glimpse of Hawaii's ethnic mosaic.

CHECK THE WEATHER

Kauai's environment can change in an instant, and with little or no warning. Strong ocean currents, flash floods, and rockslides are a real threat, especially during extreme weather events. If you're hiking, consult wind and rain conditions and predictions. Hurricane season runs from June to November.

SWIMMING ISN'T ALWAYS SAFE

Unfortunately, Kauai has the highest drowning rate in the state due to rocky shores, big waves, wind, and unseen rip currents. Even strong swimmers should stick to beaches with a lifeguard who knows the local currents and tides. Be particularly cautious and always check conditions before you head out at ⊕ *hawaiibeachsafety.com/kauai*. If in doubt, don't go out!

THE WATER IS GREAT; THE FOOD IS OKAY

Kauai's tap water is highly rated as it is naturally filtered through volcanic rock and has no odd taste or odor. Bringing a refillable bottle, rather than adding to the ocean plastic problem, is appreciated. The food is all safe to eat, but typical island fare is nothing too fancy. Still, there are one-of-a-kind food trucks and local holes-in-the-wall, and you must try local *laulau* (taro leaves and kalua pig) and poke (a raw ahi tuna bowl).

PRICES ARE HIGHER HERE

Almost everything is shipped in to Kauai, meaning you'll see higher prices than you're used to at the grocery store. On the other hand, the island produce and beef are fresh and good quality; find the best deals by talking to a local.

ROUTE NUMBERS ARE RARELY USED

You're more likely to hear "turn right at the old appliance store" or "turn *makai* (toward the ocean) at the big mango tree" rather than a highway route number or a street name. It's best to have a clear idea where you are going before you set off. The town areas off the highway use complicated address-numbering systems, so be prepared, especially in developments like Princeville.

MIND YOUR (ROAD) MANNERS

It's a good policy not to pass another car on any road as visibility is often diminished by the ever-present guinea grass, an invasive weed that lines the roads. Most local drivers are courteous, and they appreciate the same from you, especially in areas with one-lane bridges (alternate five cars) or scenic lookouts (park off the road). So, no tailgating, please. Horns are used rarely.

CHICKENS ARE EVERYWHERE

Kauai's unofficial bird roams the island everywhere, all the time. They beg for food at the beach, jump onto your picnic table, and, most annoyingly for the tired traveler, start crowing well before dawn.

RENEWABLE ENERGY IS A PRIORITY

Kauai is speeding toward renewable energy independence. By 2019, the electricity co-op obtained 55% of its power from renewable solar and hydro energy, some days hitting 100%. The island's goal is to reach 70% renewable energy by 2030 and 100% in 20 years.

USE REEF-SAFE SUNSCREEN

Sunscreens containing oxybenzone and octinoxate, ingredients that can harm coral reefs and marine ecosystems, have been banned in Hawaii since 2021. Protect the environment—and your skin—by using a product that's certified marine safe, such as TropicSport.

Getting Here and Around

Air

Flying time is about 10 hours from New York, 8 hours from Chicago, and 5 hours from Los Angeles.

Some of the major airline carriers serving Hawaii fly directly from the U.S. mainland to Kauai, allowing you to bypass connecting flights out of Honolulu. Although Lihue Airport is smaller and more casual than Honolulu International, it can also be quite busy during peak times.

Plants and plant products are subject to regulation by the Department of Agriculture, on both entering and leaving Hawaii. Upon leaving the Islands, you'll have to have your bags x-rayed and tagged at one of the airport's agricultural inspection stations before you proceed to check-in. Pineapples and coconuts with the packer's agricultural inspection stamp pass freely; papayas must be treated, inspected, and stamped. All other fruits are banned for export to the U.S. mainland. Flowers pass—except for gardenias, rose leaves, jade vine, and mauna loa. Also banned are insects, snails, soil, cotton, cacti, sugarcane, and all berry plants.

You'll have to leave dogs and other pets at home. A 120-day quarantine is imposed to keep out rabies, which is nonexistent in Hawaii. If specific pre- and post-arrival requirements are met, animals may qualify for a 30-day or 5-day-or-less quarantine.

AIRPORTS
On Kauai, visitors fly into Lihue Airport (LIH), on the East Side of the island. Visitor information booths are outside each baggage-claim area. Visitors will also find a newsstand, flower shop, Starbucks, bar, restaurant, and gift shop in the terminal.

For most domestic and international flights, however, Honolulu International Airport (HNL) is the main stopover. From Honolulu, interisland flights to Kauai depart regularly from early morning until evening. In addition, some carriers offer nonstop service directly from the U.S. mainland to Lihue Airport.

To travel interisland from Honolulu on Hawaiian Air, you will depart from the connected interisland terminal (Terminal 1). Southwest Airlines flies out of Terminal 2. A free bus service, the Wiki Wiki Shuttle, operates between terminals.

GROUND TRANSPORTATION
Some major hotels provide airport shuttles to and from Lihue Airport. In addition, travelers who've booked a tour with Kauai Island Tours, Roberts Hawaii, IMI Tours, or Polynesian Adventure Tours will be picked up at the airport.

SpeediShuttle offers transportation between the airport and hotels, resorts, and time-share complexes on the island. There is an online reservation and fare quote system for information and bookings. Another option is to hire a taxi or limousine. Cabs are available curbside at baggage claim. Cab fares to locations around the island are estimated as follows: Poipu $35–$42, Wailua–Waipouli $18–$20, Lihue–Kukui Grove $10–$15, Princeville–Haena $75–$95. Kauai Luxury Transportation & Tours offers service to Lihue Airport. Kauai Taxi Company also will deliver groceries from your list.

Uber and Lyft are somewhat recent arrivals on the island. You can expect to pay around $75–$80 for a ride from the airport to Princeville (approximately 30 miles).

FLIGHTS

Although flight schedules have changed frequently due to the pandemic, several major carriers consistently have served Lihue Airport: Alaska Airlines (Seattle, Portland), American Airlines (Los Angeles, Honolulu, Maui, and Hawaii Island), Delta (Los Angeles, Honolulu, Maui), and United Airlines (Denver, Los Angeles, San Francisco, Honolulu, Maui, and Hawaii Island). WestJet flies from Vancouver, BC, Canada, in the winter. Hawaiian offers a daily, nonstop Los Angeles–Lihue flight; all other mainland flights require a connection in Honolulu except Southwest Airlines, which has limited direct flights to Lihue from Oakland.

INTERISLAND FLIGHTS

Hawaiian Airlines and Southwest service Kauai regularly. In addition to offering a discount for booking online, free frequent-flier programs entitle you to rewards and upgrades the more you fly. Be sure to compare prices offered by interisland carriers. If you are somewhat flexible with your days and times for island-hopping, you should have no problem getting a round-trip ticket.

🚲 Bicycle

With few marked bike lanes, poor shoulders, and busy roads, Kauai is not ideal to tour by bicycle. There is a recreational cycling scene, however, and local shops rent cruisers for exploring resort areas and the East Side's coastal path, mountain bikes for challenging trail rides, and skinny-tire road bicycles. An annual race (⊕ pedaltothemeadow.com) heads from Kekaha up the 16 miles and 3,800 feet to Kokee; the spandex crowd trains for it year-round, so share the mountain road with aloha.

🚌 Bus

On Kauai, the County Transportation Agency operates the Kauai Bus, which provides service between Hanalei and Kekaha. It also provides limited service to the airport and to Koloa and Poipu. The fare is $2 for adults, and frequent-rider passes are available. The new North Shore Shuttle now operates to Kee Beach from either Waipa or Princeville, depending on road construction. Updates about fares, routes, and a hop-on, hop-off option are posted at ⊕ gohaena.com. The website ⊕ getaroundkauai.com has information about resources for sustainable transportation choices.

🚗 Car

The independent way to experience all of Kauai's stunning beauty is to get in a car and explore. The 15-mile stretch of Napali Coast, with its breathtaking, verdant-green sheer cliffs, is the only outer part of the island that's not accessible by car. Otherwise, one main road can get you from Barking Sands Beach on the West Side to Haena on the North Shore.

Asking for directions will almost always get a helpful explanation from the locals, but you should be prepared for an island term or two. Instead of using compass directions, remember that Hawaii residents refer to places as being either mauka (toward the mountains) or makai (toward the ocean) from one another.

Hawaii has a strict seat-belt law. All those riding in the vehicle must wear a seat belt; on Kauai, the fine for not wearing one is $112. There is also a law forbidding the use of handheld devices while driving. Drivers must leave at least 3 feet of space when passing cyclists. Jaywalking

Getting Here and Around

is common in the Islands, so please pay careful attention to the roads. It also is considered rude to honk your horn, so be patient if someone is turning or proceeding through an intersection.

While driving on Kauai, you will come across several one-lane bridges. If you are the first to approach a bridge, the car on the other side will wait while you cross. If a car on the other side is closer to the bridge, then you should wait while the driver crosses. If you're enjoying the island's dramatic views, pull over to the shoulder so you don't block traffic.

Do consider some drive-free days, however … both to fully unplug and relax and to give this Eden a break from added cars.

GASOLINE
You can count on having to pay more at the pump for gasoline on Kauai than in the continental U.S. There are no gas stations past Princeville on the North Shore, none in Poipu, and none past Waimea on the West Side, so fuel up before heading out to the end of the road.

PARKING
Only recently has Kauai instituted parking fees for nonresidents at a few popular tourist areas, and these fees are collected for upkeep. Under consideration at the time of writing is a daily fee of $10 for nonresidents to park at high-use county beach parks. There is a $10 fee for nonresidents to park at Kee Beach, and a $10 fee for nonresidents covers the four fantastic lookouts over Waimea Canyon and in Kokee. Otherwise, there are parking meters at only a couple of state office buildings but no pay-to-park garages, tags, or lots. If there's room on the side of the road, you probably can park there as long as your vehicle isn't hanging into the road or blocking someone's driveway.

ROAD CONDITIONS
Kauai has a relatively well-maintained highway running south from Lihue to Barking Sands Beach; a spur at Waimea takes you up Waimea Canyon Drive to Kokee State Park. A northern route also winds its way from Lihue to the end of the road at Haena, the beginning of rugged and roadless Napali Coast. Extreme weather in recent years caused landslides past Princeville, so ask if repairs are still in progress. Opt for a four-wheel-drive vehicle if dirt-road exploration holds any appeal.

ROADSIDE EMERGENCIES
If you find yourself in an emergency or accident while driving on Kauai, pull over if you can. If you have a cell phone with you, call the roadside assistance number on your rental-car contract or AAA Help. If you find that your car has been broken into or stolen, report it immediately to your rental-car company and an agent can assist you. If it's an emergency and someone is hurt, call 911 immediately and stay there until first responders arrive.

CAR RENTAL
While on Kauai, you can rent anything from an econobox to a Tesla. Rates are usually better if you reserve through a rental agency's website. It's wise to make reservations far in advance and make sure that a confirmed reservation guarantees you a car, especially if you're visiting during peak seasons or for major events. Rates have risen sharply and can begin at about $80 a day for an economy car with air-conditioning, automatic transmission, and unlimited mileage. This may not include the airport concession fee, general excise tax, rental-vehicle surcharge, or vehicle license fee. When you reserve a car, ask about cancellation penalties. Many rental companies in

Hawaii offer coupons for discounts at various attractions that could save you money later on in your trip.

In Hawaii you must be 21 years of age to rent a car, and you must have a valid driver's license and a major credit card. Those under 25 will pay a daily surcharge of $15–$35. Request car seats and extras when you book. Hawaii's Child Passenger Restraint Law requires that all children three years and younger be in an approved child safety seat in the back seat of a vehicle. Children ages four to seven must be seated in a rear booster seat or child restraint, such as a lap and shoulder belt. Rentals of car seats and boosters range from $5 to $8 per day.

Your unexpired driver's license is valid for rental for up to 90 days.

Since the main road around the island is mostly only two lanes, allow plenty of time to return your car before your departure flight. Traffic can be slow during morning and afternoon rush hours. Give yourself about an hour before check-in time for the return process.

ISLAND DRIVING TIMES

It might not seem as if driving from the North Shore to the West Side, say, would take much time, as Kauai is smaller than Oahu, Maui, and certainly the Big Island. But it will take longer than you'd expect, and Kauai roads are subject to some heavy traffic, especially going through Kapaa and Lihue.

🏍 Motorcycle

Once you've transported luggage and settled into your room, heading out by motorcycle is an option that has gained popularity. Renters must hold a valid motorcycle license, be over 21, and have

Island Driving Times	
Haena to Hanalei	8 miles/15 mins
Hanalei to Princeville	4 miles/10 mins
Princeville to Kilauea	5 miles/10 mins
Kilauea to Anahola	8 miles/15 mins
Anahola to Kapaa	5 miles/15 mins
Kapaa to Lihue	10 miles/25 mins
Lihue to Poipu	13 miles/25 mins
Poipu to Kalaheo	8 miles/15 mins
Kalaheo to Hanapepe	4 miles/10 mins
Hanapepe to Waimea	7 miles/15 mins

operating experience. Passengers must be over 18. Closed-toe shoes, eye protection, and a Department of Transportation–approved helmet are required in Hawaii. Kauai Motorsports offers various makes and models.

🚗 Ride-Sharing

Ride-sharing apps like Uber and Lyft are newcomers to the Kauai transportation scene; they usually offer a slightly cheaper rate than traditional taxis or car services.

🚕 Taxi

Kauai has always had taxi service, though it's never been a major transportation choice. Upon arrival, you can catch a cab from the small lot near the baggage claim. Kauai Taxi Company, City Cab, and Princeville Taxi head the Kauai fleet. During shortages of rental cars, it's wise to book cabs at least two days ahead.

Essentials

📍 Communications

With cell-phone reception spotty in many remote areas, you can't always rely on connectivity, no matter the data plan. With that said, most major hotels and resorts offer high-speed Wi-Fi access in rooms and/or lobbies. If you're staying at a condo or B&B without service, ask the proprietor for the nearest café with wireless access.

🍴 Dining

Hawaii is a melting pot of cultures, and nowhere is this more apparent than in its cuisine. From luau and "plate lunch" to sushi and steak, there's no shortage of interesting flavors and presentations. It's always a good idea to make dining reservations if you want to eat at particular restaurants.

⇨ *For information about the restaurants in each area of Kauai, see the Planning section at the start of each regional chapter.*

WHAT IT COSTS in U.S. Dollars			
$	$$	$$$	$$$$
RESTAURANTS			
under $17	$17–$26	$27–$35	over $35
HOTELS			
under $180	$180–$260	$261–$340	over $340

➕ Health

In addition to being the Aloha State, Hawaii is known as the Health State. The life expectancy here is 83 years, the longest in the nation. Balmy weather makes it easy to remain active year-round, and the low-stress aloha attitude certainly contributes to general well-being. When you are visiting the Islands, however, there are a few health issues to keep in mind.

The Hawaii State Department of Health recommends that you drink 16 ounces of water per hour to avoid dehydration when hiking or spending time in the sun. Use sunscreen, wear UV-reflective sunglasses, and protect your head with a visor or hat for shade. If you're not acclimated to warm, humid weather, allow plenty of time for rest stops and refreshments.

When visiting freshwater streams, be aware of the tropical disease leptospirosis, which is spread by animal urine and carried into streams and mud. Symptoms include fever, headache, nausea, and red eyes; they may not appear immediately. If left untreated, it can cause liver and kidney damage, respiratory failure, internal bleeding, and even death. To avoid this, don't swim or wade in freshwater streams or ponds if you have open sores, and don't drink from any freshwater streams or ponds, especially after heavy rains.

On the Islands, fog is a rare occurrence, but there often can be "vog," an airborne haze of gases released from volcanic vents on Hawaii Island. During certain weather conditions such as "Kona Winds," the vog can settle over the Islands and wreak havoc with respiratory conditions, especially asthma or emphysema. If susceptible, stay indoors and get emergency assistance if needed.

The Islands have their share of bugs and insects that enjoy the tropical climate as much as visitors do. Most are harmless but annoying. When planning to spend time outdoors in hiking areas, wear long-sleeved clothing and pants and use mosquito repellent containing DEET. In very damp places you may encounter the dreaded local centipede. On the Islands they usually come in one of three colors: brown, blue, or bright orange. They range from the size of a worm to an 8-inch cigar. Their sting is very painful, and the reaction is similar to bee- and wasp-sting reactions. If stung, immediately run very hot water over the wound for 20 minutes or so. When camping, shake out your sleeping bag before climbing in, and check your shoes in the morning, as the centipedes like cozy places. If planning on hiking or traveling in remote areas, always carry a first-aid kit and appropriate medications for sting reactions.

COVID-19 AND TRAVEL

COVID-19 brought all travel to a virtual standstill in the first half of 2020. Although the COVID-19 illness is mild in most people, severe or even life-threatening complications can occur in older adults, unvaccinated people, and those with weaker immune systems or certain medical conditions. Once travel started up again, Hawaii residents and visitors were asked to be particularly careful about hygiene and to avoid unnecessary trips.

Kauai officials have been extra cautious as the island has very limited ICU beds, and all supplies must be flown or shipped in. Kauai County posts updates at ⊕ *kau-ai.gov/covid-19*. At time of writing, a mask still may be required indoors at healthcare facilities, on public transportation, and at specific businesses and events.

Check with your airline and official websites to keep abreast of current vaccination, testing, and quarantine guidelines.

As of late March 2022, there were no COVID-related requirements for arriving domestic passengers, but this could change quickly if COVID cases increase. Voluntary post-travel testing is encouraged for 3–5 days after arrival. For more information, visit ⊕ *hawaiicovid19.com*. All travelers arriving in Hawaii directly from international airports must comply with any U.S. federal requirements; check with your airline.

Starting two weeks before a trip, anyone planning to travel should be on the lookout for some of the following symptoms: cough, fever, chills, trouble breathing, muscle pain, sore throat, or new loss of smell or taste. If you experience any of these symptoms, you should not travel at all, contact your physician, and get tested. Be honest if you've been exposed, and remember that you can be infectious without having any symptoms.

To protect yourself and others during travel, wear a mask that fits well over your nose and mouth, wash your hands often with soap and water, avoid contact with people showing symptoms, and limit your time in crowds. You may wish to bring extra supplies, such as disposable masks, disinfecting wipes, hand sanitizer, and a first-aid kit with a thermometer. Rapid test kits would be a bonus.

Given how abruptly travel was curtailed in 2020 and how quickly travel restrictions can change, it is wise to protect yourself by purchasing a travel insurance policy that will reimburse you for cancellation costs. Not all travel insurance policies protect against pandemic-related cancellations, so always read the fine print.

Essentials

🕐 Hours of Operation

Even people in paradise have to work. Generally, local business hours are weekdays 8–5. Banks are usually open Monday–Thursday 8:30–4 and until 6 on Friday. Some banks have Saturday morning hours.

Many self-serve gas stations stay open around the clock, with full-service stations usually open from around 7 am until 9 pm. The larger U.S. post offices are open weekdays 8:30 am–4:30 pm and Saturday 8:30–noon. Check operating hours for smaller post offices.

Most museums generally open their doors between 9 am and 10 am and stay open until 5 pm Tuesday–Saturday. Many museums operate with afternoon hours only on Sunday and close on Monday. Visitor-attraction hours vary throughout the state, but most sights are open daily, with the exception of major holidays such as Christmas. Check local publications upon arrival for attraction hours and schedules if visiting over holiday periods. The local dailies carry a listing of local cultural events for those time periods.

Stores in resort areas sometimes open as early as 8, with shopping-center opening hours varying from 9:30 to 10 on weekdays and Saturday, a bit later on Sunday. Bigger malls stay open until 9 weekdays and Saturday and close at 5 on Sunday. Boutiques in resort areas may stay open to catch after-dinner shoppers.

✏️ Immunizations

International travelers planning to visit the United States should check ⊕ *www. cdc.gov* for current federal requirements for COVID-19 vaccination and testing.

🛏️ Lodging

There are several top-notch resorts on Kauai, as well as a wide variety of condos, vacation rentals, and bed-and-breakfasts to choose from. Selecting vacation lodging is a tough decision, but fret not—our expert writers and editors have done most of the legwork.

Looking for a tropical forest retreat, a big resort, or a private vacation rental? We'll give you all the details you need to book a place that suits your style.

■ TIP→ **Reserve your room far in advance. Be sure to ask about discounts and special packages (hotel websites often have online-only deals).**

⇨ *For information about lodgings in each area of Kauai, see the Planning section at the start of each regional chapter.*

📷 Packing

Hawaii is casual: sandals, bathing suits, and comfortable, informal clothing are the norm. In summer, synthetic slacks and shirts, although easy to care for, can be uncomfortably sticky. If you're visiting in winter, bring a sweater or light- to medium-weight jacket. A polar fleece pullover is ideal and makes a great impromptu travel pillow.

One of the most important things to tuck into your suitcase is reef-safe sunscreen, though it is readily available at most stores.

As for clothing in the Hawaiian Islands, there's a saying that when a man wears a suit, he's either applying for a loan or he's a lawyer trying a case. Only a few upscale restaurants in Honolulu require a jacket for dinner. The aloha shirt is accepted dress in Hawaii for business

Where to Stay on Kauai

	LOCAL VIBE	PROS	CONS
The North Shore	Properties here have the "wow" factor with ocean and mountain beauty; laid-back Hanalei and Princeville set the high-end pace.	When the weather is good, this area has it all. Epic winter surf, gorgeous waterfalls, and verdant vistas create some of the best scenery in Hawaii.	Frequent winter rain (being green has a cost) means you may have to travel south to find the sun; expensive restaurants and shopping offer few deals.
The East Side	The most reasonably priced area to stay for the practical traveler; lacks the pizzazz of expensive resorts on North and South Shores; more traditional beach hotels.	The best travel deals show up here; more direct access to the local population; plenty of decent restaurants with good variety, along with delis in food stores.	Beaches aren't the greatest (rocky, reefy) at many of the lodging spots; congested traffic at times; some crime issues in parks.
The South Shore	Resort central; plenty of choices where the consistent sunshine is perfect for those who want to do nothing but play golf or tennis and read a book by the pool.	Beautiful in its own right; many enchanted evenings with stellar sunsets; summer surf a bit easier for beginners to handle.	Though resorts are lush, surrounding landscape is desert-like with scrub brush; travel time to North Shore sights is long.
The West Side	There are few options for lodging in this mostly untouristed setting, with contrasts such as the extreme heat of an August day in Waimea to a frozen winter night up in Kokee.	A gateway area for exploration into the wilds of Kokee or for boating trips on Napali Coast; main hub for boat and helicopter trips; outstanding sunsets.	Least convenient side for most visitors; daytime is languid and dry; river runoff can ruin ocean's clarity.

Essentials

and social occasions. Shorts are acceptable daytime attire, along with a T-shirt or polo shirt. There's no need to buy expensive sandals on the mainland—here you can get flip-flops for a couple of dollars and off-brand sandals for $20.

Golfers should remember that many courses have dress codes requiring a collared shirt; call courses you're interested in for details. If you're not prepared, you can pick up appropriate clothing at resort pro shops.

⊕ Passport

All visitors to the United States require a passport that is valid for six months beyond your expected period of stay.

⊕ Safety

Hawaii is generally a safe tourist destination, but it's still wise to follow the same common-sense safety precautions you would normally follow in your own hometown. Don't leave valuables in the car even if they are in the trunk, and don't leave them unattended on the beach.

Be wary of those hawking "too good to be true" prices on everything from car rentals to attractions. Many of these offers are just a lure to get you in the door for time-share presentations. When handed a flier, read the fine print before you make your decision to participate.

⑤ Taxes

Kauai County has a 4.5% sales tax on all purchases, including food. The state sales tax plus the hotel room tax (13.25%) add approximately 18% to

your hotel bill. A $5-per-day road tax is assessed on each rental car ($3 with Hawaii driver's license).

⊙ Time

Hawaii is on Hawaiian Standard Time (HST), five hours behind New York and two hours behind Los Angeles for the winter months.

While the U.S. mainland uses daylight savings time from March until November, Hawaii does not, so add an extra hour's difference between the Islands and U.S. mainland destinations. You may also find that things generally move more slowly here. That has nothing to do with your watch—it's just the laid-back way called Hawaiian time.

⑤ Tipping

Tip cabdrivers 15% of the fare. Standard tips for restaurants and bar tabs run from 15% to 20% of the bill, depending on the level of service. Bellhops at hotels usually receive $1 per bag, more if you have bulky items such as golf clubs and surfboards. Tip the hotel room cleaner $1 or more per night, paid daily. Tip door workers $1 for assistance with taxis; tips for concierges vary depending on the service. For example, tip more for "hard-to-get" tickets or dining reservations.

For single-day guided activities like a boat trip to Napali, a zip-lining tour, or surf lessons, you should tip each guide at least $10–$20 if you feel they enhanced your experience. Often, the tour company takes the bulk of your booking price, and the locals who are sharing their alohas with you are depending on your tips.

🧭 Tours

Globus has two Hawaii itineraries that include Kauai, one of which is an escorted cruise on Norwegian Cruise Line's *Pride of America* that includes two days on the Garden Island. Tauck offers an 11-night "Best of Hawaii" tour that includes two nights on Kauai with leisure time for either relaxation or exploration.

Atlas Cruises & Tours sells more than a dozen Hawaii trips ranging from 7 to 12 nights; these are operated by various guided-tour companies. Several trips include two to three nights on Kauai.

SPECIAL-INTEREST TOURS
BIRD-WATCHING

More than 150 species of birds live in the Hawaiian Islands. Field Guides has a three-island (Oahu, Kauai, and the Big Island), 10-day guided bird-watching trip for 14 enthusiasts that focuses on endemic land birds and specialty seabirds. While on Kauai, birders will visit Kokee State Park, Alakai Wilderness Preserve, and Kilauea Point National Wildlife Refuge. The trip costs about $6,725 per person and includes accommodations, meals, ground transportation, interisland air, an eight-hour pelagic boat trip, and guided bird-watching excursions. Travelers must purchase their own airfare to and from their gateway city.

Victor Emanuel Nature Tours, the largest company in the world specializing in bird-watching tours, has two nine-day trips that include Kauai. "Spring Hawaii" is the theme of the late February/early March birding trip, when seabird diversity on the island is at its peak. Birders will see the *koloa* (Hawaiian duck), one of Hawaii's most endangered wetland birds, as well as Laysan albatrosses, red- and white-tailed tropicbirds, red-footed boobies, wedge-tailed shearwaters, great frigatebirds, brown boobies, and possibly even red-billed tropicbirds. Participants in the "Fall Hawaii" birding trip will visit Oahu, Kauai, and the Big Island in October. Birders will see Kauai honey-creepers and Hawaiian short-eared owls at Kokee State Park and Alakai Swamp and seabirds at the National Wildlife Refuges at Kilauea and Hanalei. Both the "Spring Hawaii" and "Fall Hawaii" tours cost about $6,995 per person. The trips include accommodations, meals, interisland air, ground transportation, and guided excursions. Travelers must purchase their own airline ticket to Honolulu and home from Hilo.

CULTURE

Road Scholar, a nonprofit educational travel organization, offers several guided tours for adults over 50 that focus on Hawaiian culture. With all the tours listed, travelers must purchase their own airline tickets to Hawaii.

"Tropical Splendor" is an 11-day ocean voyage that focuses on the history of the Islands with visits to *heiau* (sacred temples) and museums along with a visit to a royal palace. On Kauai, participants visit Waimea Canyon and sail along the rugged Napali Coast. The cost of this tour starts at $5,199 per person and includes accommodations, meals, ground transportation, and admission fees, as well as tipping charges and a travel assistance plan.

"The Best of Hawaii, Maui, Oahu, and Kauai" is a more adventurous 21-day tour that includes eight nights on the Big Island of Hawaii, four nights on Maui, four nights on Kauai, and four nights on Oahu. Exploring the natural beauty of these islands, travelers visit Volcanoes National Park and the Hamakua Coast on

Essentials

Hawaii Island (the Big Island), Haleakala National Park on Maui, Kilauea Point National Wildlife Refuge and the National Tropical Botanical Garden on Kauai, and Pearl Harbor and Iolani Palace on Oahu, learning about these islands' diverse birdlife, marine life, forests, volcanoes, and more. Prices start at $8,499 per person and include accommodations, meals, ground transportation, admission fees, and interisland air travel between Kauai and Hawaii Island.

HIKING

"Wild Kauai" is the theme of a weeklong trip to Kauai sponsored by Sierra Club Outings. In addition to daylong hikes of 5 to 9 miles through many of the rain forests in Kokee State Park, participants will have opportunities for ocean kayaking, snorkeling, and swimming at secluded beaches, as well as bird-watching. Hikers will help in the maintenance of some trails. Accommodations are in shared cabins and, as with all Sierra Club Outings, participants are expected to help prepare some of the meals using only local, fresh ingredients. The trip costs about $2,675 per person and includes accommodations, meals, and ground transportation. Travelers must purchase their own tickets to and from their gateway city.

Another Sierra Club trip emphasizes "Service and Culture," with visitors helping propagate seeds of the ohia tree, the threatened "backbone" of the Hawaiian forest, on which many endangered birds depend. That tour costs $1,395 per person, has a low difficulty rating, and offers poi-making, snorkeling, hiking, and more. Travelers purchase their own airfare.

🛂 Visa

Except for citizens of Canada and Bermuda, most visitors to the United States must have a visa. If you are from one of the 40 designated members of the Visa Waiver Program, then you only require an ESTA (Electronic System for Travel Authorization) as long as you are staying for 90 days or less.

Nationals of Visa-Waiver nations who have traveled to Democratic People's Republic of Korea, Iran, Iraq, Libya, Somalia, Sudan, Syria, or Yemen no longer qualify for ESTA. Also, if you have been denied a visa to visit the United States, your application for the ESTA program most likely will be denied.

📍 Visitor Information

Before you go, check the Kauai Visitors Bureau website (⊕ www.gohawaii.com/islands/kauai) for a free travel planner with information on accommodations, transportation, sports and activities, dining, arts and entertainment, and culture. You can also take a virtual tour of the island that includes great photos and helpful planning information. The Hawaii Tourism Authority's website (⊕ www.hawaiitourismauthority.org) offers tips on everything from packing to flying around the state.

The Hawaii Department of Land and Natural Resources site (⊕ dlnr.hawaii.gov) has information on hiking, fishing, and camping permits and licenses; state parks; hiking safety and mountain and ocean preservation; and details on volunteer programs.

Go Haena (⊕ *gohaena.com*) has details about the reservations and fees required to visit the popular park, beaches, and trails at the end of the road on Kauai's North Shore; there's also info about shuttle service.

Keep your beach time safe by checking out Hawaiian Beach Safety (⊕ *hawaiibeachsafety.com*) online before you head out.

📅 When to Go

Kauai is beautiful in every season, but if you must have good beach weather, you should plan to visit between June and October. The rainy season runs from November through February, with the windward, or east and north, areas of the island receiving most of the rainfall. Nights can be cool from November through March. Rain is possible throughout the year, of course, but it rarely rains everywhere on the island at once. If it's raining where you are, head to another side of the island, usually south or west.

Big surf can make many North Shore beaches unswimmable during winter months, while the South Shore gets its large swells in summer. February is the best month to see humpback whales, though they arrive as early as October and a few may still be around in early April. In winter, Napali Coast boat tours can be rerouted due to high seas, the

Kalalau Trail can become very muddy or impassable, and sea kayaking is not an option. If you have your heart set on visiting Kauai's famed Napali Coast, you may want to visit in the drier, warmer months (May–September).

■ TIP➔ **The slowest months for tourism on Kauai tend to be May and September, so you'll have more elbow room at the beach, fewer folks on trails, and an easier time getting dinner reservations.**

HAWAII HOLIDAYS

If you happen to be in the Islands on March 26 or June 11, you'll notice light traffic and busy beaches—these are state holidays. March 26 recognizes the birthday of Prince Jonah Kuhio Kalanianaole, a member of the royal line who served as a delegate to Congress and spearheaded the effort to set aside homelands for Hawaiian people. June 11 honors the first island-wide monarch, Kamehameha I; locals drape his statues with lei and stage elaborate parades. May 1 isn't an official holiday, but "May Day is Lei Day in Hawaii Nei," when schools and civic groups celebrate the quintessential Islands gift, the flower lei. Statehood Day is the third Friday in August (Hawaii became the 50th state on August 21, 1959).

Hawaiian Vocabulary

Although an understanding of Hawaiian is by no means required on a trip to the Aloha State, a *malihini,* or newcomer, will find plenty of opportunities to pick up a few of the local words and phrases. Traditional names and expressions are widely used in the Islands. You're likely to read or hear at least a few words each day of your stay.

Simplifying the learning process is the fact that the Hawaiian language contains only seven consonants—*H, K, L, M, N, P, W,* and the silent *'okina,* or glottal stop, written '—plus one or more of the five vowels. All syllables, and therefore all words, end in a vowel. Each vowel, with the exception of a few diphthongized double vowels, such as *au* (pronounced "ow") or *ai* (pronounced "eye"), is pronounced separately. Thus *'Iolani* is four syllables (ee-oh-la-nee), not three (yo-la-nee). Although some Hawaiian words have only vowels, most also contain some consonants, but consonants are never doubled.

Pronunciation is simple. Pronounce *A* "ah" as in *father; E* "ay" as in *weigh; I* "ee" as in *marine; O* "oh" as in *no; U* "oo" as in *true.*

Consonants mirror their English equivalents, with the exception of *W.* When the letter begins any syllable other than the first one in a word, it is usually pronounced as a *V. 'Awa,* the Polynesian drink, is pronounced "ava," *'ewa* is pronounced "eva."

Almost all long Hawaiian words are combinations of shorter words; they are not difficult to pronounce if you segment them. *Kalaniana'ole,* the highway running east from Honolulu, is easily understood as *Kalani ana 'ole.* Apply the standard pronunciation rules—the stress falls on the next-to-last syllable of most two- or three-syllable Hawaiian words—and Kalaniana'ole Highway is as easy to say as Main Street.

Now about that fish. Try *humu-humu nuku-nuku āpu a'a.*

The other unusual element in Hawaiian language is the *kahakō,* or macron, written as a short line (ˉ) placed over a vowel. Like the accent (´) in Spanish, the kahakō puts emphasis on a syllable that would normally not be stressed. The most familiar example is probably *Waikīkī.* With no macrons, the stress would fall on the middle syllable; with only one macron, on the last syllable, the stress would fall on the first and last syllables. Some words become plural with the addition of a macron, often on a syllable that would have been stressed anyway. No Hawaiian word becomes plural with the addition of an *S,* since that letter does not exist in the language.

⇨ *Note that Hawaiian diacritical marks are not printed in this guide.*

PIDGIN
You may hear Pidgin English, the unofficial language of Hawaii. It is a Creole language, with its own grammar, evolved from the mixture of English, Hawaiian, Japanese, Portuguese, and other languages spoken in 19th-century Hawaii, and it is heard everywhere.

GLOSSARY
What follows is a glossary of some of the most commonly used Hawaiian words. Hawaiian residents appreciate visitors who at least try to pick up the local language.

'a'ā: rough, crumbling lava, contrasting with *pāhoehoe,* which is smooth.

'ae: yes.

aikane: friend.

āina: land.

akamai: smart, clever, possessing savoir faire.

akua: god.

ala: a road, path, or trail.

ali'i: a Hawaiian chief, a member of the chiefly class.

aloha: love, affection, kindness; also a salutation meaning both greetings and farewell.

'ānuenue: rainbow.

'a'ole: no.

'apōpō: tomorrow.

'auwai: a ditch.

auwē: alas, woe is me!

'ehu: a red-haired Hawaiian.

'ewa: in the direction of 'Ewa plantation, west of Honolulu.

hala: the pandanus tree, whose leaves (*lau hala*) are used to make baskets and plaited mats.

hālau: school.

hale: a house.

hale pule: church, house of worship.

hana: to work.

haole: foreigner. Since the first foreigners were Caucasian, *haole* now means a Caucasian person.

hapa: a part, sometimes a half; often used as a short form of *hapa haole*, to mean a person who is part-Caucasian.

hau'oli: to rejoice. *Hau'oli Makahiki Hou* means Happy New Year. *Hau'oli lā hānau* means Happy Birthday.

heiau: an outdoor stone platform; an ancient Hawaiian place of worship.

he mea iki or **he mea 'ole:** you're welcome.

holo: to run.

holoholo: to go for a walk, ride, or sail.

holokū: a long Hawaiian dress, somewhat fitted, with a yoke and a train. It was worn at court, and at least one local translates the word as "expensive muumuu."

holomū: a post–World War II cross between a *holokū* and a mu'umu'u, less fitted than the former but less voluminous than the latter, and having no train.

honi: to kiss; a kiss. A phrase that some tourists may find useful, quoted from a popular hula, is *Honi Ka'ua Wikiwiki:* Kiss me quick!

honu: turtle.

ho'omalimali: flattery, a deceptive "line," bunk, baloney, hooey.

huhū: angry.

hui: a group, club, or assembly. A church may refer to its congregation as a *hui* and a social club may be called a *hui.*

hukilau: a seine; a communal fishing party in which everyone helps to drive the fish into a huge net, pull it in, and divide the catch.

hula: the dance of Hawaii.

iki: little.

ipo: sweetheart. Commonly seen as "ku'uipo," or "my sweetheart."

ka: the. This is the definite article for most singular words; for plural nouns, the definite article is usually *nā.* Since there is no *S* in Hawaiian, the article may be your only clue that a noun is plural.

Hawaiian Vocabulary

kahuna: a priest, doctor, or other trained person of old Hawaii, endowed with special professional skills that often included prophecy or other supernatural powers.

kai: the sea, saltwater.

kalo: the taro plant from whose root *poi* (paste) is made.

kamā'aina: literally, a child of the soil; it refers to people who were born in the Islands or have lived there for a long time.

kanaka: originally a man or humanity, it is now used to denote a male Hawaiian or part-Hawaiian, but is occasionally taken as a slur when used by non-Hawaiians. *Kanaka maoli* is used by some Native Hawaiian rights activists to embrace part-Hawaiians as well.

kāne: a man, a husband. If you see this word (or *kane*) on a door, it's the men's room.

kapa: also called by its Tahitian name, *tapa,* a cloth made of beaten bark and usually dyed and stamped with a repeat design.

kapakahi: crooked, cockeyed, uneven. You've got your hat on *kapakahi.*

kapu: keep out, prohibited. This is the Hawaiian version of the more widely known Tongan word *tabu* (taboo).

kēia lā: today.

keiki: a child; *keikikāne* is a boy, *keikiwahine* a girl.

kōkua: to help, assist. Often seen in signs like "Please *kōkua* and throw away your trash."

kona: the leeward side of the Islands, the direction (south) from which the *kona* wind and *kona* rain come.

kula: upland.

kuleana: a homestead or small plot of ground on which a family has been installed for some generations without necessarily owning it. By extension, *kuleana* is used to denote any area or department in which one has a special interest or prerogative. You'll hear it used this way: "If you want to hire a surfboard, see Moki; that's his *kuleana.*"

kupuna: grandparent; elder.

lā: sun.

lamalama: to fish with a torch.

lānai: a porch, a balcony, an outdoor living room.

lani: heaven, the sky.

lauhala: the leaf of the *hala,* or pandanus tree, widely used in handicrafts.

lei: a garland of flowers.

lōlō: feeble-minded, crazy.

luna: a plantation overseer or foreman.

mahalo: thank you.

mahina: moon.

makai: toward the ocean.

mālama: to take care of, preserve, protect

malihini: a newcomer to the Islands.

mana: the spiritual power that the Hawaiians believe inhabits all things and creatures.

manō: shark.

manuahi: free, gratis.

mauka: toward the mountains.

mauna: mountain.

mele: a Hawaiian song or chant, often of epic proportions.

Mele Kalikimaka: Merry Christmas (a transliteration from the English phrase).

Menehune: a Hawaiian pixie. The Menehune were a legendary race of little people who accomplished prodigious work, such as building fishponds and temples in the course of a single night.

moana: the ocean.

mu'umu'u: the voluminous dress in which the missionaries enveloped Hawaiian women. Culturally sensitive locals have embraced the Hawaiian spelling but often shorten the spoken word to "mu'u." Most English dictionaries include the spelling "muumuu."

nani: beautiful.

nui: big.

'ohana: family.

'ono: delicious.

pāhoehoe: smooth, unbroken, satiny lava.

palapala: document, printed matter.

pali: a cliff, precipice.

pānini: prickly pear cactus.

paniolo: a Hawaiian cowboy, a rough transliteration of *español,* the language of the Islands' earliest cowboys.

pau: finished, done.

pilikia: trouble. The Hawaiian word is much more widely used here than its English equivalent.

pū: large conch shell used to trumpet the start of luau and other special events.

puka: a hole.

pule: prayer, blessing. Often performed before a meal or event.

pupule: crazy, like the celebrated Princess Pupule. This word has replaced its English equivalent in local usage.

pu'u: volcanic cinder cone.

tūtū: grandmother

waha: mouth.

wahine: a female, a woman, a wife, and a sign on the ladies' room door; the plural form is *wāhine.*

wai: freshwater, as opposed to saltwater, which is *kai.*

wailele: waterfall.

wikiwiki: to hurry, hurry up (since this is a reduplication of *wiki,* quick, neither *W* is pronounced as a *V*).

2

Travel Smart HAWAIIAN VOCABULARY

Great Itineraries

Road Trip: The Best of Kauai in 8 Days

Kauai is small, but its major byways generally circumnavigate the island with no through-roads, so it can take more time than you expect to get around. Taking a boat ride along Napali Coast, hiking the Kalalau Trail, kayaking the Wailua River, marveling at a waterfall, watching whales at Kilauea Lighthouse, shopping for gifts at Koloa Town shops—there's so much to see and do. Rather than trying to check everything off your list in one fell swoop, choose your favorites and devote a full day to the experiences, allowing time to relax.

DAY 1: SETTLE IN ON THE EAST SIDE

The East Side of the island is a convenient area to make a home base. Stay here, and you'll have the easiest access to most of the island's top attractions. Fresh off a long flight, you'll likely want to relax by the pool at your hotel/condo or walk the coastal path at **Kealia Beach Park,** just north of funky Kapaa Town. The far end near the rock jetty is for safe swimming and easy bodysurfing. There are plenty of welcoming, casual dining options around Kapaa, or try **Hukilau Lanai** for a fantastic first meal.

Logistics: Wailua/Kapaa traffic can be a nightmare, so avoid rush and midday times. It's 10 miles from the airport to Kapaa, but drive times can vary from 15 to 35 minutes. Kealia Beach is three minutes north of Kapaa and has plenty of parking.

DAY 2: TAKE IT ALL IN

For an incredible, and literal, overview of Kauai's beaches, forests, canyons, waterfalls, and ocean, take a morning helicopter trip out of Lihue with **Blue Hawaiian Helicopters** or **Jack Harter Helicopters**. These are expensive trips, but the images of the rolling verdant carpet far below will linger long in your memory. A rainy-day way to get a good island overview is with a visit to the **Kauai Museum.** Afternoon is free for beach time or laid-back shopping in Kapaa Town. An alternative is to have lunch in Lihue and lounge on **Kalapaki Beach.**

Logistics: Kalapaki Bay is five minutes south of Lihue.

DAY 3: EAST SIDE OFFERINGS

Check out the Kapaa/Wailua area, which has a little something for everyone. Rent a bike at **Kauai Cycle** and this time coast along Ke Ala Hele Makalae, enjoying the coastal path's ocean views and invigorating fresh air. Or take a moderate, 2-mile (one-way) hike on the **Sleeping Giant Trail** for panoramic vistas of the entire East Side. Then get back on the main road for a short drive up to **Opaekaa Falls,** one of the Wailua River's mightiest displays, and nearby temple ruins.

Logistics: From mid-Kapaa to the starting point of the Sleeping Giant Trail is 3 miles; just avoid rush hours.

DAY 4: SOUTH SHORE SIGHTS

Start with a hike on the **Mahaulepu Heritage Trail** near Poipu for wondrous ocean-side views of pristine beaches and craggy ledges. A quick dip at **Poipu Beach Park** will refresh your limbs after your hike. Grab lunch in Poipu or Koloa, then drive down Lawai Road to **Spouting Horn,** Kauai's version of Old Faithful. Across the road is the **National Tropical Botanical Garden,** where you can tour beautiful grounds of exotic flora and learn about biodiversity in Hawaii and the Pacific.

Logistics: The Mahaulepu Trail is about 10 minutes from Koloa Town. From there to Spouting Horn is about another 10-minute drive.

DAY 5: AT SEA ON NAPALI COAST

Choose your preferred watercraft (Zodiac for adventure rafting or catamaran for pleasure cruising) and depart from the boat harbor in Eleele for an unforgettable journey along the breathtakingly scenic Napali Coast. Most trips are about four hours and usually include a light snack; some include drinks. Don't schedule anything too demanding afterward, as you'll likely be pleasantly tired, and you'll want to savor the memories of the sights you just beheld. If you wish, though, just a mile from Eleele is Hanapepe, an artsy, historic small town that's great for a stroll and some browsing in locally owned shops and galleries; don't miss the Swinging Bridge.

Logistics: Eleele is about 16 miles west of Lihue Airport.

DAY 6: EXPLORE NATURAL WONDERS

In the mountains of Kokee on the West Side, you'll enjoy the splendor of the mountains, the ocean, the sunlight, and the crisper air. Stop along the way at the scenic overlooks of **Waimea Canyon** and be dazzled by the interplay of light and shadow as the sun moves across this spectacular landscape. Take a break at Kanaloahuluhulu Meadow to have lunch at **Kokee Lodge** and check out the **Kokee Natural History Museum** next door (a big trail map is on the porch). Continue another 5 miles or so to the postcard-worthy **Kalalau Lookout.**

Logistics: Drive up from Waimea Town and come down on the Kekaha side, which is less steep and best for sunset watching. It's about 30 minutes straight up to the meadow, but scenic stops stretch it out.

DAY 7: NORTH SHORE PLAYGROUND

The North Shore's plentiful sights and activities include swimming, surfing, golf, tennis, botanical gardens, hiking, and horseback riding. Visit **Limahuli Garden & Preserve** in Haena, which features an ancient Hawaiian layout of a typical self-sufficient community, or **Na Aina Kai Botanical Gardens & Sculpture Park**, with its artistic side and working-farm focus. At **Kilauea Lighthouse,** behold the cliffs, exotic birds, and magnificent coastal view. Spend the rest of your day at **Hanalei Bay** swimming, taking a surf lesson, or just strolling the 2-mile crescent-shape beach. For the family, a round of minigolf at **Anaina Hou Community Park** in Kilauea can be joyful and instructive: the 18-hole layout reveals Hawaii's story through its landscaping.

Logistics: Limahuli is about a 15-minute ride west of Hanalei/Waipa by car or on the shuttle.

DAY 8: HIKE PART OF THE KALALAU TRAIL

Now experience Napali Coast from land. The moderate trek to Hanakapiai Beach offers incredible views peering straight down over the sea, a visit to a dramatic beach (don't swim), and a hike up a stream to a 300-foot waterfall. You won't be taking the arduous 11-mile journey (one-way) of the entire coastal Kalalau Trail, so take your time and enjoy Kauai's scenery. Be sure to secure a permit if you plan to hike beyond Hanakapiai or camp.

Logistics: Well ahead of your trip, check ⊕ *gohaena.com* for the latest reservation information for accessing the park and trailhead. It's a roller-coaster 2 miles to Hanakapiai Beach; allow an hour one-way. The hike up the valley is also 2 miles—but plan on 90 minutes each way. Factor in time to return, wear sturdy shoes, stay hydrated, and only do this hike if you're fit.

Contacts

✈ Air

AIRPORTS Honolulu International Airport (HNL). ✉ *Honolulu* ☎ *808/836–6413* ⊕ *www.hidot.hawaii. gov/airports.* **Lihue Airport (LIH).** ✉ *Lihue* ☎ *808/274–3800* ⊕ *www.hidot.hawaii. gov/airports.*

AIRPORT GREETINGS Alii Greeting Service. ✑ *res@aliigreeting-service.com* ⊕ *www. aliigreetingservice.com.* **LeiGreeting.com.** ✉ *Honolulu* ☎ *800/665–7959* ⊕ *leigreeting.com.*

GROUND TRANSPORTA-TION Kauai Luxury Transportation & Tours. ✉ *Lihue* ☎ *808/634–7260* ⊕ *kauai-luxurytransportation.com.* **SpeediShuttle.** ✉ *Lihue* ☎ *877/242–5777* ⊕ *www. speedishuttle.com.*

🚌 Bus

Kauai Bus. ✉ *Lihue* ☎ *808/246–8110* ⊕ *www. kauai.gov/transportation.*

🚗 Car

State of Hawaii Department of Transportation. ✉ *Honolulu* ☎ *808/241–3000 to report a highway problem or check traffic and roadwork* ⊕ *hidot.hawaii.gov/ highways/roadwork/kauai.*

✚ Health

Kauai Urgent Care. ✉ *4484 Pahee St., Lihue* ☎ *808/245–1532* ⊕ *www. hawaiipacifichealth.org/ wilcox.* **Kauai Veterans Memorial Hospital.** ✉ *4643 Waimea Canyon Dr., Waimea (Kauai County)* ☎ *808/338–9431* ⊕ *kauai. hhsc.org.* **Wilcox Memorial Hospital.** ✉ *3-3420 Kuhio Hwy., Lihue* ☎ *808/245–1100* ⊕ *www.hawaiipaci-chealth.org/wilcox.*

🛏 Lodging

County of Kauai Camping. ✉ *Lihue* ☎ *808/241–4463 for permits* ⊕ *www.kauai. gov.*

🧭 Tours

RECOMMENDED COMPA-NIES Atlas Cruises & Tours. ☎ *800/942–3301* ⊕ *www. atlastravelweb.com.* **Globus.** ☎ *866/755–8581* ⊕ *www.globusjourneys. com.* **Tauck.** ☎ *800/788–7885* ⊕ *www.tauck.com.*

BIRD-WATCHING Field Guides. ☎ *800/728–4953* ⊕ *www.fieldguides.com.* **Victor Emanuel Nature Tours.** ☎ *800/328–8368* ⊕ *www. ventbird.com.*

CULTURE Road Scholar. ☎ *800/454–5768* ⊕ *www. roadscholar.org.*

HIKING Sierra Club Outings. ☎ *415/977–5522* ⊕ *www. sierraclub.org/outings.*

◉ Visitor Information

GoHaena.com. ✉ *Haena* ⊕ *GoHaena.com.* **Hawaii Beach Safety.** ✑ *kauail-ifeguards@gmail.com* ⊕ *hawaiibeachsafety.com, www.kauailifeguards. org.* **Hawaii Department of Land and Natural Resources.** ⊕ *dlnr.hawaii.gov.* **Hawaii Tourism Authority.** ✉ *1801 Kalakaua Ave., 1st floor, Honolulu* ☎ *808/973–2255* ⊕ *www.gohawaii.com.* **Kauai Vacation Explorer.** ⊕ *www.kauaiexplorer. com.* **Kauai Visitors Bureau.** ✉ *4334 Rice St., #101, Lihue* ☎ *808/245–3971* ⊕ *www.gohawaii.com/ kauai.*

Chapter 3

THE NORTH SHORE

Updated by
Cheryl Crabtree

● Sights	🍴 Restaurants	🛏 Hotels	👜 Shopping	🍸 Nightlife
★★★★★	★★☆☆☆	★★☆☆☆	★★★☆☆	★☆☆☆☆

WELCOME TO THE NORTH SHORE

TOP REASONS TO GO

★ **Napali Coast.** Whether you choose to hike the stunning Napali Coast or take a boat, the views will stay with you forever.

★ **Surfing paradise.** Beautiful Hanalei Bay has spawned some of the greatest surfers in the world. Lie on the fine sand or walk the beach, stopping to picnic at the legendary Hanalei Pier.

★ **Kilauea Point National Wildlife Refuge.** Known for its lighthouse and stunning ocean views, the area is also home to numerous exotic bird colonies, including the albatross and nene (Hawaiian goose).

★ **Beaches and trails.** End-of-the-road Kee Beach is also the beginning of the Kalalau Trail. The beach is safe for novices in the summer, and snorkeling is good.

★ **Lush gardens.** In one of the most biodiverse valleys of Hawaii, the Limahuli Garden & Preserve hosts an impressive array of native Hawaiian plants and birds.

The North Shore stretches westward 17 miles along Route 56 from Kilauea Town on the island's northeastern tip to the end of the road at Kee Beach. It continues another 15 miles (no roads here, just trails) beneath the steep cliffs of iconic Napali Coast to remote Polihale State Park.

On the North Shore are the hubs of Princeville and Hanalei, plus Haena, the rural district west of Hanalei Town. Beaches, including secluded pockets with steep paths down cliffs to the shore and the sprawling 2-mile park at Hanalei Bay, line the shore. Hanalei Stream flows from the mountains down to the bay and demarcates the North Shore's east and west sides.

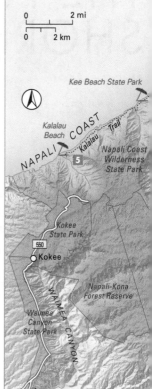

1 Hanalei. With magical waterfalls and a classic bay, Hanalei is a top draw on Kauai even if the town center can become overcrowded.

2 Haena. Deep-blue surf and a refurbished visitor area make Haena a great choice for nature walks. In summer, bring your snorkel.

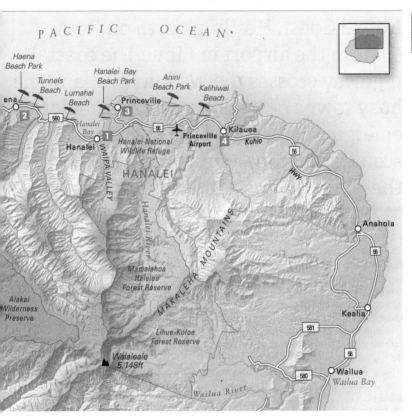

3 Princeville. This upscale community is the place to golf, play tennis, surf, and access isolated beaches. There's also a small shopping center.

4 Kilauea. The former plantation town has grown into more than a bedroom community. The standout Kilauea Lighthouse attracts endangered birds.

5 Napali Coast. On the northwest side of the island, Kauai's unforgettable coastline—a dramatic series of emerald-green cliffs and waterfalls—can be seen by hiking, boat, or helicopter ride.

The North Shore of Kauai includes the environs of Kilauea, Princeville, Hanalei, and Haena, as well as the world-famous Napali Coast. Heading north on Route 56 from the airport in Lihue, the coastal highway crosses the Wailua River and the busy towns of Wailua and Kapaa before emerging into a decidedly rural and scenic landscape, with expansive views of the island's rugged interior mountains.

As the two-lane highway turns west and narrows, it winds through spectacular scenery and passes the posh resort community of Princeville before dropping down into Hanalei Valley. Here it narrows further and becomes a federally recognized scenic roadway, replete with one-lane bridges (the local etiquette is for five to seven cars to cross at a time, before yielding to those on the other side), hairpin turns, and heart-stopping coastal vistas. The road ends at Haena State Park and Kee Beach, where the ethereal rain forests and fluted sea cliffs of Napali Coast Wilderness State Park begin. Seeing Napali Coast by boat, on foot, or by helicopter is a highlight of any trip to Kauai.

Floods in 2018 caused major physical changes to the North Shore, including landslide areas and general infrastructure chaos. One result is a permitting system for visitors to Haena State Park, which begins with a check-in system at the park. Rules limit vehicles to 900 per day, compared with the previous average of 2,000 per day. The result is a less crowded and calmer atmosphere at Kee Beach.

From Kee Beach, you can hike 2 miles to Hanakapiai Beach on Napali Coast, and as long as you've come this far, you might as well take the 2-mile hike into Hanakapiai Valley to a towering 300-foot waterfall. Along the way you'll see mind-blowing scenes of coastal beauty.

In winter, Kauai's North Shore receives more rainfall than other areas of the island. Don't let this deter you from visiting. The clouds drift over mountains, including Namolokama, creating a mysterious mood, and then, in a blink, disappear, rewarding you with mountains laced with a dozen waterfalls or more. The views of the mountain—as well as the sunsets over the ocean—from Hanalei Bay and Kee Beach are fantastic.

The North Shore attracts all kinds—from celebrities to surfers. In fact, the late Andy Irons, three-time world surfing champion, along with his brother Bruce and legend Laird Hamilton, grew up riding waves along the North Shore.

Planning

Planning Your Time

Plan to spend at least two days exploring North Shore attractions, and perhaps some extra time to lounge on the sand or by a resort pool or to join a boat or helicopter trip along Napali Coast. Count on a full day to experience Haena and the west, where you can hike in Haena State Park, stroll out to Kee Beach, visit Limahuli Garden, and stop in Hanalei Town to shop, dine, and wander along the bay. Head to the east side another day to check out Kilauea Point National Wildlife Refuge and Kilauea Lighthouse, historic Kilauea Town, and the Princeville area golf courses and restaurants.

Getting Here and Around

Route 56 goes from Lihue on the East Side to the North Shore, where only one road leads beyond Princeville to Kee Beach at the western end of the North Shore: Route 560. Hanalei's commercial stretch fronts this route, and there is parking at the shopping compounds on each side of the road. After Hanalei, parking is restricted to two main areas, Haena Beach Park and a lot at Haena State Park, and Route 560 has few pull-out areas. Traffic and parking have become major concerns as the North Shore has gained popularity, so be prepared to be patient.

There is no access by car to Napali Coast; you have to hike, take a boat, or view it from a helicopter. See ⊕ *getaroundkauai.com* for information on various transportation options on the island, including shuttles, buses, rideshares, bike and motorbike rentals, and walking guides.

Beaches

North Shore beaches are famed for their drop-dead gorgeous scenery, and beachgoers set up chairs and towels everywhere to gaze at white sands and turquoise waters set against a backdrop of mountains, streams, and waterfalls. Keep in mind that reservations are needed if you want to visit popular Kee Beach and Haena State Park; see ⊕ *gohaena. com.*

The waves on the North Shore can be big—and we mean huge—in winter, drawing crowds to witness nature's spectacle. By contrast, in summer the waters can be completely serene. But treacherous currents easily pull people out to sea at any time of year. Some beaches, including Hanalei Bay, Kee, and Anini, have lifeguards, showers, and more crowds, while others with fewer amenities attract those seeking more seclusion. ■ **TIP→ Avoid swimming and water activities unless a lifeguard is present, and heed all warning signs posted at the beach.**

Parking lots often fill quickly; it's best to arrive early to get a spot, and do not park on residents' lawns or block their driveways or you'll pay a hefty fine. One final tip: the rule of thumb is to head south or west when it rains in the north.

Hotels

The North Shore is mountainous and wet, which accounts for its rugged, lush landscape. Posh resorts and condominiums await you at Princeville, a community with dreamy views, an excellent golf course, and lovely sunsets. It maintains the lion's share of North Shore accommodations—primarily luxury hotel rooms and condos built on a plateau overlooking the sea. The St. Regis Princeville Resort here was sold to 1 Hotels; after extensive remodeling it will reopen in fall 2022 as 1 Hotel Hanalei Bay. Hanalei, a bayside town in a broad valley, has a smattering of hotel rooms and numerous vacation rentals, many within walking distance of the beach. Prices tend to be high in this resort area. If you want to do extensive sightseeing on other parts of the island, be prepared for a long drive—one that's very dark at night.

Hotel and restaurant reviews have been shortened. For full information, see Fodors.com. Hotel prices in the reviews are the lowest cost of a standard double room in high season. Restaurant prices in the reviews are the average cost of a main course at dinner, or if dinner is not served, at lunch.

WHAT IT COSTS in U.S. Dollars			
$	$$	$$$	$$$$
RESTAURANTS			
under $17	$17–$26	$27–$35	over $35
HOTELS			
under $180	$180–$260	$261–$340	over $340

Restaurants

Because of the North Shore's isolation, restaurants have enjoyed a captive audience of visitors who don't want to make the long, dark trek into Kapaa Town on the East Side for dinner. As a result, dining has been characterized by expensive fare that isn't especially memorable. Fortunately, the situation is slowly improving as new restaurants open and others change hands or menus.

Still, dining on the North Shore can be pricier than on other parts of the island, and not especially family-friendly. Most of the restaurants are found in Hanalei Town or the Princeville resorts. Consequently, you'll encounter delightful mountain and ocean views, but just one restaurant with

oceanfront dining. In a pinch, you can pick up poke bowls, sushi, hot entrées, sandwiches, and salads at the well-stocked Foodland grocery store in the Princeville Shopping Center.

Hanalei, Haena, and West

Hanalei is 32 miles northwest of Lihue; Haena is 5 miles northwest of Hanalei.

Crossing the historic one-lane bridge into Hanalei reveals old Hawaii, including working taro farms, poi making, and evenings of throwing horseshoes at Black Pot Beach Park—the latter found unmarked (as many places are on Kauai) at the east end of Hanalei Bay Beach Park. Although the current real-estate boom on Kauai has attracted mainland millionaires to build estate homes on the few remaining parcels of land in Hanalei, there's still plenty to see and do. It's *the* gathering place on the North Shore. Restaurants, shops, and people-watching here are among the best on the island, and you won't find a single brand-name, chain, or big-box store around—unless you count surf brands like Quiksilver and Billabong.

The beach and river at Hanalei offer swimming, snorkeling, bodyboarding, surfing, and kayaking. Those hanging around at sunset often congregate at the Hanalei Pavilion, where a husband-and-wife slack-key-guitar–playing combo makes impromptu appearances. There's an old rumor, since quashed by the local newspaper, the *Garden Island,* that says Hanalei was the inspiration for the song "Puff, the Magic Dragon," performed by the 1960s singing sensation Peter, Paul, and Mary. Even with the newspaper's clarification, some tours still point out the shape of the dragon carved into the mountains encircling the town.

Once you pass through Hanalei Town, the road shrinks even more as you skirt

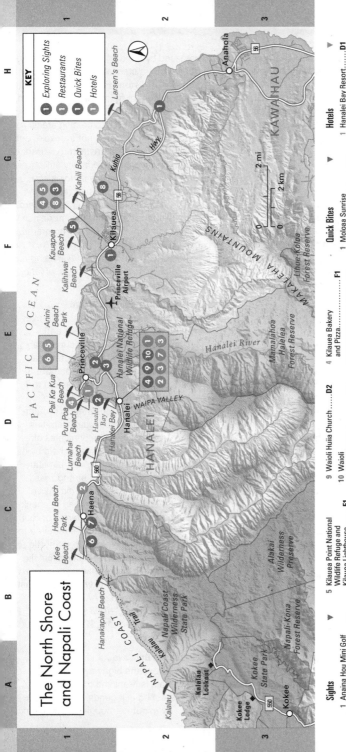

The North Shore and Napali Coast

KEY

1 Exploring Sights
1 Restaurants
1 Quick Bites
1 Hotels

PACIFIC OCEAN

NAPALI COAST

Larsen's Beach

Kahili Beach

Kauapea Beach

Kalihiwai Beach

Anini Beach Park

Pali Ke Kua Beach

Puu Poa Beach

Lumahai Beach

Haena Beach Park

Kee Beach

Hanakapiai Beach

Princeville

Princeville Airport

Hanalei

Hanalei Bay

Haena

Anahola

Kilauea

Kalalau

Kokee

WAIPA VALLEY

HANALEI

Hanalei River

Hanalei National Wildlife Refuge

MAKALEHA MOUNTAINS

Mamalahoa Halelea Forest Reserve

Lihue-Koloa Forest Reserve

KAWAIHAU

Napali-Kona Forest Reserve

Napali Coast Wilderness State Park

Alakai Wilderness Preserve

Kokee State Park

Kalalau Lookout

Kokee Lodge

Kokee

Kuhio Hwy

560

56

2 mi

2 km

0

0

Sights

1 Anaina Hou Mini Golf & Gardens.........F1
2 Hanalei Pier.............D1
3 Hanalei Valley Overlook.........E1
4 Hoopulapula Haraguchi Rice Mill.........D2
5 Kilauea Point National Wildlife Refuge and Kilauea Lighthouse.........F1
6 Limahuli Garden & Preserve.........C1
7 Maniniholo Dry Cave.........C1
8 Na Aina Kai Botanical Gardens & Sculpture Park.........G1
9 Waioli Huiia Church.........D2
10 Waioli Mission House.........D2

Restaurants

1 Bar Acuda.........D2
2 Hanalei Dolphin.........D2
3 Hanalei Gourmet.........D2
4 Kilauea Bakery and Pizza.........F1
5 Kilauea Market + Cafe...F1
6 Nanea Restaurant and Bar.........E1
7 Postcards Café.........D2
8 Sushi Girl Kauai.........F1

Quick Bites

1 Moloaa Sunrise Juice Bar & Fruit Stand..H2
2 North Shore General Store.........E1
3 Trilogy.........F1

Hotels

1 Hanalei Bay Resort.....D1
2 Hanalei Colony Resort...C1
3 Hanalei Inn.........D2
4 1 Hotel Hanalei Bay.....D1
5 Westin Princeville Ocean Resort Villas.....E1

the coast and pass through Haena. Blind corners, quick turns, and one-lane bridges force slow driving along this scenic stretch across the Lumahai and Wainiha Valleys. The road ends at Kee Beach and the Haena State Park entrance and parking lot.

◉ Sights

Hanalei Pier

MARINA/PIER | FAMILY | Built in 1892, the historic Hanalei Pier can be seen from miles across the bay and is a great spot for photos or taking a leisurely stroll; it attracts a gathering every sunset. The pier came to fame when it was featured in the award-winning 1957 movie *South Pacific*. Fishers fish here, and picnickers picnic. The pier was refurbished after flooding in 2018. ⊠ *Weke Rd., Hanalei.*

★ Hanalei Valley Overlook

VIEWPOINT | Dramatic mountains and a patchwork of neat taro farms bisected by the wide Hanalei River make this one of Hawaii's loveliest views, even with the flood damage it sustained in 2018. The fertile Hanalei Valley has been planted with taro since perhaps AD 700, save for an 80-year-long foray into rice that ended in 1960. (The historic Haraguchi Rice Mill is all that remains of that era.) Many taro farmers lease land within the 900-acre Hanalei National Wildlife Refuge, helping to provide wetland habitat for four species of endangered Hawaiian waterbirds. ⊠ *Rte. 56, across from Foodland, Princeville.*

Hoopulapula Haraguchi Rice Mill

FARM/RANCH | FAMILY | Rice grew in the taro fields of Hanalei Valley for almost 80 years—beginning in the 1880s and ending in the early 1960s—and today this history is embodied in the Haraguchi family, whose ancestors threshed, hulled, polished, separated, graded, and bagged rice in their 3,500-square-foot rice mill. It was demolished once by fire and twice by hurricanes, and was damaged by flooding in 2018 and 2021. Rebuilt to the standards of the National Register of Historic Places, the mill—with neighboring taro fields—is typically open for tours on a limited schedule mainly due to endangered-bird nesting areas. At this writing, tours were not available, but check the website or Instagram (@HanaleiTaro) for updates. The family still farms taro on the one-time rice paddies and also operates the Hanalei Taro & Juice kiosk in Hanalei Town; see ⊕ *hanaleitaro. com*. All proceeds from the historic rice mill go to nonprofit education programs. ⊠ *5–5070 Kuhio Hwy., Hanalei* ✚ *Next to Kayak Kauai* ☎ *808/651–3399* ⊕ *haraguchiricemill.org* ⚏ *$70 tour by reservation when available.*

★ Limahuli Garden & Preserve

GARDEN | FAMILY | Narrow Limahuli Valley, with its fluted mountain peaks and ancient stone taro terraces, creates an unparalleled setting for this botanical garden and nature preserve, one of the most gorgeous spots on Kauai and the crown jewel of the National Tropical Botanical Garden. Dedicated to protecting native plants and unusual varieties of taro, it represents the principles of conservation and stewardship held by its founder, Juliet Rice Wichman. Limahuli's primordial beauty and strong *mana* (spiritual power) eclipse the extensive botanical collection. Call ahead to check if guided tours are being offered, or tour on your own. A reservation is required to park here, though North Shore Shuttle riders are exempt. ◼ **TIP→ Check out the quality gift shop and revolutionary compost toilet, and be prepared to walk a somewhat steep hillside.** ⊠ *5–8291 Kuhio Hwy., Hanalei* ☎ *808/826–1053* ⊕ *www.ntbg. org* ⚏ *Self-guided tour $25, guided tour $100 (when available).*

Maniniholo Dry Cave

CAVE | Across the highway from Haena Beach Park is Maniniholo Dry Cave, a place steeped in legends. You can walk for a few minutes through a 30-yard-long cave, which darkens and becomes more claustrophobic as you glide across its sandy floor, hearing the drips down the walls and wondering at its past. Legend has it that Maniniholo was the head fisherman of the Menehune—Kauai's quasi-mythical first inhabitants. After gathering too much food to carry, Maniniholo's men stored the excess under a cliff overnight. When he returned in the morning, the food had vanished, and he blamed the imps living in the cliff's cracks. He and his men dug into the cliff to find and destroy the imps, leaving behind the dry cave. ⊠ *Rte. 560, Haena* 🎟 *Free.*

Waioli Huiia Church

CHURCH | Like the Waioli Mission House behind it, this little church is an exquisite representation of New England architecture crossed with Hawaiian thatched buildings. Designated a National Historic Landmark, the church—affiliated with the United Church of Christ—doesn't go unnoticed right alongside Route 560 in downtown Hanalei, and its doors are often wide open (from 10 am to 2 pm, give or take), inviting inquisitive visitors in for a look around. During Hurricane Iniki's visit in 1992, which brought sustained winds of 160 mph and wind gusts up to 220 mph, the church was lifted off its foundation but, thankfully, it has been lovingly restored. Services are held at 10 am on Sunday, with many hymns sung in Hawaiian and often accompanied by piano, ukulele, and hula. ⊠ *5–5363A Kuhio Hwy., Hanalei* 🕿 *808/826–6253* ⊕ *www.waiolihuiiachurch.org.*

Waioli Mission House

HISTORIC HOME | Built by missionaries William and Mary Alexander, this 1837 home has tidy New England–style architecture and formal koa-wood furnishings that epitomize the prim and proper missionary influence. Informative guided tours offer a fascinating peek into the private lives of Kauai's early white residents. One-hour private guided tours are available for a requested donation; reservations are required, so call to reserve a day and time. ⊠ *5–5373 Kuhio Hwy., Hanalei* 🕿 *808/826–1528* ⊕ *grovefarm.org/waioli-imissionhouse* 🎟 *$10 requested tour donation.*

🏖 Beaches

★ Haena Beach Park

BEACH | This drive-up beach park favored by campers year-round has a wide bay named Makua bordered by two large reef systems, creating favorable waves for skilled surfers during peak winter conditions. Entering the water can be dangerous in winter when the big swells roll in. In July and August, waters at this same beach are usually as calm as a lake, and throughout summer this is a premier snorkeling site. It's not unusual to find a food vendor parked here, selling sandwiches and drinks out of a converted bread van. Adjacent to this beach is Tunnels Beach.

Parking is extremely limited (the lot typically fills up by 8:30 am), and all vehicles illegally parked outside of designated parking zones are subject to fees and towing. You can also park your car in the shuttle parking lot in Waipa, west of Hanalei Town, and board the North Shore Shuttle for a ride to the beach park ($35 round-trip with seven stops); see ⊕ *go-haena.com* for details and reservations. **Amenities:** food and drink; lifeguards; parking (free); showers; toilets. **Best for:** snorkeling; surfing; walking. ⊠ *Near end of Rte. 560, Haena* ✛ *Across from Maniniholo Dry Cave* 🎟 *Free.*

Hanakapiai Beach

BEACH | If you're not up for the full 11-mile haul to Kalalau Beach, you can see part of Napali Coast via a 2-mile hike to Hanakapiai Beach, which fronts a tropical valley. It'll take about two hours from the starting point at the Kee Beach parking area in Haena State Park, and you'll have plenty of company on the trail. You cannot hike

the Kalalu Trail beyond this beach without a permit. This is no longer a secluded beach, although it is still wilderness, and you'll find no amenities except pit toilets.

We do not recommend swimming or any water activities at this beach. The ocean here is what locals like to call "confused," and Hanakapiai Bay has been the site of numerous drownings. In winter, surf often eats up the beach, exposing lava-rock boulders backing the sand. Be cautious when crossing the stream that runs through the valley, as it can quickly flood, stranding hikers on the wrong side. This has resulted in helicopter rescues and even deaths, as people are swept out to sea while attempting to cross. ■ TIP→ **A new bridge makes the passage easier, but don't attempt to cross during heavy rain. Amenities:** toilets. **Best for:** sunset. ⊠ *Napali Coast State Wilderness Park, Kalalau Trail, End of Rte. 560, 7 miles west of Hanalei, Haena* ⊕ *dlnr.hawaii. gov/dsp* ⊠ *$5 nonresident entrance fee for Haena State Park; $10 per vehicle for parking for nonresidents* ⊊ *Trailhead for hike to beach starts at Kee Beach; see* ⊕ *gohaena.com for information about parking reservations.*

★ **Hanalei Bay**

BEACH | FAMILY | This 2-mile crescent beach cradles a wide bay in a setting that is quintessential Hawaii: the sea is on one side, and behind you are the mountains, often ribboned with waterfalls and changing color in the shifting light. In winter, Hanalei Bay boasts some of the biggest onshore surf breaks in the state, attracting world-class surfers, and the beach is plenty wide enough for sunbathing and strolling. In summer, the bay is transformed—calm waters lap the beach, sailboats moor in the bay, and outrigger-canoe paddlers ply the sea. Pack the cooler, haul out the beach umbrellas, and don't forget the beach toys because Hanalei Bay is worth scheduling for an entire day, maybe two. Several county beach parks, some with pavilions, can be found along the bay: Waioli, Black Pot, and Hanalei Pavilion (with ample facilities). **Amenities:** lifeguards; parking (free); showers; toilets. **Best for:** sunset; surfing; swimming; walking. ⊠ *Weke Rd., Hanalei* ⊠ *Free.*

★ **Kee Beach**

BEACH | Highway 560 on the North Shore literally dead-ends at this beach, pronounced "*kay*-eh," which is also the start of the challenging, permit-required 11-mile Kalalau Trail on Napali Coast and a culturally significant area to Native Hawaiians, who still use an ancient *heiau* (a stone platform used as a place of worship) dedicated to hula. (It's not appropriate to hang out on the platform or leave offerings there; stay at a respectful distance.) The setting is gorgeous, with Makana (a prominent peak that Hollywood dubbed "Bali Hai" in the blockbuster musical *South Pacific*) imposing itself on the lovely coastline and lots of lush tropical vegetation.

The small beach is protected by a reef—except during high surf—creating a small, sandy-bottom lagoon that's a popular snorkeling spot. There can be a strong current in winter. A mandatory permit system limits guests and prevents overcrowding. Unless you are a Hawaii resident with identification, you must reserve a spot online (reservations open 30 days prior); the prized spaces sell out weeks in advance. See ⊕ *gohaena.com* for reservations. Passes are valid during specified time periods. The parking area is ⅓ mile from the beach on a path partially on a boardwalk, so be prepared to lug your beach gear. Kee Beach is a great place to watch the sunset lighting up Napali Coast. **Amenities:** lifeguards; parking (fee); showers; toilets. **Best for:** snorkeling; sunset; swimming; walking. ⊠ *Haena State Park, end of Rte. 560* ✛ *7 miles west of Hanalei* ⊕ *dlnr.hawaii.gov/ dsp* ⊠ *$5 per person nonresident entry fee, plus $10 for nonresident vehicle parking.*

Hanalei Bay attracts big-wave surfers in the winter and then becomes a calm haven for swimmers in the summer.

Lumahai Beach

BEACH | Famous as the beach where Nurse Nellie washed that man right out of her hair in *South Pacific,* Lumahai is picturesque, with a river and ironwood grove on the western end and stands of hala (pandanus) trees and black lava rock on the eastern side. In between is a long stretch of olivine-flecked sand that can be wide or narrow, depending on the surf. The beach can be accessed in two places from the highway; one involves a steep hike from the road. Avoid swimming and water activities here—the ocean can be dangerous, with a snapping shore break year-round and monster swells in the winter; in addition, the current can be strong near the river. Parking is very limited, along the road or in a rough dirt lot near the river. **Amenities:** none. **Best for:** solitude; sunset; walking. ⊠ *Hanalei* ✛ *On winding section of Rte. 560, near mile marker 5* ⬚ *Free.*

🍴 Restaurants

⭐ Bar Acuda

$$$$ | **TAPAS** | Hip and pricey, this tapas bar is a top place in Hanalei in terms of flavor and creativity, with food that's often organic and consistently remarkable. The dining room is super-casual but chic, with a welcoming bar and a nice porch for outdoor dining. **Known for:** interesting wine list; sophisticated, eclectic cuisine; short, often-changing menu with innovative specials. ⑤ *Average main: $40* ⊠ *Hanalei Center, 5–5161 Kuhio Hwy., Hanalei* ☎ *808/826–7081* ⊕ *www.cudahanalei.com* ⊘ *No lunch. Closed Sun. and Mon.*

⭐ The Hanalei Dolphin

$$$ | **SEAFOOD** | Fresh fish caught in local waters by local fishers take star billing at this upscale, tropical-theme restaurant and sushi lounge on the banks of the Hanalei River. There are also many land-based dishes on the menu, including Hawaiian and *haole* (white-person) chicken, beef tenderloin, and steaks. **Known for:** fresh local ingredients; extensive wine and sake list; on-site fish market also carries cheeses and steaks. ⑤ *Average main: $28* ✉ *5–5016 Kuhio Hwy., Hanalei* ☎ *808/826–6113* ⊕ *www.hanaleidolphin.com* ◷ *No lunch Mon.–Sat.*

The Hanalei Gourmet

$$ | AMERICAN | Hanalei's restored old schoolhouse holds an airy restaurant offering dolphin-safe tuna, low-sodium meats, fresh-baked breads, and homemade desserts, as well as a casual atmosphere where both families and the sports-watching crowd can feel equally comfortable. Lunch and dinner menus feature sandwiches, burgers, hearty salads, a variety of *pupus* (appetizers), and nightly specials of fresh local fish. **Known for:** fish taco nights; friendly bar; consistently good food. ⑤ *Average main: $26* ✉ *Hanalei Center, 5–5161 Kuhio Hwy., Hanalei* ☎ *808/826–2524* ⊕ *www.hanaleigourmet.com.*

Postcards Café

$$$$ | AMERICAN | This plantation-cottage restaurant has a menu full of seafood but also offers additive-free vegetarian and vegan options. Top menu picks include crispy leek salad with buckwheat noodles, miso-chocolate beef short ribs, and grilled yucca. **Known for:** desserts with no refined sugar; meat-free options; local-market fish; cozy dining room in historic setting. ⑤ *Average main: $38* ✉ *5–5075A Kuhio Hwy., Hanalei* ☎ *808/826–1191* ⊕ *postcardscafe.com* ◷ *No lunch. Closed Sun. and Mon.*

🛏 Hotels

Hanalei Colony Resort

$$$$ | RESORT | The only true beachfront resort on Kauai's North Shore, Hanalei Colony is a laid-back, go-barefoot kind of resort sandwiched between towering mountains and the sea. **Pros:** well-maintained units with Hawaiian-style

---

Mai Tais 🍸

Hard to believe, but the cocktail known around the world as the mai tai has been around only since 1944. While the recipe has changed slightly over the years, the original formula, created by bar owner Victor J. "Trader Vic" Bergeron, included 2 ounces 17-year-old J. Wray & Nephew rum over shaved ice, ½ ounce Holland DeKuyper orange curaçao, ¼ ounce Trader Vic's rock candy syrup, ½ ounce French Garnier orgeat syrup, and the juice of one fresh lime. Done the right way, this tropical drink still lives up to the name "mai tai!"— Tahitian for "out of this world!"

---

furnishings; kitchens in units; private, quiet property. **Cons:** no TVs, room phones, or air-conditioning (rooms have ceiling fans); damp in winter; weak cell-phone reception. ⑤ *Rooms from: $475* ✉ *5–7130 Kuhio Hwy., Haena* ☎ *808/826–6235, 800/628–3004* ⊕ *www.hcr.com* ➹ *48 units* ☺ *No Meals.*

Hanalei Inn

$ | APARTMENT | If you're looking for lodgings that won't break the bank and put you just a block from gorgeous Hanalei Bay, look no further, as this is literally the only choice among the town's pricey vacation rentals. **Pros:** coin-operated laundry on-site; quick walk to beach, bus stop, and shops; full kitchen. **Cons:** older property; daytime traffic noise; strict cancellation policy. ⑤ *Rooms from: $179* ✉ *5–5468 Kuhio Hwy., Hanalei* ☎ *808/826–9333, 877/769–5484* ⊕ *www.hanaleiinn.net* ➹ *4 studios* ☺ *No Meals.*

🍸 Nightlife

The Hanalei Gourmet Bar

BARS | The sleepy North Shore stays awake—until 10:30, that is—each evening in this small, convivial deli and bar inside Hanalei's restored old school building. There's local live Hawaiian, jazz, rock, and folk music on Saturday and Sunday evenings. ⊠ *Hanalei Center, 5–5161 Kuhio Hwy., Hanalei* ☎ *808/826–2524* ⊕ *www.hanaleigourmet.com.*

Tahiti Nui

BARS | This venerable and funky institution in sleepy Hanalei still offers its famous luau at 5 on Tuesday and Wednesday evenings, although the bar is the big attraction. The spirits of locals and visitors alike are always high at this popular hangout, which features live nightly entertainment and Hawaiian music on Friday evening. It's open until 1 am on weekends. ⊠ *5–5134 Kuhio Hwy., Hanalei* ☎ *808/826–6277* ⊕ *www.thenui. com.*

🎟 Performing Arts

Hanalei Slack Key Concerts

CONCERTS | Relax to the instrumental music form created by Hawaiian *paniolo* (cowboys) in the early 1800s. Shows are Wednesday in Kapaa at All Saints' Church and Tuesday at the Princeville Community Center. If you're looking for a scenic setting, though, head to Hale Halawai Ohana O Hanalei on Friday and Sunday; it's *mauka* (toward the mountains) down a dirt access road across from St. William Catholic Church (Malolo Road) and then left down another dirt road. ⊠ *5–5299 Kuhio Hwy., Hanalei* ☎ *808/826–1469* ⊕ *www.hawaiianslackkeyguitar.com* 🎫 *From $10.*

🛍 Shopping

Hanalei's two shopping centers, directly across from each other, offer more than you might expect in a remote, relaxed town. The boutiques, eateries, and services are mostly locally owned.

Ching Young Village

SHOPPING CENTER | This popular, family-run shopping center has its roots in the Chinese immigrants who came to Hawaii in the early 19th century. Hanalei's only full-service grocery store is here, along with other shops useful to locals and visitors, such as a music shop selling ukuleles and CDs, jewelry stores, art galleries, a surf shop, a variety store, and several smallish restaurants. ⊠ *5–5190 Kuhio Hwy., near mile marker 2, Hanalei* ☎ *808/826–7222* ⊕ *chingyoungvillage. com.*

Crystal & Gems Gallery

JEWELRY & WATCHES | Sparkling crystals of every shape, size, type, and color, as well as locally made jewelry and paintings, are sold in this amply stocked boutique. The knowledgeable staff can help you choose crystals for specific healing purposes. ⊠ *4489 Aku Rd., Hanalei* ☎ *808/826–9304* ⊕ *www.crystals-gems.com.*

Hanalei Center

SHOPPING CENTER | Once an old Hanalei schoolhouse, the Hanalei Center now houses a bevy of boutiques and restaurants. You can dig through '40s and '50s vintage memorabilia, find Polynesian artifacts, or search for that unusual gift, including fine jewelry and paper art jewelry. Buy beach gear as well as island wear and women's clothing. A full-service salon and a yoga studio are in the two-story modern addition to the center. ⊠ *5–5161 Kuhio Hwy., near mile marker 2, Hanalei* ☎ *808/826–7677.*

🏃 Activities

SPAS
Hanalei Day Spa

SPAS | The single-lane bridges may be one reason life slows down as you travel past tony Princeville; another is this boutique day spa on the grounds of the Hanalei Colony Resort in Haena, with in-spa and beachside spa services. Owner Darci Frankel is an Ayurveda practitioner with three decades of experience. Spa treatments include body wraps, scrubs, and packages for individuals and couples. Its specialty is massage: lomilomi (a traditional Hawaiian-style massage), deep tissue, relaxation, and a special four-hand massage. ⊠ *Hanalei Colony Resort, 5–7132 Kuhio Hwy., Haena* ✛ *6 miles past Hanalei* ☎ *808/826–6621* ⊕ *www. hanaleidayspa.com* ⌸ *Massages from $228.*

Princeville and Kilauea

Princeville is 4 miles northeast of Hanalei; Kilauea is 5 miles east of Princeville.

Built on a bluff offering gorgeous sea and mountain vistas, including Hanalei Bay, Princeville is the creation of a 1970s resort development. A few large hotels, world-class golf courses, and lots of condos and time-shares anchor the area.

Five miles east down Route 56, Kilauea, a former sugar plantation town, maintains its rural flavor in the midst of unrelenting gentrification encroaching on all sides. Especially noteworthy are its historic lava-rock buildings, including Christ Memorial Episcopal Church on Kolo Road and, on Keneke Street at Kilauea Road (commonly known as Lighthouse Road), the former Kong Lung Company, which is now an expensive shop.

GETTING HERE AND AROUND

There is only one main road, Route 56, through the Princeville resort area, so maneuvering a car here can be a nightmare. If you're trying to find a smaller lodging unit, get specific driving directions. Parking is available at the Princeville Shopping Center at the entrance to the resort. Kilauea, about 5 miles east on Route 56, has a public parking lot in the town center as well as parking at the end of Kilauea Road for access to the lighthouse.

◉ Sights

Anaina Hou Community Park

MINIATURE GOLF | FAMILY | The island's first miniature-golf course comes with a small botanical garden and a 300-seat theater/arts center. The 18-hole course was designed to be challenging, beautiful, and family-friendly. Replacing the typical clown's nose and spinning wheels are some water features and tropical tunnels. Surrounding each hole is plant life that walks players through different eras of Hawaiian history.

The Porter Pavilion hosts concerts, plays, private parties, and community meetings. A children's playground made from recycled materials is also on-site, and a gift shop with local products and a concessions counter make this place a fun activity for any time of day. On Saturday morning, a farmers' market adjacent to the course sells fresh Kauai produce and local goods. ⊠ *5–273 Kuhio Hwy., Kilauea* ☎ *808/828–2118* ⊕ *www.anainahou. org* ⌸ *$19, $15 kids 4–12* ⊘ *Closed Mon.–Wed.*

★ Kilauea Point National Wildlife Refuge and Kilauea Lighthouse

WILDLIFE REFUGE | FAMILY | A beacon for sea traffic since it was dedicated in 1913, this National Historic Landmark has the world's largest clamshell lens in a lighthouse and stands within a wildlife refuge where thousands of seabirds soar on the trade winds and nest on the steep ocean cliffs. It's well worth the site's modest entry fee to see nene geese (the state bird, a threatened species), white- and red-tailed tropicbirds, and more (identifiable by educational signboards), as well as native plants, dolphins, humpback whales (in season), huge winter surf, and gorgeous North Shore views. The gift shop has a great selection of books about the island's natural history and an array of unique merchandise, with all proceeds benefiting education and preservation efforts. Advance reservations are

Kilauea Lighthouse is located in Kilauea Point National Wildlife Refuge, a sanctuary for seabirds.

required via ⊕ *recreation.gov.* ⊠ *Kilauea Lighthouse Rd., Kilauea* ☎ *808/828–0384* ⊕ *www.fws.gov/kilaueapoint, www. kilaueapoint.org* 🎫 *$10, kids under 16 free* ☉ *Closed Sun.–Wed.; reservations required via* ⊕ *recreation.gov.*

★ Na Aina Kai Botanical Gardens & Sculpture Park

GARDEN | Joyce and Ed Doty's love for plants and art spans the 240 acres here and includes many different gardens, a hardwood plantation, an *ahupuaa* (a Hawaiian land division), a re-created Navajo compound, an Athabascan village, a Japanese teahouse, a hedge maze, a waterfall, and access to a sandy beach. Throughout the grounds are more than 200 bronze sculptures, one of the nation's largest collections. One popular feature is a children's garden with a 16-foot-tall Jack and the Beanstalk bronze sculpture, gecko maze, tree house, kid-size train, and, of course, a tropical jungle. Located in a residential neighborhood and hoping to maintain good neighborly relations, the nonprofit organization

limits tours (guided only). Tour lengths vary from 1½ to 5 hours. Reservations are required. ⊠ *4101 Wailapa Rd., Kilauea* ☎ *808/828–0525* ⊕ *www.naainakai.org* 🎫 *Tours from $40.*

🏖 Beaches

Anini Beach Park

BEACH | **FAMILY** | A great family park, Anini features one of the longest and widest fringing reefs in all Hawaii, creating a shallow lagoon that is good for snorkeling and kids splashing about, even though there are no lifeguards. It is safe except when surf is raging outside the reef and strong currents are created. A rip current exists between the two reefs where the boats enter and exit the beach ramp, so avoid swimming there. The entire reef follows the shoreline for some 2 miles and extends 1,600 feet offshore at its widest point. There's a narrow ribbon of sandy beach, with lots of grass and shade, as well as a county campground at the western end and a small boat ramp. **Amenities:** parking (free); showers;

County and State Beach Parks

Kauai has all kinds of beaches, from family-friendly strands to beaches best for surfers. Some are great for swimming; others are for a beach stroll.

If restrooms, covered picnic areas, showers, and easy accessibility are important to you, stick to these county and state beach parks in areas located around the island:

- Anahola Beach Park, East Side

- Anini Beach Park, North Shore

- Haena State Park, North Shore

- Hanalei Pavilion Beach Park, North Shore

- Kekaha Beach Park, West Side

- Kukuiula Small Boat Harbor, South Shore

- Lydgate State Park, East Side

- Poipu Beach Park, South Shore

- Salt Pond Beach Park, West Side

toilets. **Best for:** sunrise; swimming; walking. ⊠ *Anini Rd., off Rte. 56, Princeville* 🖃 *Free.*

Kahili Beach (*Rock Quarry Beach*)
BEACH | You wouldn't know it today, but this beach on Kilauea Bay was once an interisland steamer landing and a rock quarry. Today, it's a fairly quiet beach, although when the surf closes out many other North Shore surf spots, the break directly offshore from Kilauea Stream near the abandoned quarry is still rideable. For the regular ocean goer, summer's the best bet, although the quickly sloping ocean bottom makes for generally treacherous swimming. The stream estuary is quite beautiful, and the ironwood trees and false kamani growing in the generous sand dunes at the rear of the beach provide protection from the sun. It's a wonderful place to observe seabirds. **Amenities:** none. **Best for:** solitude; surfing; walking. ⊠ *Off Wailapa Rd., Kilauea* ✛ *Turn left on dirt road and follow to end.*

Kalihiwai Beach
BEACH | A winding road leads down a cliff face to picture-perfect Kalihiwai Beach, which fronts a bay of the same name. It's another one of those drive-up

beaches, so it's very accessible. Most people park under the grove of ironwood trees, near the stream, where young kids like to splash and older kids like to bodyboard. ⚠ **The stream carries leptospirosis, a potentially lethal bacteria that can enter through open cuts. In winter months, beware of a treacherous shore break. Summer is the only truly safe time to swim.** The local-favorite winter surf spot off the eastern edge of the beach is for advanced surfers only. Toilets here are the portable kind, and there are no showers. **Amenities:** parking (free); toilets. **Best for:** solitude; surfing; swimming; walking. ⊠ *Kalihiwai Rd., on Kilauea side of Kalihiwai Bridge, Kilauea* 🖃 *Free.*

Kauapea Beach (*Secret Beach*)
BEACH | This beach was relatively unknown—except by local fishers, of course—for a long time, hence the common reference to it as "Secret Beach." You'll understand why once you stand on the coarse white sands of Kauapea and see the solid wall of rock that runs the length of the beach, making it fairly inaccessible. For the hardy, there is a steep hike down the western end. From there, you can walk for a long way in either direction in summer. During winter,

The upscale community of Princeville is home to golf courses and isolated beaches.

big swells cut off access to sections of the beach. You may witness dolphins just offshore, and it's a great place to see seabirds, as Kilauea Point National Wildlife Refuge and its historic lighthouse lie at the eastern end. Nudity is not uncommon, though it is illegal in Hawaii. A consistent onshore break makes swimming here typically very dangerous. On big-surf days, don't go near the shoreline. **Amenities:** parking (free). **Best for:** solitude; sunrise; walking. ⊠ *Kalihiwai Rd., just past turnoff for Kilauea, Kilauea* ⌖ *Free.*

Larsen's Beach

BEACH | The long, wide fringing reef here is this beach's trademark. The waters near shore are generally too shallow for swimming; if you go in, wear a rash guard to protect against prickly sea urchins and sharp coral on the bottom. This area is known for its tricky currents, especially during periods of high surf, and has been the site of numerous drownings. It can be dangerous to snorkel here. There's some nudity at the western end.

Accessing this long strand of coarse, white sand requires hiking down a steep, rocky trail that is slippery when wet. **Amenities:** parking (free). **Best for:** solitude; sunrise; walking. ⊠ *Off Koolau Rd., Kilauea* ⌖ *Look for dirt road and "Beach Access" sign* ⌖ *Free.*

Pali Ke Kua Beach (*Hideaways*)

BEACH | This is actually two very small pocket beaches separated by a slender, rocky point, and the narrow beach area can all but disappear in wintertime. However, in summer, the steep, rocky trail (don't trust the rusty handrails and rotting ropes) that provides access reduces the number of beachgoers, at times creating a deserted beach feel. Winter's high surf creates dangerous conditions. The parking lot is small. ■**TIP**➔ **Don't attempt the trail after a heavy rain—it turns into a mudslide. Amenities:** parking (free). **Best for:** sunset; surfing. ⊠ *End of Ka Haku Rd., Princeville* ⌖ *On dirt trail between parking lot and condominium complex* ⌖ *Free.*

Beach Safety on Kauai

Hawaii's world-renowned, beautiful beaches can be extremely dangerous at times due to large waves, wind, and strong currents—so much so that the state rates wave hazards using three signs: a yellow square (caution), a red stop sign (high hazard), and a black diamond (extreme hazard). Signs are posted and updated three times daily or as conditions change.

Visiting beaches with lifeguards is strongly recommended, and you should swim only when there's a normal caution rating. Never swim alone or dive into unknown water or shallow breaking waves. If you're unable to swim out of a rip current, tread water and wave your arms in the air to signal for help.

Even in calm conditions, there are other dangerous things in the water to be aware of, including razor-sharp coral, jellyfish, eels, and sharks, to name a few.

Jellyfish cause the most ocean injuries, and signs are sometimes posted along beaches when they're present. Reactions to a sting are usually mild (burning sensation, redness, welts); however, in some cases they can be severe (breathing difficulties). If you're stung, pick off the tentacles, rinse the affected area with water, and apply ice.

The chances of getting bitten by a shark in Hawaiian waters are very low; sharks attack swimmers or surfers three or four times per year. Of the 40 species of sharks found near Hawaii, tiger sharks are considered the most dangerous because of their size and indiscriminate feeding behavior. They're easily recognized by their blunt snouts and vertical bars on their sides.

Here are a few tips to reduce your shark-attack risk:

■ Swim, surf, or dive with others at beaches patrolled by lifeguards.

■ Avoid swimming at dawn, dusk, and night, when some shark species may move inshore to feed.

■ Don't enter the water if you have open wounds or are bleeding.

■ Avoid murky waters, harbor entrances, areas near stream mouths (especially after heavy rains), channels, or steep drop-offs.

■ Don't wear high-contrast swimwear or shiny jewelry.

■ Don't swim near dolphins, which are often prey for large sharks.

The website ⊕ *hawaiibeachsafety. com* provides beach hazard maps as well as weather and surf advisories, and ⊕ *hioceansafety.com* has good general safety information.

Puu Poa Beach

BEACH | The coastline along the community of Princeville is primarily made up of sea cliffs with a couple of pocket beaches. The sea cliffs end with a long, narrow stretch of beach just east of the Hanalei River. Public access is via 100-plus steps around the back of 1 Hotel Hanalei Bay (scheduled to open in late 2022); hotel guests can take the elevator to sea level. The beach itself is subject to the hazards of winter's surf, narrowing and widening with the surf height. On calm days, snorkeling is good thanks to a shallow reef system pocked with sand. Sometimes a shallow sandbar extends across the river to Black Pot Beach Park, part of the Hanalei Beach system, making it easy to cross the river. On high-surf days, the outer edge of the reef near the river draws internationally ranked surfers. The 1 Hotel Hanalei Bay pool is off-limits to nonguests, but the hotel's restaurants and bars are not. Note that parking is limited. **Amenities:** food and drink; parking (free). **Best for:** snorkeling; sunset; surfing. ⊠ *End of Ka Haku Rd., off Rte. 560, Princeville* ⌀ *Free.*

🍴 Restaurants

A rough few years have diminished the restaurant selection in Princeville and Kilauea, starting in 2018 with the massive floods and continuing through 2021 with closures due to the coronavirus. Restaurants at 1 Hotel Hanalei Bay, the former St. Regis Princeville Resort, will open in fall 2022. Though it may not offer what it once did, this area still has a number of good spots—after all, people need to eat. You'll find everything from inexpensive holes-in-the-wall to relatively sophisticated, expensive establishments.

Kilauea Bakery & Pizzeria
$$ | AMERICAN | FAMILY | Open from 6:30 am, the bakery serves coffee drinks, delicious fresh pastries, bagels, and breads in the morning, but late risers should beware: breads and pastries sell out quickly. Pizza (including a gluten-free dough option), soup, and salads can be ordered for lunch or dinner. **Known for:** fresh chocolate chip cookies made in-house daily; its starter of Hawaiian sourdough made with guava; specialty pizzas topped with eclectic ingredients. ⓢ *Average main: $20* ⊠ *Kong Lung Center, 2484 Keneke St., Kilauea* ☎ *808/828–2020* ⊕ *www.kilaueabakery.com.*

Kilauea Market + Café
$$ | HAWAIIAN | Order freshly prepared Hawaiian and American meals—breakfast, lunch, and dinner—snacks, beer, and wine at the counter at this casual, contemporary restaurant, coffee bar, and beer and wine bar in an upscale grocery store. The extensive and eclectic menus include something for everyone, from *loco moco* (white rice topped with a hamburger patty, brown gravy, and fried egg), plate lunches, and fresh-catch fish-and-chips to pizzas, burgers, salads, and sandwiches. **Known for:** indoor and outdoor seating; daily specials; convenient stop on the way to and from lighthouse and beaches. ⓢ *Average main: $19* ⊠ *2555 Ala Namahana Pkwy., Kilauea* ☎ *808/828–2837* ⊕ *www.kilaueamarket.com.*

Nanea Restaurant & Bar
$$$ | HAWAIIAN | FAMILY | The signature restaurant of the Westin Princeville Ocean Resort Villas has casual, open-air seating that perfectly complements an island-style menu sure to please a wide range of diners. Grilled rib eye is served with bacon and sour cream mashed potatoes, while the chicken—smoked kalua style—is accompanied by Molokai sweet potatoes. **Known for:** local ingredients; kids eat free; inventive cocktails. ⓢ *Average main: $35* ⊠ *Westin Princeville Ocean Resort Villas, 3838 Wyllie Rd., Princeville* ☎ *808/827–8808* ⊕ *www.marriott.com.*

Sushigirl Kauai
$ | SUSHI | Pick up some of Kauai's tastiest made-to-order rolls, sushi burritos, and poke bowls with ahi, smoked salmon, and (sometimes) ono at this modest trailer. Dine in the adjacent courtyard (snag a table with an umbrella) or picnic at the beach. **Known for:** entire menu is gluten-free; veggie and vegan options; fresh, local, organic ingredients. ⓢ *Average main: $13* ⊠ *Kong Lung Center, 2484 Kaneke St., Kilauea* ☎ *808/320–8646* ⊕ *www.sushigirlkauai.com.*

☕ Coffee and Quick Bites

Moloaa Sunrise Juice Bar & Fruit Stand
$ | AMERICAN | Don't let the name fool you; they don't open at sunrise (more

like 7:30 am, so come here after you watch the sunrise elsewhere). And it's not just a fruit stand: fill up on bagels, pancakes, smoothies, and coffee drinks in the morning; homemade salads, burritos, panini, and sandwiches for lunch; and tropical-style fresh juices, such as pineapple, carrot, watermelon, and guava, anytime. **Known for:** fresh, natural ingredients; local fruits and vegetables for sale; great spot to stretch your legs and pick up food for a picnic. $ *Average main: $10* ⊠ *6011 Koolau Rd., at Kuhio Hwy., Kilauea* ☎ *808/822–1441* ⊕ *www. moloaasunrisefruitstand.com* ☾ *Closed weekends. No dinner.*

North Shore General Store

$ | **AMERICAN** | Attached to a gas station and small-items store, this classic hole-in-the-wall has the best deals for a take-out breakfast or lunch on the North Shore. Darron's local-beef burgers have a loyal following, and you may have to get in line for his lunchtime favorite, chili-pepper chicken. **Known for:** food truck at Anini Beach on weekdays; espresso bar and homestyle breakfast and lunch plates; closes at 6:30 pm. $ *Average main: $10* ⊠ *Princeville Shopping Center, 5–4280 Kuhio Hwy., Princeville* ☎ *808/826–1122* ⊕ *pizzakauai.com* ☾ *No dinner.*

Trilogy

$ | **CAFÉ** | A tiny café with a huge local following, Trilogy serves artisanal coffee, tea, chai, adaptogenic elixirs (with ingredients that may reduce the effects of stress on the body), and other blends, plus an array of sweet and savory treats, from avocado toast with macadamia nut pesto and za'atar seasoning to cakes and cookies. **Known for:** lilikoi (passion fruit) mousse; organic, raw, gluten-free, vegan, and vegetarian options; adaptogenic elixirs and other creative blends. $ *Average main: $13* ⊠ *Kilauea Plantation Center, 4270 Kilauea Rd., Kilauea* ⊕ *www.trilogy-coffeekauai.com* ☾ *No dinner.*

Hotels

Hanalei Bay Resort

$$$$ | **RESORT** | **FAMILY** | The nicest feature of this three-story condominium resort overlooking Hanalei Bay is its upper-level pool with authentic lava-rock waterfalls, an open-air hot tub, and a kid-friendly sand beach. **Pros:** lively lounge; beautiful views; pool, tennis courts, and fitness center on property. **Cons:** long walk to beach; some units far from main building and restaurant; steep walkways. $ *Rooms from: $422* ⊠ *5380 Honoiki Rd., Princeville* ☎ *808/826–6522, 877/344–0688* ⊕ *www.hanaleibayresort. com* ⮱ *134 units* ‖○‖ *No Meals.*

1 Hotel Hanalei Bay

$$$$ | **RESORT** | **FAMILY** | Set to open in late 2022 and not available for final viewing at the time of this writing, this swanky wellness resort—the newly renovated former St. Regis Princeville—offers expansive views of the sea and mountains, including Makana, the landmark peak immortalized as mysterious Bali Hai in the film *South Pacific.* **Pros:** attractive lobby area; state-of-the-art spa; numerous dining options. **Cons:** expensive even for the area; beach not ideal for swimming; minimal grounds. $ *Rooms from: $1900* ⊠ *5520 Ka Haku Rd., Princeville* ☎ *808/826–9644, 833/623–2111* ⊕ *www.1hotels.com* ⮱ *252 rooms* ‖○‖ *No Meals.*

★ Westin Princeville Ocean Resort Villas

$$$$ | **RESORT** | **FAMILY** | Spread out over 18½ acres on a bluff above Anini Beach, this Westin property marries the comforts of spacious condominium living with the top-notch service and amenities of a luxurious hotel resort. **Pros:** kids' program; on-site minimarket; ocean views. **Cons:** units can be far from parking; whirlpool tub is small; path to the nearby beach is a steep six- to seven-minute walk. $ *Rooms from: $356* ⊠ *3838 Wyllie Rd., Princeville* ☎ *808/827–8700* ⊕ *www. marriott.com* ⮱ *366 units* ‖○‖ *No Meals.*

▼ Nightlife

★ Happy Talk Lounge

BARS | You can sip an umbrella cocktail while you gaze at the original Bali Hai from this lounge, open on two sides and offering breezy views across Hanalei Bay to plush emerald mountains. If you think the scene looks familiar, maybe you've seen the classic movie *South Pacific*, filmed here. The Hollywood version of Bali Hai is actually Kauai's Mt. Makana. Order a tropical cocktail and *pupu* (Hawaiian hors d'oeuvres) and enjoy a truly enchanted evening as the sun sets over the sparkling waters. Local musicians entertain guests Thursday through Monday. ■TIP→ **Nearby Tunnels Beach (aka Haena Beach and Mākua) is often called Nurses' Beach, where Mitzi Gaynor sang about washing that man right outta her hair; Hanalei Bay is where Bloody Mary sang "Bali Hai."** ⊠ *Hanalei Bay Resort, 5380 Honoiki Rd., Princeville* ☎ *808/431–4084* ⊕ *www.happytalklounge.com.*

🛍 Shopping

Princeville Shopping Center is a bustling little mix of businesses, necessities, and some unique, often pricey, shops. Kilauea is a bit more sprawled out and offers a charming, laid-back shopping scene with a neighborhood feel.

Kong Lung Trading

SOUVENIRS | Sometimes called the Gump's of Kauai, this store sells elegant clothing, glassware, books, gifts, and artwork—all very lovely and expensive. The shop is housed in a beautiful 1892 stone building in the heart of Kilauea. It's the showpiece of the pretty little Kong Lung Center, where everything from handmade soaps to hammocks can be found. A great bakery and pizza joint (Kilauea Bakery & Pizzeria) rounds out the center's offerings, along with an exhibit of historical photos. ⊠ *Kong Lung Center, 2484 Keneke St., Kilauea* ☎ *808/828–1822* ⊕ *www.konglungkauai.com.*

Princeville Shopping Center

SHOPPING CENTER | The big draws at this small center are a full-service grocery store and a hardware store, but there's also the North Shore General Store (famed for its burgers and other food to go), a fun toy store, a bar, a mailing service, a nice sandal boutique, women's clothing, and an ice cream shop. This is also the last stop for gas and banking when you're heading west along the North Shore. ⊠ *5–4280 Kuhio Hwy., near mile marker 28, Princeville* ☎ *808/826–9497* ⊕ *www.princevillecenter.com.*

Napali Coast

Napali Coast is considered the jewel of Kauai, and for all its greenery, it would surely be an emerald. After seeing the coast, many are at a loss for words because its beauty is so overwhelming. Others resort to poetry. Pulitzer Prize–winning poet W. S. Merwin wrote a novel-in-verse, *The Folding Cliffs*, based on a true story set in Napali. *Napali* means "the cliffs," and while that sounds like a simple name, it's quite an apt description. The coastline is cut by a series of small valleys, like fault lines, running to the interior, with the resulting cliffs seeming to bend back on themselves like an accordion-folded fan made of green velvet. More than 5 million years old, these sea cliffs rise as high as 4,000 feet above the Pacific, and every shade of green is represented in the vegetation that blankets their lush peaks and folds. At the base of the cliffs there are caves, secluded beaches, and waterfalls to explore.

Let's put this in perspective: even if you had only one day on Kauai, we'd still recommend heading to Napali Coast on Kauai's northwest side. Once you're there, you'll understand why no road traverses this series of folding-fan cliffs. That leaves three ways to experience the

Continued on page 98

NAPALI COAST: EMERALD QUEEN OF KAUAI

If you're coming to Kauai, Napali ("the cliffs" in Hawaiian) is a major must see. More than 5 million years old, these sea cliffs rise thousands of feet above the Pacific, and every shade of green is represented in the vegetation that blankets their lush peaks and folds. At their base, there are caves, secluded beaches, and waterfalls to explore.

The big question is how to explore this gorgeous stretch of coastline. You can't drive to it, through it, or around it. You can't see Napali from a scenic lookout. You can't even take a mule ride to it. The only way to experience its magic is from the sky, the ocean, or the trail.

FROM THE SKY

If you've booked a helicopter tour of Napali, you might start wondering what you've gotten yourself into on the way to the airport. Will it feel like being on a small airplane? Will there be turbulence? Will it be worth all the money you just plunked down?

Your concerns will be assuaged on the helipad, once you see the faces of those who have just returned from their journey: Everyone looks totally blissed out. And now it's your turn.

Climb on board, strap on your headphones, and the next thing you know the helicopter gently lifts up, hovers for a moment, and floats away like a spider on the wind—no roaring engines, no rumbling down a runway. If you've chosen a flight with music, you'll feel as if you're inside your very own IMAX movie.

Pinch yourself if you must, because this is the real thing. Your pilot shares history, legend, and lore. If you miss something, speak up: pilots love to show off their island knowledge. You may snap a few pictures (not too many or you'll miss the eyes-on experience!), nudge a friend or spouse, and point at a whale breeching in the ocean, but mostly you stare, mouth agape. There is simply no other way to take in the immensity and greatness of Napali but from the air.

(left) The Napali Coast is a breathtaking stretch of Kauai coastline lined by sea cliffs rising thousands of feet into the sky. (bottom) Helicopter tours over Napali Coast

GOOD TO KNOW

Helicopter companies depart from the north, east, and west sides of the island. Most are based in Lihue, near the airport.

If you want more adventure—and air—choose one of the helicopter companies that flies with the doors off.

Some companies offer flights without music. Know the experience you want ahead of time. Some even sell a video of your flight, so you don't have to worry about taking pictures.

Wintertime rain grounds some flights; plan your trip early in your stay in case the flight gets rescheduled.

IS THIS FOR ME?

Taking a helicopter trip is the most expensive way to see Napali—as much as $340 for an hour-long tour.

Claustrophobic? Choose a boat tour or hike. It's a tight squeeze in the helicopter, especially in one of the middle seats.

Short on time? Taking a helicopter tour is a great way to see the island.

WHAT YOU MIGHT SEE

■ Nualolo Kai (an ancient Hawaiian fishing village) with its fringed reef

■ The 300-foot Hanakapiai Falls

■ A massive sea arch formed in the rock by erosion

■ The 11-mile Kalalau Trail threading its way along the coast

■ The amazing striations of *aa* and *pahoehoe* lava flows that helped push Kauai above the sea

FROM THE OCEAN

Napali from the ocean is two treats in one: spend a good part of the day on (or in) the water, and gaze up at majestic green sea cliffs rising thousands of feet above your head.

There are three ways to see it: a mellow pleasure-cruise catamaran allows you to kick back and sip a mai tai; an adventurous raft (Zodiac) tour will take you inside sea caves under waterfalls, and give you the option of snorkeling; and a daylong outing in a kayak is possible in the summer.

Any way you travel, you'll breathe ocean air, feel spray on your face, and see pods of spinner dolphins, green sea turtles, flying fish, and, if you're lucky, a rare Hawaiian monk seal.

Napali stretches from Kee Beach in the north to Polihale beach on the West Side. You'll be heading towards the lush Hanakapiai Valley, where within a few minutes, you'll see caves and waterfalls galore. About halfway down the coast just after the Kalalau Trail ends, you'll come to an immense arch—formed where the sea eroded the less dense basaltic rock—and a thundering 50-foot waterfall. And as the island curves near Nualolo State Park, you'll begin to notice less vegetation and more rocky outcroppings.

(Left and top right) Kayaking on Napali Coast
(Bottom right) Dolphins off Napali Coast

GOOD TO KNOW

If you want to snorkel, choose a morning rather than an afternoon tour—preferably during a summer visit—when seas are calmer.

If you're on a budget, choose a non-snorkeling tour.

If you want to see whales, take any tour, but be sure to plan your vacation for December through March.

You can only embark from the North Shore in summer. If you're staying on the South Shore, it might not be worth your time to drive to the north, so head to the West Side.

IS THIS FOR ME?

Boat tours are several hours long, so if you have only a short time on Kauai, a helicopter tour is a better alternative.

Even on a small boat, you won't get the individual attention and exclusivity of a helicopter tour.

Prone to seasickness? A large boat can be surprisingly rocky, so be prepared. Afternoon trips are rougher because the winds pick up.

WHAT YOU MIGHT SEE

■ Hawaii's state fish—the humuhumunukunukuapuaa—otherwise known as the reef triggerfish

■ Waiahuakua Sea Cave, with a waterfall coming through its roof

■ Tons of marine life, including dolphins, green sea turtles, flying fish, and humpback whales, especially in February and March

■ Waterfalls—especially if your trip is after a heavy rain

FROM THE TRAIL

If you want to be one with Napali—feeling the soft red earth beneath your feet, picnicking on the beaches, and touching the lush vegetation—hiking the Kalalau Trail is the way to do it.

Most people hike only the first 2 miles of the 11-mile trail and turn around at Hanakapiai. This 4-mile round-trip hike takes three to four hours. It starts at sea level and doesn't waste any time gaining elevation. (Take heart—the uphill lasts only a mile and tops out at 400 feet; then it's downhill all the way.) At the half-mile point, the trail curves west and the folds of Napali Coast unfurl.

Along the way you might share the trail with feral goats and wild pigs. Some of the vegetation is native; much is introduced.

After the 1-mile mark the trail begins its drop into Hanakapiai. You'll pass a couple of streams of water trickling across the trail, and maybe some banana, ginger, the native uluhe fern, and the Hawaiian ti plant. Finally the trail swings around the eastern ridge of Hanakapiai for your first glimpse of the valley and then switchbacks down the mountain. You'll have to boulder-hop across the stream to reach the beach. If you like, you can take a 4-mile, round-trip fairly strenuous side trip from this point to the gorgeous Hanakapiai Falls.

(Left) View along Napali Coast
(Top right) Feral goats in Kalalau Valley
(Bottom right) Napali Coast

GOOD TO KNOW

Wear comfortable, amphibious shoes. Unless your feet require extra support, wear a self-bailing sort of shoe (for stream crossings) that doesn't mind mud.

During winter the trail is often muddy, so be extra careful; sometimes it's completely inaccessible.

Don't hike after heavy rain—flash floods are common.

If you plan to hike the entire 11-mile trail (most people do the shorter hike described at left) you'll need a permit to go past Hanakapiai.

Hikers must carry out all their trash.

IS THIS FOR ME?

Of all the ways to see Napali (with the exception of kayaking the coast), this is the most active. You need to be in decent shape to hit the trail.

If you're vacationing in winter, this hike might not be an option due to flooding—whereas you can take a helicopter year-round.

WHAT YOU MIGHT SEE

- Big dramatic surf right below your feet

- Amazing vistas of the cool blue Pacific

- The spectacular Hanakapiai Falls; if you have a permit don't miss Hanakoa Falls, less than ½ mile off the trail

- Wildlife, including goats and pigs

- Zany-looking hala trees, with aerial roots and long, skinny serrated leaves known as lauhala. Early Hawaiians used them to make mats, baskets, and canoe sails.

coastline—by air, by water, or on foot. We recommend all three, in that order—each one gets progressively more sensory. A helicopter tour is your best bet if you're strapped for time; we recommend Jack Harter Helicopters (*see Aerial Tours in the Activities and Tours chapter for more information*). Boat tours are great for family fun and a day on the water; hiking, of course, is the most budget-friendly option, though it's physically challenging.

Whatever way you choose to visit Napali, you might want to keep this awe-inspiring fact in mind: at one time, thousands of Hawaiians lived self-sufficiently in these valleys.

GETTING HERE AND AROUND

Napali Coast runs 15 miles from Kee Beach (one of Kauai's more popular snorkeling spots) on the island's North Shore to Polihale State Park (the longest stretch of beach in the state) on the West Side of the island. How do you explore this gorgeous stretch of coastline? You can't drive to it, through it, or around it. You can't see Napali from a scenic lookout. You can't even take a mule ride to it. The only way to experience its magic is from the sky, the ocean, or the trail. The Kalalau Trail can be hiked from the "end of the road" at Kee Beach, where the trailhead begins in Haena State Park at the northwest end of Kuhio Highway (this part is Route 560). There's no need to hike the trail's entire, challenging 11 miles (one-way) to get a full experience. Doing that requires a camping permit, which you can apply for up to 90 days in advance of your planned trip (see ⊕ *dlnr. hawaii.gov/dsp*).

An option for seeing Napali Coast on foot is to hike the first 2 miles into **Hanakapiai Beach** and then another 2 miles up that valley; that is allowed without a permit. The beach is accessed from a trailhead in the parking lot at Kee Beach; check ⊕ *gohaena.com* before you travel for information about reservations and shuttle service. The beach is a small jewel, but swimming and other water activities are not recommended because there are no lifeguards; the shore break is often dangerous. It's more for sunning and relaxing.

⊕ Beaches

★ Kalalau Beach

BEACH | Located at the end of the trail with the same name, Kalalau is a remote beach in spectacular Napali Coast State Wilderness Park, and reaching it requires an arduous 11-mile hike along sea cliff faces (permit required), through steaming tropical valleys, and across sometimes-raging streams. The trail has no to limited cell phone service and is recommended for experienced hikers only. Another option is to paddle a kayak to the beach—summer only, though, or else the surf is way too big. All boat and kayak tours must be through a permitted, guided company. The beach is anchored by a *heiau* (a stone platform used as a place of worship) on one end and a waterfall on the other.

The safest time to come is summer, when the trail is dry and the beach is wide, cupped by low, vegetated sand dunes and a large walk-in cave on the western edge. Day hikes into the valley offer waterfalls, freshwater swimming pools, and wild, tropical fruits. Though state camping permits are required, the valley often has a significant illegal crowd, which has strained park facilities and degraded much of its former peaceful solitude. Helicopter overflights are near-constant in good weather. **Amenities:** none. **Best for:** sunset; walking; solitude. ⊠ *Napali Coast State Wilderness Park* ⊹ *Trailhead starts at end of Rte. 560, 7 miles west of Hanalei* ⊕ *www.hawaiistateparks.org*.

THE EAST SIDE

4

Updated by
Joan Conrow

⊙ Sights	🍴 Restaurants	🛏 Hotels	🛍 Shopping	🍸 Nightlife
★★★★☆	★★★☆☆	★★★☆☆	★★★★☆	★★☆☆☆

WELCOME TO THE EAST SIDE

TOP REASONS TO GO

★ **Golden beaches.** With open fields and a large pool for snorkeling, Lydgate State Park is great for picnics and safe swimming. A beautiful seaside pathway, Ke Ala Hele Makalae, starts here.

★ **Mountain hikes.** Trek up to the Sleeping Giant (Nounou Mountain) for a great view of the island from high up. Variations in terrain make the East Side suitable for hikers of all abilities.

★ **Scenic waterfalls.** You can watch water tumble hundreds of feet down from mighty Opaekaa Falls and get great views of the Wailua River Valley here.

★ **Location, location, location.** Reasonably priced restaurants, affordable lodging prices, and a central location close to Kauai's airport make the East Side a practical place to stay. It's also a great place to meet the locals.

★ **Kapaa Town.** Kapaa's vintage plantation-style buildings now house boutiques and eateries as well as art shops. Side streets offer a reminder of Kauai before commercialization.

Though it has no exact boundaries, the East Side starts in Lihue, where planes and cruise ships bring visitors to the island. The region meanders a few miles west to include Puhi but primarily extends northward, encompassing the communities of Hanamaulu, Wailua, and Kapaa. It's an area with plenty of the necessities travelers need.

This is the windward side of the island, which means the prevailing trade winds blow on shore. While the trades help keep temperatures cool, they also bring frequent showers—and rainbows—and the ocean can get a little rough when they're blowing briskly. The beautiful coastline here is dominated by fringing coral reefs, and these make the ocean too shallow for swimming in some spots.

1 Kapaa. This colorful former plantation town recalls an earlier era. Its small shops, eateries, and art shops are good for a lively stroll around town.

2 Wailua. Great places to stay, eat, and shop on an affordable budget, plus a central location, make this area of the Coconut Coast hard to beat.

3 Lihue. The island's "capital," as well as its business and commercial center, is where you'll fly into Kauai. Busy during the workday, it's quiet in the evening except for a few nightspots.

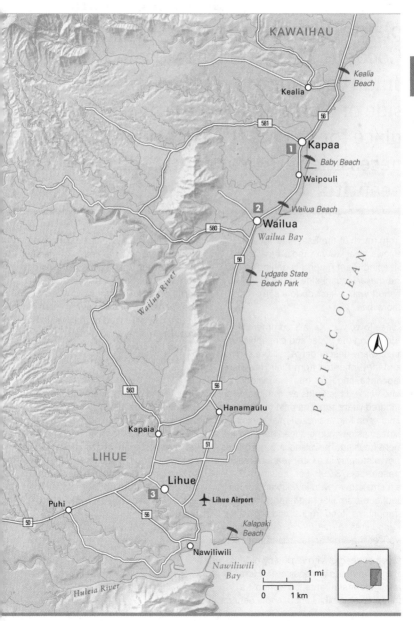

The East Side encompasses Kapaa, Wailua, and Lihue. It's also known as the Royal Coconut Coast for the coconut plantation where today's aptly named Coconut Marketplace is located and the small coconut groves that still sit on each side of Kuhio Highway. It's a convenient place for the practical traveler, as all the necessities are nearby and the coast is beautiful.

From much of the East Side you can enjoy a clear view of the eternally Sleeping Giant mountain behind you. On the *makai* (ocean) side of the highway, a short walk takes you to a semi-rocky shoreline.

Kapaa Town was Kauai's commercial hub during the sugar and pineapple eras. Many descendants still live on the land they inherited from their Hawaiian, Japanese, and Portuguese ancestors who worked the fields as immigrants a hundred years ago. The past few decades have seen Kapaa's residential areas expand as newcomers lead demand for more housing. The island population has grown steadily in recent years to reach its present-day 73,298. For the visitor, Kapaa is a small town with jewelry and dress boutiques, smaller restaurants, tourist emporiums, food trucks, and shops. It's a good area to meet local people who work at the smaller establishments.

Kapaa connects with Wailua by means of the ill-defined Waipouli area. Here you'll find restaurants, bike shops, a chiropractor, a bikini shop, and a general assortment of small businesses. The Wailua area, now marked with the shell of the former Coco Palms Hotel across from Wailua Beach, was the traditional home of Kauai's famous *alii*, rulers of the commoners. Much of Kauai's Hawaiian history can be traced to the Wailua River area. More recently, Sinatra and Presley graced the coast while filming movies and enjoying the laid-back scene of old Kauai.

Lihue is the county seat, and the whole East Side is the island's center of commerce, so early-morning and late-afternoon drive times (or rush hours) can get very congested in what's known locally as Kapaa Krawl. If you're driving, take advantage of the Kapaa bypass, which can take you from northern Kapaa Town all the way past Wailua, avoiding most of the traffic.

Planning

Planning Your Time

Given the area's many recreational activities, it's easy to spend two or three days on the East Side. Take one of several mountain hikes or rent a bicycle and cruise Ke Ala Hele Makalae, a pathway that runs along the coast. Plan to spend some time soaking up the sun and surf at the numerous beaches, including several, like Lydgate State Park, that are excellent for children. You can enjoy two beautiful waterfalls from roadside pullouts, including Wailua Falls, or visit cultural sites that reflect ancient Hawaii, such as Poliahu Heiau. Shoppers will find small, unique stores to browse in Kapaa and elsewhere, and there are good local options when hunger hits.

Getting Here and Around

The island's major airport is in Lihue, making the East Side a practical base for travelers to Kauai. Turn to the right out of the airport at Lihue for the road to Wailua. Careful, though—the zone between Lihue and Wailua has been the site of many car accidents. Two bridges—under which the culturally significant Wailua River gently flows—mark the beginning of Wailua. It quickly blends into Kapaa via Waipouli; there's no real demarcation. Pay attention and drive carefully, always knowing where you are going and when to turn off.

Route 56 leads into Lihue from the north, and Route 50 comes here from the south and west. The road from the airport (where Kauai's car rental agencies are) leads to the middle of Lihue. Many of the area's stores and restaurants are on and around Rice Street, which also leads to Kalapaki Bay and Nawiliwili Harbor.

The website ⊕ *getaroundkauai.com* presents some sustainable transportation options for getting around the island, though a car is the most practical option for exploring.

Beaches

The East Side of the island is considered the "windward" side, a term you'll often hear in weather forecasts. It simply means the side of the island receiving most of the onshore winds. The wind helps break down rock into sand, so there are plenty of beaches here. Unfortunately, only a few of those beaches are protected, so many are not ideal for beginning ocean goers, though they are perfect for long sunrise ambles. On super-windy days, kiteboarders sail along the eastern shore, sometimes jumping waves and performing acrobatic maneuvers in the air.

Hotels

Location, location, location. The East Side, or Coconut Coast, is a good centralized home base if you want to see and do it all on the island. This is also one of the few resort areas on Kauai where you can actually walk to the beach, restaurants, and stores from your condo, hotel, or vacation-rental unit. It's not only convenient but also comparatively cheap. You pay less for lodging, meals, services, merchandise, and gas here—mainly because much of the coral-reef coastline isn't as ideal as the sandy-bottom bays that front the fancy resorts. We think the shoreline is just fine. There are pockets in the reef to swim in, and the coast is uncrowded and boasts spectacular views. ■TIP→ **Traffic on the main highway can be bumper-to-bumper in the afternoon.** All in all, though, it's a good choice for families because the prices are right and there's plenty to keep everyone happy and occupied.

Hotel and restaurant reviews have been shortened. For full information, see Fodors.com. Hotel prices in the reviews are the lowest cost of a standard double room in high season. Restaurant prices are the average cost of a main course at dinner, or if dinner is not served, at lunch.

WHAT IT COSTS in U.S. Dollars

	$	$$	$$$	$$$$
RESTAURANTS				
	under $17	$17–$26	$27–$35	over $35
HOTELS				
	under $180	$180–$260	$261–$340	over $340

Restaurants

Because the East Side is the island's largest population center, it presents a wide selection of restaurants. It's also a good place to get both cheaper meals and the local-style cuisine that residents favor.

Most of the eateries are along Kuhio Highway between Kapaa and Wailua; a few are tucked into shopping centers and resorts. In Lihue, it's easier to find lunch than dinner because many restaurants cater to the business crowd.

You'll find all the usual fast-food joints in both Kapaa and Lihue, as well as virtually every international cuisine available on Kauai. Although fancy gourmet restaurants are less abundant in this part of the island, there's plenty of good, solid food, and a few stellar attractions. But unless you're staying on the East Side, or passing through, it's probably not worth the long drive from the North Shore or Poipu resorts to eat here.

Tours

Roberts Hawaii Tours
BUS TOURS | The Round-the-Island Tour, sometimes called the Waimea Canyon–Fern Grotto Tour, gives a good overview of half the island, including Fort Elizabeth and Opaekaa Falls. Guests are transported in air-conditioned, 25-passenger minibuses. The trip includes a boat ride up the Wailua River to the Fern Grotto and a visit to the lookouts above Waimea Canyon. Roberts also offers a Kauai Movie Tour. ✉ *3–4567 Kuhio Hwy., Hanamaulu* ☎ *808/245–9101, 800/831–5541* ⊕ *www.robertshawaii.com/kauai* ✉ *From $98.*

Kapaa and Wailua

Kapaa is 16 miles southeast of Kilauea; Wailua is 3 miles southwest of Kapaa.

Old Town Kapaa was once a sugar and pineapple plantation town, which is no surprise—most of the larger towns on Kauai once were. It's where you'll find the best selection of shops in the area, most of them tucked into a quaint collection of wooden-front shops, some built by plantation workers and still run by their progeny today. Kapaa houses two grocery stories: a large Safeway and locally owned Big Save. It also offers plenty of dining options and easy access to the ocean and a walking-biking trail that runs along the coast. If the timing is right, plan to cruise the town on the first Saturday evening of each month, when the bands are playing and the town's wares are on display. To the south, Wailua comprises a few restaurants, shops, and resorts along the coastline, as well as Lydgate State Park, with its wonderful playground and safe swimming areas.

Sights

Fern Grotto

NATURE SIGHT | Though it's really not much to look at, visitors seem to like this longtime attraction, perhaps because of the serenity of just cruising up and down the Wailua River, accompanied by Hawaiian music, to see it. The grotto itself is nothing more than a yawning lava tube swathed in lush fishtail ferns 3 miles up the river. Though it was significantly damaged after Hurricane Iniki in 1992 and again after heavy rains in 2006, the greenery has completely recovered. The Smith's Kauai tour group is the only way to legally see the grotto. You can access the entrance with a kayak, but if boats are there, you may not be allowed to land. ⊠ *Rte. 56, just south of Wailua River, Kapaa* ☎ *808/821–6895* ⊕ *smithskauai.com* ⊠ *$30.*

★ Ke Ala Hele Makalae

TRAIL | Running from the southern end of Lydgate Park north to Donkey Beach, between Kealia and Anahola, this 8-mile seaside path is a favorite of visitors and locals alike. Sea breezes, gorgeous ocean views, smooth pavement, and friendly smiles from everyone as they bike, walk, skate, and run add to the pleasures of the trail. The path has many entry points, and you'll have your choice of bike shops just off the trail. ⊠ *1121 Moanakai Rd., Kapaa* ⊕ *www.kauaipath. org/kauaicoastalpath.*

Keahua Arboretum

GARDEN | Tree-lined and grassy, this arboretum in the Lihue-Koloa Forest Reserve is a perfect spot for a picnic—and there are lots of picnic tables scattered throughout the parklike setting. A typically shallow, cascading stream makes for a fun spot for kids to splash, although the water's a bit chilly. After crossing the stream on the bridge, the 1-mile walking trail meanders through mango, monkeypod, and exquisite rainbow eucalyptus trees. This is an exceptionally peaceful place—good for yoga and meditation—that is, unless the resident roosters decide to crow. ⊠ *Kuamoo Rd., Wailua (Kauai County)* ⊠ *Free.*

Kealia Scenic Viewpoint

VIEWPOINT | This ocean overlook is perfect for spotting whales during their winter migration. In fact, on three Saturdays in winter, the Hawaiian Islands Humpback Whale National Marine Sanctuary conducts its annual whale count from this spot. It's easy to hop on the cement bike-and-walking path just below for a coastal stroll or ride. Most days you can see clear to Lihue and beyond. If you packed them, bring your binoculars. ⊠ *Rte. 56, Kapaa* ✢ *Between mile markers 9 and 10.*

Lydgate Farms

FARM/RANCH | **FAMILY** | Hawaii is the only state in the country where *Theobroma cacao* grows—the tree whose seeds become chocolate—and the Lydgates are on a mission to grow enough cacao on their family farm that one day they will produce an identifiable Kauai homegrown chocolate. For now, you can tour this organic farm (in addition to cacao, they grow vanilla, timber trees, bamboo, and many tropical fruits) and learn how chocolate is made, "from branch to bar," as they put it. The three-hour tour includes, of course, plenty of chocolate tastings. Reservations are required for the morning tour, which runs weekdays at 9 am. ⊠ *5730 Olohena Rd., Kapaa* ☎ *808/821–1857* ⊕ *lydgatefarms.com* ⊠ *Tour $125; kids 6 and under free.*

Opaekaa Falls

WATERFALL | **FAMILY** | The mighty Wailua River produces many dramatic waterfalls, and Opaekaa (pronounced "oh-pie-*kah*-ah") is one of the best, plunging hundreds of feet to the pool below. It can be easily viewed from a scenic overlook with ample parking. Opaekaa means "rolling shrimp," which refers to tasty native crustaceans that were once so

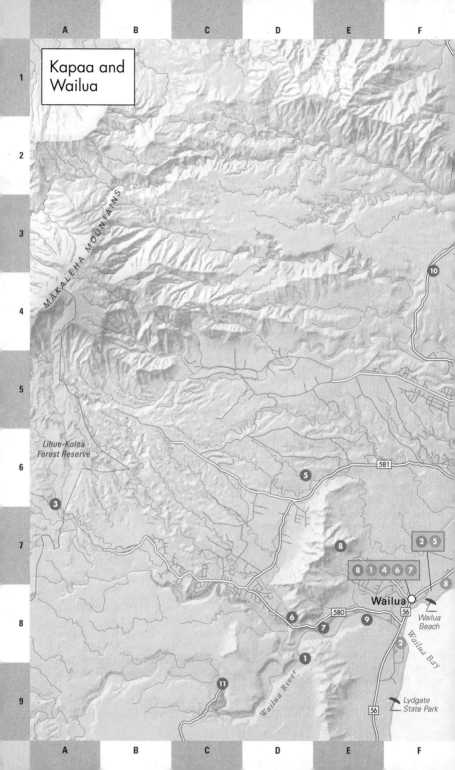

Kapaa and
Wailua

MAKALEHA MOUNTAINS

Lihue-Koloa
Forest Reserve

581

5

3

8

2 5

8 1 4 6 7

Wailua

8

Wailua
Beach

580

9

56

6

7

56

2

Wailua Bay

1

11

Wailua River

Lydgate
State Park

56

10

KEY

1 *Exploring Sights*
1 *Restaurants*
1 *Quick Bites*
1 *Hotels*

0 ____ 1 mi
0 ____ 1 km

abundant they could be seen tumbling in the falls. Do not attempt to hike down to the pool. ■TIP→ **Just before reaching the parking area for the waterfall, turn left into a scenic pullout for great views of the Wailua River and its march through the valley to the sea.** ✉ *Kuamoo Rd., Wailua (Kauai County)* ✛ *From Rte. 56, turn mauka (toward the mountains) onto Kuamoo Rd. and drive 1½ miles.*

★ **Poliahu Heiau**

RELIGIOUS BUILDING | Storyboards near this ancient *heiau* (sacred site) recount the significance of the many sacred structures found along the Wailua River. It's unknown exactly how the ancient Hawaiians used Poliahu Heiau—one of the largest pre-Christian temples on the island—but legend says it was created by the Menehune, the legendary race of little people who were quick builders, because of the unusual stonework found in its walled enclosures. From this site, drive downhill toward the ocean to *pohaku hanau,* a two-piece birthing stone said to confer special blessings on all children born there, and *pohaku piko,* whose crevices were a repository for umbilical cords left by parents seeking a clue to their child's destiny, which reportedly was foretold by how the cord fared in the rock. ■TIP→ **Some Hawaiians feel these sacred stones shouldn't be viewed as tourist attractions, so always treat them with respect. Never stand or sit on the rocks or leave any offerings.** ✉ *5558–5568 Kuamoo Rd., Wailua (Kauai County)* ✑ *Free.*

Sleeping Giant

MOUNTAIN | Although its true name is Nounou, this landmark mountain ridge is more commonly known as the Sleeping Giant because of its resemblance to a very large man sleeping on his back. Legends differ on whether the giant is Puni, who was accidentally killed by rocks launched at invading canoes by the Menehune, or Nunui, a gentle creature who has not yet awakened from the nap

he took centuries ago after building a massive temple and enjoying a big feast. The ridge can be experienced up close via one of several trails that traverse the giant's body (*see Hiking in the Activities and Tours chapter*). ✉ *Rte. 56, Kapaa* ✛ *About 1 mile north of Wailua River.*

Smith's Tropical Paradise

GARDEN | FAMILY | Nestled next to Wailua Marina along the mighty Wailua River, this 30-acre botanical and cultural garden offers a glimpse of distinctive foliage, including fruit orchards, a bamboo rain forest, and tropical lagoons. Enjoy a stroll along a mile of pathways. It's a popular spot for wedding receptions and other large events, and its luau is one of the island's oldest and best. ✉ *3–5971 Kuhio Hwy., Kapaa* ✛ *Just south of Wailua River* ☎ *808/821–6895* ⊕ *smithskauai.com* ✑ *$10* ⏱ *Closed weekends, Tues., and Thurs.*

Spalding Monument

VIEWPOINT | The Colonel Zephaniah Spalding monument commemorates the Civil War veteran who purchased this splendid property overlooking an area from Anahola to Kapaa in 1876 and soon established what became the Kealia Sugar Plantation. Turn onto Kealia Road just after mile marker 10 for an off-the-beaten-track scenic detour. Immediately on your right are a small post office and a food truck and, on your left, rodeo grounds often in use on summer weekends. The road ascends, and 2½ miles later you'll reach a grassy area with the concrete remains of a monument. It's a nice place to picnic or to simply look at the nearby grazing horses. If you're an early riser, this is a great spot to watch the sun rise; if not, check the local newspaper for the next full moon. It's possible to continue on for another very bumpy 2 miles, where you'll reconnect with Highway 56 near the town of Anahola, but your bike or car will not thank you for it. You're better off doubling back. ✉ *Kealia Rd., Kapaa.*

Did You Know?

Beautiful Wailua Falls is best known for appearing in the opening credits of *Fantasy Island*. It's easily accessible from the road.

★ **Wailua Falls**

WATERFALL | FAMILY | Kauai has plenty of noteworthy waterfalls, but this one is especially gorgeous, easy to find, and easy to photograph. You may recognize the impressive cascade from the opening sequences of the *Fantasy Island* television series. To reach it, drive north from Lihue following Maalo Road in Hanamaulu, then travel uphill for 3 miles. ⊠ *Maalo Rd., off Rte. 580, Lihue.*

🏊 Beaches

Aliomanu Beach

BEACH | This narrow beach is lined with homes, most of them set back a bit and screened with vegetation that blocks access along the sand in a number of places when the surf is up or tide is high. The waters off Aliomanu Beach are protected by the fringing reef 100 yards or so out to sea, and there are pockets for swimming. However, currents can be tricky, especially near the stream tucked in the beach's elbow toward the northern end and at the river mouth on the southern end that demarcates neighboring Anahola Beach. This beach is in Hawaiian Homelands, an area held in trust for Native Hawaiians by the State of Hawaii, and is frequently used by fishers and local families for camping. **Amenities:** parking (free). **Best for:** solitude; sunrise. ⊠ *Aliomanu Rd., north of mile marker 14, Anahola* ⧉ *Free.*

Anahola Beach Park

BEACH | Anahola is part of the Hawaiian Home Lands on Kauai, so this beach park is definitely a locals' hangout, especially for families with small children. The shallow and calm water at the beach road's end is tucked behind a curving finger of land and perfect for young ones. As the beach winds closer to the river mouth, there's less protection and a shore break favorable for bodyboarders if the trade winds are light or *kona* (south) winds are present. The long, sandy beach is nice for a morning or evening stroll, but the

campground often makes this beach busier in summer. **Amenities:** lifeguards; parking (free); showers; toilets. **Best for:** surfing; swimming; walking. ⊠ *Anahola Rd., south of mile marker 14, Anahola* ⧉ *Free.*

Baby Beach

BEACH | FAMILY | There aren't many safe swimming beaches on Kauai's East Side; however, this one usually ranks highly with parents because there's a narrow, lagoonlike area between the beach and the near-shore reef perfect for small children. In winter, watch for east and northeast swells that would make this not such a safe option. There are minimal beach facilities—and no lifeguards—so watch your babies. There is an old-time shower spigot (cold water only) along the roadside available to rinse off the salt water. **Amenities:** parking (free); showers. **Best for:** sunrise; swimming. ⊠ *Moanakai Rd., Kapaa* ⧉ *Free.*

Donkey Beach (*Paliku Beach*)

BEACH | This beach gets its unusual name from the former Lihue Plantation Company, which once kept a herd of mules and donkeys in the pasture adjacent to the beach. If the waves are right, bodyboarders and surfers might be spotted offshore. However, the waters here are usually rough and not recommended for swimming and snorkeling. Instead, we suggest a morning walk along the easy trail that overlooks the coast, starting at the northern end of Kealia Beach. It's not uncommon to see nude sunbathers here. **Amenities:** none. **Best for:** solitude; sunrise; surfing. ⊠ *Rte. 56, north of Kealia Kai subdivision, Kealia* ⧉ *Free.*

Kealia Beach

BEACH | Adjacent to the highway heading north out of Kapaa, ½-mile-long Kealia Beach attracts bodyboarders and surfers year-round. It's a favorite with locals and visitors alike. Kealia is not generally a great beach for swimming, but it's a place to sunbathe and enjoy the beach scene. The safest area to swim is at the

Best Beaches by Activity

He says "to-*mah*-toe," and she says "to-*may*-toe." When it comes to beaches on Kauai, the meaning behind that axiom holds true: people are different. What thrills one person may leave another cold. Here are some suggestions for choosing a beach that's right for you.

Best for Families

Lydgate State Park, East Side. The kid-designed playground, the protected swimming pools, and Kamalani Bridge guarantee you will not hear these words from your child: "Mom, I'm bored."

Poipu Beach Park, South Shore. The *keiki* (children's) pool and lifeguards make this a safe spot for kids. The near-perpetual sun isn't so bad, either.

Best Stand-Up Paddling

Anini Beach Park, North Shore. The reef and long stretch of beach give beginners a calm place to try stand-up paddling. You won't get pummeled by waves here.

Wailua Beach, East Side. The Wailua River bisects the beach and heads inland 2 miles, providing stand-up paddlers with a long and scenic stretch of water before they have to figure out how to turn around.

Best Surfing

Hanalei Bay, North Shore. In winter, Hanalei Bay offers a range of breaks, from beginner to advanced. Surfing legends Laird Hamilton and the Irons brothers grew up surfing the waters of Hanalei.

Waiohai Beach, South Shore. Surf instructors flock to this spot with their students for its gentle,

near-shore break. Then, as students advance, they can paddle out a little farther to an intermediate break—if they're ready.

Best Sunsets

Kee Beach, North Shore. Even in winter, when the sun sets in the south and out of view, you won't be disappointed here because "golden hour," as photographers call the time around sunset, paints Napali Coast with a warm, gold light. Plan ahead, as reservations are required and visitor numbers are limited: ⊕ *gohaena.com*.

Polihale State Park, West Side. This due-west-facing beach may be tricky to get to, but it does offer the most unobstructed sunset views on the island. The fact that it's so remote means you won't have strangers in your photos, but you will have the island of Niihau in view. Do plan to depart right after sunset or risk getting spooked in the dark.

Best for Celeb Spotting

Haena Beach Park, North Shore. Behind those gated driveways and heavily foliaged yards that line this beach live—at least, part time—some of the world's most celebrated music and movie moguls. Plan ahead and reserve at ⊕ *gohaena.com*.

Hanalei Bay, North Shore. We know we tout this beach often, but it deserves the praise. It's a mecca for everyone—regular Joes, surfers, fishers, young people, older folks, locals, visitors, and, especially, the famous. You may also recognize Hanalei Bay from the 2011 movie *The Descendants*.

Nothing beats fruit-flavored shave ice (no, not "shaved" ice) on a hot Hawaiian day.

far north end of the beach, protected by a lava rock sea wall. The waters are often rough and the waves crumbly due to an onshore break (no protecting reef) and northeasterly trade winds. A scenic lookout on the southern end, accessed off the highway, is a superb location for saluting the morning sunrise or spotting whales during winter. A level, paved section of the Ke Ala Hele Makalae bike path, with small, covered pavilions, runs along the coastline here and is popular for walking and biking. **Amenities:** lifeguard; parking (free); showers; toilets. **Best for:** sunrise; surfing; swimming; walking. ⊠ *Rte. 56, at mile marker 10, Kealia* 🕮 *Free.*

Lydgate State Park

BEACH | FAMILY | This is by far the best family beach park on Kauai: the waters off the beach are protected by a hand-built breakwater, creating two boulder-enclosed saltwater pools for safe swimming and snorkeling most of the year. Heavy rains upriver do occasionally deposit driftwood, clogging the pools. The smaller of the two pools is perfect for *keiki* (children). Behind the beach is Kamalani Playground; children of all ages—that includes you—enjoy the swings, lava-tube slides, tree house, and open field. Picnic tables abound in the park, and pavilions for day use and overnight camping are available by permit. The Kamalani Kai Bridge is a second playground, south of the original. (The two are united by the Ke Ala Hele Makalae bike and pedestrian coastal path.) Note that at this writing, plans were under way to institute a $10 parking fee for nonresidents. ■**TIP→ This park system is perennially popular; the quietest times to visit are early mornings and weekdays. Amenities:** lifeguards; parking (free); showers; toilets. **Best for:** partiers; sunrise; swimming; walking. ⊠ *Leho Dr., Wailua (Kauai County)* ✛ *Just south of Wailua River* 🕮 *Free.*

Shave Ice

Nothing goes down quite as nicely as shave ice on a hot day. This favorite island treat has been likened to a sno-cone, but that description doesn't do a good shave ice justice. Yes, it is ice served up in a cone-shape cup and drenched with sweet syrup, but the similarities end there.

As its name implies, the ice should be feathery light—the texture of snowflakes, not frozen slush. And alongside the standard cherry and grape, you'll find all sorts of island flavorings, such as passion fruit, pineapple, coconut, mango, and, of course, a rainbow mix or snow topping of condensed milk.

Not all shave ice meets these high standards, and when you're hot, even the average ones taste great. A few places are worth seeking out. On the East Side, the best is **Hawaiian Blizzard** (⊠ *Kapaa Shopping Center, 4–1105 Kuhio Hwy.*), a true shave-ice stand that opens up weekday afternoons next to the Big Save grocery store in Kapaa. In Koloa on the South Shore, try **Waikomo Shave Ice** (⊠ *2827 Poipu Rd.*), with all-natural syrups made from fruit purees and organic sugar or Kauai honey. It's open noon to 5 pm daily. On the hot, dry West Side, make a beeline for **JoJo's** (⊠ *9734 Kaumualii Hwy.*), open on the main drag in Waimea from 11 am to 5 pm daily. All three places have benches where you can sit and slurp.

Wailua Beach

BEACH | At the mouth of Hawaii's only navigable river, Wailua Beach has considerable cultural significance. At the river's mouth, petroglyphs carved on boulders are sometimes visible during low surf and tide conditions. Surfers and stand-up paddlers enjoy this beach, and many families spend the weekend days under the Wailua Bridge at the river mouth, even hauling out their portable grills and tables to go with their beach chairs. The great news about Wailua Beach is that it's almost impossible to miss; however, parking can be a challenge. The best parking for the north end of the beach is on Papaloa Road behind the Shell station. For the southern end of the beach, park at Wailua River State Park. **Amenities:** parking (free); showers; toilets. **Best for:** surfing; swimming; walking; windsurfing. ⊠ *Kuhio Hwy., Wailua (Kauai County)* 🅼 *Free.*

🍴 Restaurants

In recent years, the most affordable, hip new eateries on the island have opened in Kapaa. Unlike the resort-dominated South and North Shores, Kapaa is local, fun, and eclectic, with food trucks on the side of the road, vegetarian venues, and bars serving up artful appetizers. Diversity is the key to this area; there is something for everyone, especially those on a budget.

Bull Shed

$$$ | **STEAKHOUSE** | The A-frame structure makes this popular restaurant look distinctly rustic from the outside, but inside, light colors and a full wall of glass highlight an ocean view that is one of the best on Kauai. The food is simple, but they know how to do surf and turf well, including prime rib and Australian rack of lamb. **Known for:** quiet bar; views of surf crashing on the rocks; combo dinner platters. ⑤ *Average main: $35* ⊠ *796 Kuhio*

Hwy., Kapaa ☎ *808/822–3791* ⊕ *www.bullshedrestaurant.com* ☽ *No lunch.*

★ Hukilau Lanai

$$$ | AMERICAN | Relying heavily on super fresh island fish and local meats and produce, this restaurant offers creatively prepared food that is a great choice for value and consistent quality on the East Side. The nightly fish specials—served grilled, steamed, or sautéed with succulent sauces—shine here. **Known for:** delicious desserts; ahi poke nachos; gluten-free options. $ *Average main: $28* ⊠ *Kauai Coast Resort, Coconut Marketplace, 520 Aleka Loop, Wailua (Kauai County)* ☎ *808/822–0600* ⊕ *www.hukilaukauai.com* ☽ *Closed Mon. No lunch.*

★ JO2 Restaurant

$$$ | FUSION | This creation of Jean-Marie Josselin, the renowned chef who brought Hawaii Regional Cuisine to Kauai in 1990, reflects his culinary growth. The food is imaginative, with its French, Japanese, and Islands influences, and it's served with flair in a chic yet casual dining room that's tucked away in a nondescript strip mall. **Known for:** excellent service; the $35 prix fixe 5–6 pm; daily-changing menu. $ *Average main: $35* ⊠ *4–971 Kuhio Hwy., Kapaa* ☎ *808/212–1627* ⊕ *www.jotwo.com* ☽ *Closed Sun. and Mon. No lunch.*

Kenji Burger

$$ | FUSION | The humble hamburger gets an Asian twist at Kenji's, a small, casual, friendly eatery that uses 100% grass-fed Kauai beef and also has plenty of nonbeef offerings. Choose the teriyaki, veggie, truffle, or hapa burger, each topped with goodies like caramelized onions, Japanese mushrooms, and tomato jam. **Known for:** sushi burritos filled with seafood; lychee soda; french fries with Japanese seasoning. $ *Average main: $19* ⊠ *4–788 Kuhio Hwy., Kapaa* ☎ *808/320–3558* ⊕ *www.kenjiburger.com* ☽ *No lunch.*

Kountry Kitchen

$ | AMERICAN | FAMILY | If you like a hearty breakfast, try this family-friendly restaurant with its cozy, greasy-spoon atmosphere and friendly service; it's a great spot for omelets, banana pancakes, waffles, and eggs Benedict in two sizes. Lunch selections include sandwiches, burgers, and *loco moco* (a popular local rice, beef, gravy, and eggs concoction). **Known for:** hearty portions; all-day breakfast; takeout options. $ *Average main: $14* ⊠ *1485 Kuhio Hwy., Kapaa* ☎ *808/822–3511* ⊕ *www.kountrystyle-kitchen.com* ☽ *Closed Tues. and Wed. No dinner.*

Lemongrass Grill

$$ | ASIAN FUSION | The decor of this restaurant known for its eclectic, Asian-influenced menu may remind you of a Pacific Rim–theme rustic tavern, with its stained-wood interior and numerous paintings and carvings. There's something for everyone here: salads, poultry, steaks and ribs, vegetarian fare, and, of course, a wide selection of seafood, all with an island flair. **Known for:** fresh fish; curries and satays; lively bar. $ *Average main: $25* ⊠ *4–871 Kuhio Hwy., Kapaa* ☎ *808/821–2888* ☽ *Closed Thurs. No lunch.*

Monico's Taqueria

$$ | MEXICAN | Monico's Taqueria is a favorite among locals and visitors due to its hearty portions and delicious, authentic cuisine including nachos and fajitas. The bright, airy dining room is cheerful, and the outdoor patio offers a view of coconut palms waving in the breeze. **Known for:** friendly service; ahi fish tacos; worthy margaritas. $ *Average main: $18* ⊠ *4–733 Kuhio Hwy., Kapaa* ☎ *808/822–4300* ☽ *Closed Sun. and Mon.*

Russell's by Eat Healthy Kauai

$$ | VEGETARIAN | A restored plantation cottage surrounded by tropical foliage is the casual setting for this island café. The vegan menu offers a limited but tasty array of plant-based options, including hummus wraps, Beyond Beef burgers, and tofu-based entrées. **Known for:** small-bites menu in afternoon; alfresco dining in leafy garden; evening music. ⑤ *Average main: $22* ✉ *4–369 Kuhio Hwy., Wailua (Kauai County)* ☎ *808/822–7990* ⊕ *eathealthykauai.com* ⊘ *Closed Sun. and Mon. No dinner Tues. and Wed.*

Shivalik Indian Cuisine
$$ | INDIAN | This eatery provides a refreshing alternative to the typical surf and turf offerings at most of Kauai's restaurants. Offering a variety of Indian regional styles, this hideaway in a small plaza turns out biryani and tandoori dishes, light and flavorful naan, and many vegetarian items, as well as curries and chicken and lamb dishes. **Known for:** extensive menu; Friday dinner buffet; tandoor oven. ⑤ *Average main: $19* ✉ *4–771 Kuhio Hwy., Wailua (Kauai County)* ☎ *808/821–2333* ⊕ *www.shivalikindian-cuisines.com* ⊘ *Closed Tues.*

Tiki Tacos
$ | MEXICAN | Not surprisingly, tacos take center stage here, though there are tamales and a quesadilla. The tacos are made from quality ingredients, many of which are organic and locally sourced, and you can mix and match. **Known for:** vegetarian options; large portions; house-made corn tortillas. ⑤ *Average main: $8* ✉ *4–971 Kuhio Hwy., Kapaa* ☎ *808/823–8226.*

☕ Coffee and Quick Bites

Mermaids Café
$ | ECLECTIC | Located right on the main drag of Kapaa, this café has an exterior that's a bit grimy and noisy, but it's worth a stop to order takeout and walk to the beach instead. The poke salad bowl and ahi nori wrap made of seared tuna, rice, and cucumber with wasabi cream sauce are the best picks here. **Known for:** popular spot; chicken or tofu satay; variety of satisfying salads. ⑤ *Average main: $12*

✉ *1384 Kuhio Hwy., Kapaa* ☎ *808/821–2026* ▭ *No credit cards.*

Papaya's
$ | AMERICAN | Kauai's largest natural-foods market, now in much larger digs fronting the highway in the same shopping center, offers a limited menu with decent vegan and vegetarian food at low prices. Food items change daily, but there's always a salad bar and favorites like tempeh wraps and fish tacos for lunch and dinner. **Known for:** smoothies and a juice bar; taro burgers; fresh, organic produce. ⑤ *Average main: $12* ✉ *4–901 Kuhio Hwy., Kapaa* ☎ *808/823–0190* ⊕ *www.papayasnaturalfoods.com.*

🛏 Hotels

Since Kapaa is the island's major population center, this area, including Waipouli and Wailua, has a lived-in, real-world feel. It has some of the best deals on accommodations and a wider choice of inexpensive restaurants and shops than you'll find in the resort areas. The beaches here are so-so for swimming but nice for sunbathing, walking, and watching the sun or the moon rise.

The Wailua area is rather compact, and much of it can be accessed from a coastal walking and biking path. The resorts here are attractive to middle-class travelers seeking a good bang for their buck. Wailua had a rich cultural significance for the ancient Hawaiians. Their royalty lived here, and *heiau* (ancient sacred grounds) are clearly marked.

Aston Islander on the Beach
$$$ | HOTEL | A low-rise, Hawaii-plantation-style design gives this 6-acre beachfront property a pleasant, relaxed feeling; the guest rooms are spread over eight three-story buildings, each with a lanai that looks out on lovely green lawns. **Pros:** online rate deals; convenient location near shops and restaurants; coin-operated laundries. **Cons:** no resort amenities but still charges fee; no

restaurant on the property; smallish pool. ⑤ *Rooms from: $339* ✉ *440 Aleka Pl., Wailua (Kauai County)* ☎ *808/822–7417, 866/774–2924* ⊕ *www.aquaaston.com* ⇨ *200 rooms* ⑩ *No Meals.*

Hilton Garden Inn Kauai Wailua Bay

$$$ | HOTEL | FAMILY | Nestled alongside Wailua Bay and the Wailua River, this low-key, low-rise chain hotel is a convenient place to stay as it's within walking distance of Lydgate Beach, with its lifeguard and lawns, and also close to shops and low-cost restaurants. **Pros:** oceanfront walking path near property; close to ocean; some beach- and ocean-view rooms. **Cons:** traffic is busy fronting hotel; restaurant meals are average; prices are high for modest facilities. ⑤ *Rooms from: $332* ✉ *3–5920 Kuhio Hwy., Kapaa* ☎ *808/823–6000, 888/823–5111* ⊕ *www.hilton.com* ⇨ *250 rooms* ⑩ *Free Breakfast.*

Hotel Coral Reef

$$ | HOTEL | FAMILY | In business since 1956, this small, three-story hotel is something of a Kauai beachfront landmark, with clean, comfortable rooms, some with great ocean views, and a large pool that overlooks the water; expect great sunrises. **Pros:** convenient location near restaurants and shops; free parking; oceanfront setting. **Cons:** traffic noise; ocean swimming is marginal; located in a busy section of Kapaa. ⑤ *Rooms from: $238* ✉ *4–1516 Kuhio Hwy., Kapaa* ☎ *808/822–4481, 800/843–4659* ⊕ *www.hotelcoralreefresort.com* ⇨ *27 rooms* ⑩ *Free Breakfast.*

Kapaa Sands

$$ | APARTMENT | An old rock etched with *kanji* (Japanese characters) reminds you that the site of this condominium gem was once occupied by a Shinto temple. **Pros:** turtle and monk seal sightings common; discounts for extended stays; walking distance to shops, restaurants, and beach. **Cons:** traffic noise in rear units; small bathrooms; no-frills lodging.

⑤ *Rooms from: $189* ✉ *380 Papaloa Rd., Wailua (Kauai County)* ☎ *808/822–4901, 800/222–4901* ⊕ *www.kapaasands.com* ⇨ *24 units* ⑩ *No Meals.*

★ Kauai Coast Resort at the Beachboy

$$$$ | TIMESHARE | FAMILY | Fronting an uncrowded stretch of beach, this three-story, primarily timeshare condo resort is convenient and a bit more upscale than nearby properties. **Pros:** attractive pool; central location; nice sunrises. **Cons:** daily housekeeping fee; ocean not ideal for swimming; beach is narrow. ⑤ *Rooms from: $379* ✉ *520 Aleka Loop, Wailua (Kauai County)* ☎ *808/822–3441, 866/729–7182* ⊕ *www.shellhospitality.com* ⇨ *108 units* ⑩ *No Meals.*

Kauai Shores Hotel

$$ | HOTEL | Once an oceanfront inn and now an affordable boutique hotel, this property remains no-frills lodging, but rooms have a refrigerator and are comfortable, bright, and clean. **Pros:** great sunrises; near walking path, shops, and dining; free Wi-Fi. **Cons:** daily hospitality fee; minimal amenities; coral reef makes ocean swimming marginal. ⑤ *Rooms from: $254* ✉ *420 Papaloa Rd., Wailua (Kauai County)* ☎ *808/822–4951, 800/560–5553* ⊕ *www.kauaishoreshotel. com* ⇨ *202 rooms* ⑩ *No Meals.*

Lae Nani Resort Kauai by Outrigger

$$$$ | APARTMENT | Ruling Hawaiian chiefs once returned from ocean voyages to this spot, now host to comfortable condominiums, and Outrigger has created attractive plant, water, and rock features. **Pros:** attractively furnished (though units differ due to individual ownership); nice beach; walking distance to playground. **Cons:** cleaning fee; no Wi-Fi; third floor is walk-up. ⑤ *Rooms from: $356* ✉ *410 Papaloa Rd., Wailua (Kauai County)* ☎ *808/823–1401, 866/994–1588* ⊕ *www. outrigger.com/hotels-resorts* ⇨ *84 units* ⑩ *No Meals.*

One of the best places for a luau on the East Side is at Smith's Tropical Paradise.

Plantation Hale Suites

$$ | APARTMENT | These older, plantation-style one-bedroom units with garden lanai have well-equipped kitchenettes and are clean and comfortable, with a queen-size pullout sofa for extra guests. **Pros:** walking distance to shops, restaurant, beach; free high-speed Internet; three pools. **Cons:** older units; coral reef makes ocean swimming challenging; traffic noise in mountain-view units. ⑤ *Rooms from: $233* ⊠ *525 Aleka Loop, Wailua (Kauai County)* ☎ *808/822–4941, 800/775–4253* ⊕ *www.plantation-hale. com* ⇴ *104 units* ¡⊙¡ *No Meals.*

Sheraton Kauai Coconut Beach Resort

$$$ | RESORT | One of the few true oceanfront properties on Kauai, this popular hotel sits on a ribbon of sand in Kapaa and has bright, spacious rooms that face the ocean or pool. **Pros:** pleasant grounds; access to coastal path; near shops and restaurants. **Cons:** high daily parking fee; small pool; coastline not conducive to swimming. ⑤ *Rooms from: $269* ⊠ *650 Aleka Loop, Wailua (Kauai County)* ☎ *808/822–3455, 800/760–8555* ⊕ *www.marriott.com* ⇴ *311 rooms* ¡⊙¡ *No Meals.*

▼ Nightlife

BARS

★ Hukilau Lanai Bar

BARS | Trade winds waft through this modest little open-air bar, which looks out onto a coconut grove. The bar and restaurant is on the property of the Kauai Coast Resort but operates independently. If the mood takes you, go on a short walk to the sea, or recline in big, comfortable chairs in Wally's Bar in the lobby while listening to Hawaiian slack key guitar. Live music plays from Wednesday through Saturday evenings. Poolside happy hour runs from 3 to 5. Try one of the freshly infused tropical martinis or Kauai-made mead, or choose from a good selection of wines by the glass. ⊠ *520 Aleka Loop, Wailua (Kauai County)* ☎ *808/822–0600* ⊕ *www.hukilaukauai.com.*

🎭 Performing Arts

LUAU AND POLYNESIAN REVUES

Although the commercial luau experience is a far cry from the backyard luau thrown by local residents to celebrate a wedding, graduation, or baby's first birthday, they're nonetheless entertaining and a good introduction to the Hawaiian food that isn't widely sold in restaurants. With many, you can watch a roasted pig being carried out of its *imu,* a hole in the ground used for cooking meat with heated stones. Besides the feast and free mai tais, there's often an exciting dinner show with Polynesian-style music and dancing. It all makes for a fun evening suitable for couples, families, and groups, and the informal setting is conducive to meeting other people.

Every luau is different, reflecting the cuisine and tenor of the host facility, so compare prices, menus, and entertainment before making your reservation. Most luau on Kauai are offered on a limited number of nights each week, so plan ahead to get the luau you want.

★ Smith Family Garden Luau

CULTURAL FESTIVALS | A 30-acre tropical garden on the Wailua River provides the lovely setting for this popular luau, which begins with the traditional blowing of the conch shell and *imu* (pig roast) ceremony, followed by cocktails, an island feast, great music, hula, and an international show in the amphitheater overlooking a torch-lighted lagoon. Presented Monday and Wednesday through Friday, it's fairly authentic and the oldest commercial luau on Kauai. ⊠ *Smith's Tropical Paradise, 174 Wailua Rd., Kapaa* ☎ *808/821–6895* ⊕ *www.smithskauai.com* 🍴 *$125; kids 7–13 $35, kids 3–6 $25.*

🛍 Shopping

Kapaa is the most heavily populated area on Kauai, so it's not surprising that it has the most diverse shopping opportunities on the island. Unlike the North Shore's retail scene, shops here are not neatly situated in centers; they are spread out along a long stretch of road, with many local retail gems tucked away and easy to miss if you're in a rush.

CLOTHING

a.ell atelier

MIXED CLOTHING | Clothing designer Angelique Ell sells everything from custom wedding gowns to men's aloha shirts to children's clothing, using sustainable materials and practices. Specialized home decor items are also sold in this distinctive boutique, as are soaps, jewelry, candles, handbags, and a bit of artwork by local artists. ⊠ *4–1320 Kuhio Hwy., Kapaa* ☎ *808/212–7550* ⊕ *www.aellatelier.com.*

Deja Vu Surf Hawaii: Kapaa

MIXED CLOTHING | This family operation has a great assortment of branded surf wear and clothes for outdoors fanatics, including tank tops, caps, swimwear, and Kauai-style T-shirts. They also carry bodyboards and water-sports accessories. Good deals can be found at sidewalk sales. ⊠ *4–1419 Kuhio Hwy., Kapaa* ☎ *808/320–7108* ⊕ *www.dejavusurf.com.*

Marta's Boat

MIXED CLOTHING | On display at this quirky boutique is expensive but unique clothing by husband-and-wife team Ambrose and Marta Curry. He creates silk-screen art with nontoxic paint on fabric in his studio next door, then she cuts and sews the fabric into bags and clothing for men, women, and children. Operating hours are erratic; you'll typically need to call ahead. ⊠ *4–770 Kuhio Hwy., Kapaa* ☎ *808/822–3926.*

GALLERIES

ALOHA Images

ART GALLERIES | ALOHA stands for "Affordable Location of Original Hawaiian Art." A self-proclaimed "candy store for art lovers," it represents 11 artists who produce Hawaii-theme art, ranging in

Kauai: Undercover Movie Star

Though Kauai has played itself in the movies, starring in *The Descendants* (2011), for example, much of its screen time has been as a stunt double for a number of tropical paradises. The island's remote valleys portrayed Venezuelan jungle in Kevin Costner's *Dragonfly* (2002) and a Costa Rican dinosaur preserve in Steven Spielberg's *Jurassic Park* (1993). Spielberg was no stranger to Kauai, having filmed Harrison Ford's escape via seaplane from Menehune Fishpond in *Raiders of the Lost Ark* (1981). Recently, the island stood in for parts of South America in Disney's *Jungle Cruise* (2021).

The fluted cliffs and gorges of Kauai's rugged Napali Coast play the misunderstood beast's island home in *King Kong* (1976), and a jungle dweller of another sort, in *George of the Jungle* (1997), also frolicked on Kauai. Harrison Ford returned to the island for 10 weeks during the filming of *Six Days, Seven Nights* (1998), a romantic adventure set in French Polynesia. Part-time Kauai resident Ben Stiller used the island as a stand-in for the jungles of Vietnam in *Tropic Thunder* (2008), and Johnny Depp came here to film some of *Pirates of the Caribbean: On Stranger Tides* (2011). But these are all relatively contemporary movies. What's truly remarkable is that Hollywood discovered Kauai in 1933 with the making of *White Heat*, which was set on a sugar plantation and—like *South Pacific* (also filmed on Kauai)— dealt with an interracial love story.

Then it was off to the races, as Kauai saw no fewer than a dozen movies filmed on the island in the 1950s,

though not all of them were Oscar contenders. Among them were *She Gods of Shark Reef* (1956) and *Miss Sadie Thompson* (1953), which starred Rita Hayworth.

The movie that is still immortalized on the island in the names of restaurants, real estate offices, a hotel, and even a sushi item is *South Pacific* (1957). (You guessed it, right?) That mythical place called Bali Hai is never far away on Kauai.

In the 1960s, Elvis Presley filmed *Blue Hawaii* (1961) and *Girls! Girls! Girls!* (1962) on the island. All in all, Kauai has welcomed plenty of Hollywood's A-list: John Wayne in *Donovan's Reef* (1963); Jack Lemmon in *The Wackiest Ship in the Army* (1960); Richard Chamberlain in *The Thorn Birds* (1983); Gene Hackman in *Uncommon Valor* (1983); Danny DeVito and Billy Crystal in *Throw Momma from the Train* (1987); and Dustin Hoffman, Morgan Freeman, Rene Russo, and Cuba Gooding Jr. in *Outbreak* (1995).

Kauai has also appeared on a long list of TV shows and made-for-TV movies, including *Gilligan's Island, Fantasy Island, Starsky & Hutch, Baywatch Hawaii*—even reality TV shows *The Bachelor* and *The Amazing Race 3*.

For the record, just because a movie did some filming here doesn't mean the entire movie was filmed on Kauai. *Honeymoon in Vegas* (1992) filmed just one scene here; the murder mystery *A Perfect Getaway* (2009) was set on the famous Kalalau Trail and featured beautiful Kauai backdrops, but was shot mostly in Puerto Rico.

cost from $75 up to the rare $25,000. Owner Ray Charron offers layaway plans upon request. ✉ *4504 Kukui St., Kapaa* ☎ *808/631–8026* ⊕ *www.alohaimages. com.*

Kela's Glass Gallery

ART GALLERIES | The colorful vases, bowls, and other fragile items sold in this distinctive gallery are definitely worth viewing if you appreciate quality handmade glass art. It's expensive, but if something catches your eye, they'll happily pack it for safe transport home. The gallery also ships worldwide. ✉ *4–1400 Kuhio Hwy., Kapaa* ☎ *808/822–4527* ⊕ *www.glass-art. com.*

GIFTS

Pagoda

ANTIQUES & COLLECTIBLES | The shop is tiny, but it's big on exceptional antiques, Hawaiiana, and gifts. The owner, Liane, has been collecting rare finds most of her life and now has a place to showcase them. Her inventory changes regularly, with a mix of new and vintage items. ✉ *4–369 Kuhio Hwy., Kapaa* ☎ *808/821–2172* ⊕ *www.pagodakauai.com.*

Vicky's Fabric Shop

FABRICS | Tropical and Hawaiian prints, silks, slinky rayons, soft cottons, quilting kits, and other fine fabrics fill this small store. A variety of sewing patterns and notions are featured as well, making it a must-stop for any sewing enthusiast and a great place to buy unique island-made gifts. Check out the one-of-a-kind selection of purses, aloha wear, and other quality hand-sewn items. ✉ *4–1326 Kuhio Hwy., Kapaa* ☎ *808/822–1746* ⊕ *www. vickysfabrics.com.*

HOME DECOR

Otsuka's

FURNITURE | Family-owned Otsuka's has a large clientele of visitors who appreciate its wide selection of unique furniture, artwork, candles, tropical-print pillows, accessories, rugs, and knickknacks.

Roadside Vendors 💼

Lei. Tropical flowers. Fresh fish. Rambutan. Avocados. Grilled *huli huli* chicken. Kalua pork. It's not uncommon to run across individuals selling flowers, produce, and food on the side of the road. Some are local farmers trying to make a living; others are people fundraising for the local canoe club. Don't be afraid to stop and buy. The prices are usually good, and most vendors are friendly and enjoy chatting.

✉ *4–1624 Kuhio Hwy., Kapaa* ☎ *808/822–7766* ⊕ *www.otsukas.com.*

JEWELRY

Jim Saylor Jewelers

JEWELRY & WATCHES | Jim Saylor and his team of jewelers have been designing beautiful keepsakes on Kauai since 1976. Gems from around the world, including black pearls, diamonds, and more, appear in his unusual settings, and he welcomes custom orders. ✉ *4–1318 Kuhio Hwy., Kapaa* ☎ *808/822–3591* ⊕ *www.jimsaylorjewelers.com.*

MARKET

NoKa Fair

MARKET | Open daily, the NoKa (North Kapaa) Fair outdoor market—formerly the Kauai Products Fair—has been redesigned and now features a collection of shipping containers repurposed to house vendors selling photography, art, clothing, aloha wear, jewelry, and gifts. ✉ *4–1613 Kuhio Hwy., Kapaa* ☎ *808/246–0988* ⊕ *nokafairkauai.com.*

SHOPPING CENTERS

Kauai Village Shopping Center

SHOPPING CENTER | The buildings of this Kapaa shopping village are in the style of a 19th-century plantation town. ABC Discount Store sells sundries; Safeway carries groceries and alcoholic beverages; Papaya's has health foods and a minimalist café. Also here are a small bakery, a bar, Ross Dress for Less, a UPS store, a Chinese restaurant, GNC, and Starbucks. ⊠ *4–831 Kuhio Hwy., Kapaa* ☎ *808/822–3777.*

Kinipopo Shopping Village

SHOPPING CENTER | At this tiny center on Kuhio Highway, Korean BBQ Restaurant fronts the highway, as does Goldsmiths Kauai, a gallery selling handcrafted Hawaiian-style gold jewelry. A bakery, a real estate company, and Avalon Gastropub round out the businesses here. ⊠ *4–356 Kuhio Hwy., Kapaa* ⊕ *www. kinipopovillage.com.*

Waipouli Town Center

SHOPPING CENTER | McDonald's is the focus of this small retail plaza, which fronts Kuhio Highway and also houses Shivalik Indian Cuisine, Waipouli Deli and Restaurant, and Auto Zone. ⊠ *4–771 Kuhio Hwy., Kapaa* ☎ *808/742–9003* ⊕ *waipoulitowncenter.com.*

🏃 Activities

SPAS
Golden Lotus Studio

YOGA | Tucked off the main road in Kapaa, this small studio offers a variety of yoga and dance classes, including yoga nidra and contortion yoga. Different types of massage are available by appointment, primarily reiki and a special $40 massage clinic with new massage school graduates. Check the website for special events and workshops. ⊠ *4–941A Kuhio Hwy., Kapaa* ☎ *808/823–9810* ⊕ *www. goldenlotuskauai.org* ⊒ *$80 for 1-hr massage.*

Lihue

7 miles southwest of Wailua.

The commercial and political center of Kauai County, which includes the islands of Kauai and Niihau, Lihue is home to the island's major airport, harbor, and hospital. This is where you can find the state and county offices that issue camping and hiking permits and the same fast-food eateries and big-box stores that blight the mainland. The county has revived the downtown by sprucing up Rice Street, but there's still little reason to linger in lackluster Lihue.

👁 Sights

★ Alekoko (Menehune) Fishpond

HISTORIC SIGHT | No one knows just who built this large, intricate, almost 1,000-year-old aquaculture structure in the Huleia River, but legend attributes it to the Menehune, a mythical—or real, depending on who you ask—ancient race of people known for their small stature, industrious nature, and superb stone-working skills. Volcanic rock was cut and skillfully fit together into massive walls four feet thick and five feet high, forming a centuries-old enclosure for raising mullet and other freshwater fish. Volunteers removed invasive mangroves and restored the pond to its original condition. You can view it from an overlook about 4 miles from downtown Lihue. ⊠ *End of Hulemalu Rd., Niumalu.*

Grove Farm Sugar Plantation Museum

FARM/RANCH | Guided tours of this carefully restored 80-acre country estate offer a fascinating and authentic look at how upper-class white people experienced plantation life in the mid-19th century. The tour focuses on the original home, built by the Wilcox family in 1860 and filled with a quirky collection of classic Hawaiiana. You can also see the workers'

Did You Know?

According to legend, the mythical Menehune built the Alekoko Fishpond more than 1,000 years ago, in just one night.

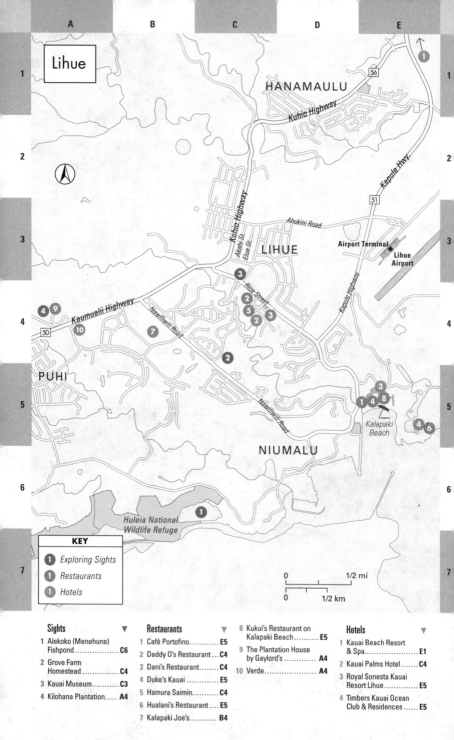

Lihue

HANAMAULU

Kuhio Highway

56

Kapule Hwy

51

Ahukini Road

LIHUE

Airport Terminal

Lihue Airport

Kuhio Highway

Akahi St.

Eiwa St.

Rice Street

Kaumualii Highway

50

Nawiliwili Road

PUHI

Kapule Highway

Nawiliwili Road

NIUMALU

Kalapaki Beach

Huleia National Wildlife Refuge

KEY
- **1** *Exploring Sights*
- **1** *Restaurants*
- **1** *Hotels*

0   1/2 mi

0   1/2 km

quarters, farm animals, orchards, and gardens that reflect the practical, self-sufficient lifestyle of the island's earliest Western inhabitants. Tours of the homestead are conducted twice a day, three days a week. To protect the historic building and its furnishings, tours may be canceled on very wet days. ■TIP➔ **With a six-person limit per tour, reservations are essential.** ✉ *4050 Nawiliwili Rd., Lihue* ☎ *808/245–3202* ⊕ *www.grovefarm.org* ✉ *$20 requested donation; tour reservations essential.*

★ Kauai Museum

HISTORY MUSEUM | Maintaining a stately presence on Rice Street, the historical museum building is easy to find and features a permanent display, "The Story of Kauai," that provides a competent overview of the Garden Island and Niihau. The exhibit traces the Islands' geology, mythology, and cultural history. Local artists are represented in changing exhibits in the second-floor Mezzanine Gallery. ■TIP➔ **The gift shop alone is worth a visit, with a fine collection of authentic Niihau shell lei, feather hatband lei, hand-turned wooden bowls, reference books, and other quality arts, crafts, and gifts—many of them locally made.** ✉ *4428 Rice St., Lihue* ☎ *808/245–6931* ⊕ *www.kauaimuseum. org* ✉ *$15* ⊙ *Closed Fri.–Sun.*

Kilohana Plantation

FARM/RANCH | FAMILY | This estate, once a much larger plantation and now a farm and visitor attraction, dates back to 1850, shortly after the "Great Mahele"—the division of land by the Hawaiian people. Plantation manager Albert Spencer Wilcox developed it as a working cattle ranch; it was also a sugar plantation. His nephew, Gaylord Parke Wilcox, took over in 1936, building Kauai's first mansion. Today the 16,000-square-foot, Tudor-style home houses specialty shops, art galleries, the Koloa Rum Company, Luau Kalamaku, and Gaylord's, a pretty restaurant with courtyard seating. Nearly half the original furnishings remain, and

the gardens and orchards were replanted according to the original plans. You can tour the grounds for free or take a 40-minute train ride that includes a chance to feed farm animals while learning the agricultural story of Kauai and viewing a working farm. A more expensive train tour includes lunch and fruit-picking in the orchard. ✉ *3–2087 Kaumualii Hwy., Lihue* ☎ *808/245–5608* ⊕ *www.kilohanakauai.com* ✉ *Grounds free; train tours $20, kids 3–12 $15.*

🜨 Beaches

Kalapaki Beach

BEACH | FAMILY | Five minutes south of the airport in Lihue, you'll find this wide beach and sandy-bottom bay fronting the Kauai Marriott. It's almost always safe from rip currents and undertows because it's around the back side of a peninsula, in its own cove. Tons of activities take place here, including all the usual water sports—beginning and intermediate surfing, bodyboarding, bodysurfing, and swimming. In addition, two outrigger canoe clubs paddle in the bay, and the Nawiliwili Yacht Club's boats sail around the harbor. Kalapaki is the only place on Kauai where double-hulled canoes are available for rent (at Kauai Beach Boys, which fronts the beach next to Duke's Kauai restaurant). Visitors can also rent snorkel gear, surfboards, bodyboards, and kayaks from Kauai Beach Boys, as well as sign up for surf lessons and sunset boat tours. A volleyball court on the beach is often used by a loosely organized group of local players; visitors are always welcome. ■TIP➔ **Avoid the stream on the south side of the beach; it often has high bacteria counts.** Duke's Kauai is one of only a couple of restaurants on the island actually on a beach. The restaurant's lower level is casual—even welcoming beach attire and sandy feet—making it perfect for lunch or an afternoon cocktail. **Amenities:** food and drink; lifeguards; parking (free); showers;

toilets; water sports. **Best for:** surfing; swimming; walking. ⊠ *Off Rice St., Lihue* ⊕ *kauaibeachboys.com* ☒ *Free.*

🍴 Restaurants

You will probably find yourself in Lihue at least a few times during your stay. When it comes to restaurants, Lihue isn't especially outstanding. There are some decent restaurants and some good low-cost eateries that feed locals and the business-lunch crowd—but nothing really stellar. If you are in town for lunch, check out some of the authentic local spots.

Café Portofino

$$$ | **ITALIAN** | The views of Kalapaki Bay and the Haupu Mountain Range are impressive at this mostly authentic northern Italian restaurant, which offers a range of pasta, meat, chicken, and fresh fish selections, as well as vegetarian entrées, a kids' menu, and pizza. Linger over coffee and ice cream–filled profiteroles or traditional tiramisu while listening to romantic music. **Known for:** open-air dining; roasted rack of lamb; romantic ambience. ⑤ *Average main: $30* ⊠ *Royal Sonesta Kauai Resort Lihue, 3481 Hoolaulea Way, Kalapaki Beach, Lihue* ☎ *808/245–2121* ⊕ *www.cafeportofino. com* ⊗ *No lunch.*

Daddy O's Restaurant

$ | **AMERICAN** | **FAMILY** | Large helpings of simple but satisfying, hearty fare are the focus at this no-frills spot in the slightly run-down Rice Shopping Center. Breakfast standards like stuffed French toast, shrimp or standard eggs Benedict, blueberry pancakes, waffles, and eggs dominate the menu and are served until closing. **Known for:** plate-lunch options; oxtail soup; island comfort food. ⑤ *Average main: $15* ⊠ *Rice Shopping Center, 4303 Rice St., Lihue* ☎ *808/245–6778* ⊕ *www.daddyoslihue.com* ⊗ *Closed Mon. No dinner.*

Dani's Restaurant

$ | **HAWAIIAN** | **FAMILY** | Kauai residents frequent this no-frills eatery near the Lihue Fire Station for hearty, local-style food at breakfast and lunch. It's a good place to try Hawaiian food, such as *laulau* (pork and taro leaves wrapped in ti leaves and steamed) or kalua pig, slow roasted in an underground oven. **Known for:** rice served with everything; Japanese options like teriyaki beef; Hawaiian comfort food at low prices. ⑤ *Average main: $9* ⊠ *4201 Rice St., Lihue* ☎ *808/245–4991* ⊗ *Closed Sun. No dinner.*

Duke's Kauai

$$$ | **SEAFOOD** | Surfing legend Duke Kahanamoku (1890–1968) is immortalized at this casual bi-level restaurant and bar on Kalapaki Beach where surfboards, photos, and other memorabilia marking Duke's long tenure as a waterman adorn the walls. Downstairs, you'll find simple, less expensive fare from fish tacos to stir-fried cashew chicken to hamburgers, served 11 am to 10:30 pm; upstairs, at dinner, fresh fish prepared in a variety of styles is the best choice, though the prime rib is a favorite among locals. **Known for:** hula pie ice-cream dessert; downstairs level good for lunch at the beach; lively bar. ⑤ *Average main: $35* ⊠ *Royal Sonesta Kauai Resort Lihue, 3610 Rice St., Kalapaki Beach, Lihue* ☎ *808/246–9599* ⊕ *www.dukeskauai. com.*

Hamura Saimin

$ | **ASIAN** | Folks just love this cash-only, old plantation-style diner, though the very simple food doesn't quite live up to the buzz. Locals and tourists still stream in and out all day long: the famous *saimin* noodle soup is the big draw, and each day the Hiraoka family dishes up about 1,000 bowls of the steaming broth and homemade noodles topped with a variety of garnishes. **Known for:** open late for Lihue; counter-style dining; grilled chicken and beef sticks. ⑤ *Average main: $9*

✉ 2956 Kress St., Lihue ☎ 808/245–3271 ⊟ No credit cards.

Hualani's Restaurant

$$ | FUSION | Hualani's is bright, airy and expansive, with an unobstructed view of the ocean, delivering diners a casual yet upscale experience that makes up for a menu that is rather limited in scope. Though it doesn't offer a wide range of choices, the food is simply and deftly prepared in an Asian fusion style. **Known for:** local ingredients; lively happy hour; kimchee fried rice with Spam. ⑤ *Average main: $25 ✉ Timbers Kauai, 3770 Alaoli Way, Lihue ☎ 808/320–7400 ⊕ www. timberskauai.com ⊘ No dinner Sun. and Mon.*

Kalapaki Joe's

$$ | AMERICAN | Both locations—in Lihue's Kukui Grove and in Poipu—appeal to sports fans who like a rip-roaring happy hour. The appetizer menu is extensive, and you can also choose from burgers, salads, sandwiches, tacos, fresh fish, and local favorites like kalua pork and cabbage. **Known for:** affordable, casual dining; plenty of TVs; boisterous bar. ⑤ *Average main: $20 ✉ 3–2600 Kaumualii Hwy., Lihue ☎ 808/245–6366 ⊕ www. kalapakijoes.com ⊘ Closed Sun. in Lihue.*

Kukui's on Kalapaki Beach

$$ | ECLECTIC | FAMILY | The meals at Kukui's feature Hawaiian, Asian, and contemporary American influences, and the open-air setting with a view of the ocean makes it a pleasant place to dine. It's spacious, making it well suited to families and those who want a relaxed setting. **Known for:** evening entertainment; garden setting; quiet atmosphere. ⑤ *Average main: $25 ✉ Royal Sonesta Kauai Resort Lihue, 3610 Rice St., Kalapaki Beach, Lihue ☎ 808/245–5050 ⊕ www.sonesta.com.*

The Plantation House by Gaylord's

$$$$ | ECLECTIC | Located in what was once Kauai's most expensive plantation estate, Gaylord's pays tribute to the elegant dining rooms of 1930s high society—candlelit tables sit on a cobblestone courtyard that surrounds a fountain and overlooks a wide lawn. The menu is eclectic, offering cioppino, sake short ribs, duck two ways, lamb shank, fresh fish, and a few vegan and vegetarian options. **Known for:** delightful outdoor seating; lavish Sunday brunch buffet; quiet dining. ⑤ *Average main: $39 ✉ Kilohana Plantation, 3–2087 Kaumualii Hwy., Lihue ☎ 808/245–9593 ⊕ www. kilohanakauai.com.*

Verde

$ | MEXICAN | Combining classic Mexican food with chile-based sauces and creations from the chef's home state of New Mexico, Verde's menu includes tostadas, enchiladas, and tacos filled with fresh fish, slow-cooked chicken, or local grass-fed beef. The garlic shrimp tacos and stacked enchilada with a choice of chicken, pork *adovada* (New Mexican red chile stew), or Kauai beef filling, smothered in red or green chile sauce, are favorites. **Known for:** red and green chile sauce; super-hot sauce; quality local ingredients. ⑤ *Average main: $14 ✉ Hokulei Village, 4454 Nuhou St., Suite 501, Lihue ☎ 808/320–7088 ⊕ www. verdehawaii.com.*

🛏 Hotels

Lihue is not the most desirable place to stay on Kauai, in terms of scenic beauty, although it does have its advantages, including easy access to the airport. Restaurants and shops are plentiful, and there's lovely Kalapaki Bay for beachgoers. Aside from the Royal Sonesta and the Kauai Beach Resort, most of the limited lodging possibilities are smaller and aimed at the cost-conscious traveler.

Kauai Beach Resort & Spa

$$$ | RESORT | This plantation-style hotel provides a relaxing, upscale oceanfront experience close to the airport, but without the noise. **Pros:** resort amenities; four pools with fun features; lawn games. **Cons:** no nearby restaurants or resorts; beach not good for swimming; high parking fee. $ *Rooms from: $269* ✉ *4331 Kauai Beach Dr., Hanamaulu* ☎ *808/246–5576* ⊕ *www.kauaibeachresortandspa. com* ⇆ *350 rooms* ⦿ *No Meals.*

Kauai Palms Hotel

$ | **HOTEL** | Not only is this low-cost alternative close to the airport, but it's also a great base for day trips to all sides of the island. **Pros:** centrally located; friendly staff; decent value for the money. **Cons:** traffic noise; smallish rooms (ask about studios and cottages); bare-bones amenities. $ *Rooms from: $154* ✉ *2931 Kalena St., Lihue* ☎ *808/246–0908* ⊕ *www. kauaipalmshotel.com* ⇆ *38 rooms* ⦿ *No Meals.*

Royal Sonesta Kauai Resort Lihue

$$$$ | **RESORT** | **FAMILY** | The former Marriott has changed hands, and its new owner, Sonesta, is conducting a $50 million refurbishment of guest rooms and common areas while the resort remains open. **Pros:** convenient location near shops and restaurants; oceanfront setting; plenty of resort amenities. **Cons:** located near an industrial area; ocean water quality can be poor at times; airport noise. $ *Rooms from: $352* ✉ *3610 Rice St., Kalapaki Beach, Lihue* ☎ *808/245–5050, 800/220–2925* ⊕ *www. sonesta.com* ⇆ *367 rooms* ⦿ *No Meals.*

Timbers Kauai Ocean Club & Residences

$$$$ | **HOUSE** | With an enviable spot along the Lihue coastline, 450 acres of landscaped grounds, and a choice of elegant homes and townhomes, Timbers Kauai is an excellent choice for those who are seeking a self-contained resort experience with an air of exclusivity. **Pros:** ocean and mountain views; private and quiet; luxurious amenities in lodgings and at resort. **Cons:** three-night minimum stay; somewhat isolated; extremely expensive. $ *Rooms from: $2900* ✉ *3770 Alaoli Way, Lihue*

☎ *855/420–9225* ⊕ *www.timberskauai. com* ⇆ *47 residences* ⦿ *No Meals.*

🍸 Nightlife

BARS

Duke's Barefoot Bar

BARS | One of the liveliest bars in Nawiliwili is this beachside bar and restaurant at Kalapaki Beach. Contemporary Hawaiian music is performed daily from 3:30 to 8 pm and from 9:30 to 11:30 am during Sunday brunch. ✉ *Royal Sonesta Kauai Resort Lihue, 3610 Rice St., Kalapaki Beach, Lihue* ☎ *808/246–9599* ⊕ *www. dukeskauai.com.*

Rob's Good Times Grill

BARS | Let loose at this popular restaurant and sports bar, which has live music Wednesday through Saturday nights. Thursday is trivia night, and sports are broadcast all weekend and Monday night. It offers local microbrews and a full menu of pub fare. ✉ *4303 Rice St., Lihue* ☎ *808/246–0311* ⊕ *www.kauaisports-barandgrill.com.*

🎭 Performing Arts

FESTIVALS

Bon Festival

CULTURAL FESTIVALS | **FAMILY** | Traditional Japanese celebrations in honor of loved ones who have died are held from late June through August at various Buddhist temples all over the island. It sounds somber, but it's really a community festival of dance, food, and socializing. To top it off, you're welcome to participate. Dance, eat, play carnival games, and hear Japanese *taiko* drumming at one of the Bon folk dances, which take place on temple lawns every Friday and Saturday night from dusk to midnight. Some dancers wear the traditional kimono; others wear board shorts and a tank top. The moves are easy to follow, the event is

Continued on page 132

HAWAII'S PLANTS 101

Tropical Hibiscus

Hawaii is a bounty of rainbow-colored flowers and plants. The evening air is scented with their fragrance. Just look at the front yard of almost any home, travel any road, or visit any local park and you'll see a spectacular array of colored blossoms and leaves. What most visitors don't know is that many of the plants they are seeing are not native to Hawaii; rather, they were introduced during the last two centuries as ornamental plants, or for timber, shade, or fruit.

Hawaii boasts nearly every climate on the planet, excluding the two most extreme: arctic tundra and arid desert. The Islands have wine-growing regions, cactus-speckled ranchlands, icy mountaintops, and the rainiest forests on earth.

Plants introduced from around the world thrive here. The lush lowland valleys along the windward coasts are predominantly populated by non-native trees including yellow- and red-fruited **guava**, silvery-leafed **kukui**, and orange-flowered **tulip trees.**

The colorful **plumeria flower**, very fragrant and commonly used in lei making, and the giant multicolored **hibiscus flower** are both used by many women as hair adornments, and are two of the most common plants found around homes and hotels. The umbrella-like **monkeypod tree** from Central America provides shade in many of Hawaii's parks including Kapiolani Park in Honolulu. Hawaii's largest tree, found in Lahaina, Maui, is a giant **banyan tree**. Its canopy and massive support roots cover about two-thirds of an acre. The native **ohia tree**, with its brilliant red brush-like flowers, and the **hapuu**, a giant tree fern, are common in Hawaii's forests and are also used ornamentally in gardens.

Naupaka, Limahuli Garden

Bougainvillea

Guava

Monkeypod

Banyan

Ohia Lehua*

Tulip Tree

Plumeria

Pandanus

Hibiscus

Anthurium

Kukui

Hapuu

*endemic to Hawaii

DID YOU KNOW?

More than 2,200 plant species are found in the Hawaiian Islands, but only about 1,000 are native. Of these, 320 are so rare, they are endangered. Hawaii's endemic plants evolved from ancestral seeds arriving in the Islands over thousands of years as baggage with birds, floating on ocean currents, or drifting on winds from continents thousands of miles away. Once here, these plants evolved in isolation, creating many new species known nowhere else in the world.

Sunshine Markets

If you want to rub elbows with the locals and purchase fresh produce and flowers at (somewhat) reasonable prices, head for Sunshine Markets, also known as Kauai's farmers' markets. These busy markets are held throughout the week, usually in the afternoon, at locations around the island—just ask any local person. They're good fun, and they support neighborhood farmers and vendors. Arrive a little early, bring dollar bills to speed up transactions and your own shopping bags to carry your produce, and be prepared for some pushy shoppers. Farmers are usually happy to educate visitors about unfamiliar fruits and veggies, especially when the crowd thins.

The pandemic affected the markets and their schedules; for current information on the Sunshine Markets, see Kauai's government website at ⊕ *www.kauai.gov.* Here are a couple in operation at this writing.

East Side Sunshine Market ⊠ *Kapaa Beach Park, Kapaa. Wednesday 3 pm.*

West Side Sunshine Market ⊠ *Hanapepe Park, Hanapepe. Thursday 3 pm.*

lively and wholesome, and it's free. A different temple hosts a dance each weekend. Watch the local paper for that week's locale. ⊕ *Island-wide* ⊕ *kauaibondance.org.*

LUAU AND POLYNESIAN REVUES

Luau Kalamaku

CULTURAL FESTIVALS | Set on the grounds of a historic sugar plantation, this luau bills itself as the only "theatrical" luau on Kauai. The luau feast is served buffet style, there's an open bar, and the performers aim to both entertain and educate about Hawaiian culture. Guests sit at tables around a circular stage; tables farther from the stage are elevated, providing unobstructed views. Additional packages offer visitors the opportunity to watch the show only, tour the 35-acre plantation via train, or enjoy special romantic perks like a lei greeting and champagne. ■ TIP→ **Check the website for days and times; the luau is not offered daily.** ⊠ *Kilohana Plantation, 3–2087 Kaumualii St., Lihue* ☎ *877/622–1780* ⊕ *www. luaukalamaku.com* 🖅 *$146, kids 13–17 $98, kids 3–12 $56.*

MUSIC AND PLAYS

Kauai Community Players

THEATER | This talented local group presents plays throughout the year in its intimate theater. ⊠ *4411 Kikowaena St., across from Kauai Community College, Lihue* ☎ *808/245–7700* ⊕ *www.kauaicommunityplayers.org* 🖅 *From $20.*

Kauai Concert Association

CONCERTS | This group offers a program of well-known classical musicians, including soloists and small ensembles, at a range of venues around the island, from hotel ballrooms to private rooms. ⊠ *Lihue* ☎ *808/652–5210* ⊕ *www.kauai-concert. org* 🖅 *Tickets from $40.*

🔴 Shopping

Lihue is the business area on Kauai, as well as home to all the big-box stores (Costco, Home Depot, and Walmart) and the only real mall. Do not mistake this town as lacking in rare shopping finds, however. Lihue is steeped in history and diversity while simultaneously welcoming new trends and establishments.

Besides informative displays, the Kauai Museum has a gift shop that is one of the best places on the island to find reasonably priced local crafts and books.

CLOTHING

Hilo Hattie, The Store of Hawaii

MIXED CLOTHING | This is the big name in aloha wear for tourists throughout the Islands, and Hilo Hattie has only one store on Kauai, located a mile from Lihue Airport. Come here for cool, comfortable muumuu and aloha shirts for men, women, and children in bright floral prints, as well as other souvenirs. Also, be sure to check out the line of Hawaii-inspired home furnishings. ⊠ *3252 Kuhio Hwy., Lihue* ☎ *808/245–3404* ⊕ *www.hilohattie. com.*

FOOD

Kauai Fruit & Flower Company (*The Pine-apple Store*)

At this shop near Lihue and five minutes away from the airport, you can buy fresh Hawaii Gold pineapples, sugarcane, ginger, tropical flowers, coconuts, and local jams, jellies, and honey, plus papayas, bananas, and mangoes from Kauai. ■ **TIP** ➜ **Note that some of the fruit sold here cannot be shipped out of state.** ⊠ *3–4684 Kuhio Hwy., Lihue* ☎ *808/320–8870*

⊕ *www.kauaifruit.com* ⊘ *Closed Sat. afternoon and Sun.*

GIFTS

★ Kapaia Stitchery

SOUVENIRS | Hawaiian quilts made by hand and machine, a beautiful selection of fabrics, quilting kits, handmade aloha shirts, and unique fabric arts fill a cute, small, red plantation-style building a mile outside Lihue. There are also many locally made gifts and quilts for sale in this locally owned store. The staff is friendly and helpful, even though a steady stream of customers keeps them busy. ⊠ *3–3551 Kuhio Hwy., Lihue* ☎ *808/245–2281* ⊕ *kapaiastitchery.com* ⊘ *Closed Sun.*

★ Kauai Museum Shop

CRAFTS | The gift shop at the museum sells some fascinating books, maps, and prints, as well as lovely authentic Niihau shell jewelry, handwoven lauhala hats, and koa wood bowls. Also featured at the Kauai Museum are tapa cloth, authentic hand-carved tiki figurines, as well as other good-quality local crafts and books at reasonable prices. ⊠ *4428 Rice St., Lihue* ☎ *808/245–6931* ⊕ *www.kauaimuseum. org* ⊗ *Closed Fri.–Sun.*

HOME DECOR

Two Frogs Hugging

HOUSEWARES | On display here are lots of interesting housewares, accessories, knickknacks, and hand-carved collectibles, as well as baskets and furniture from Indonesia, the Philippines, and China. Antiques and reproductions for the home and outdoors are available. The shop occupies expansive quarters in the Lihue Industrial Park. ⊠ *3094 Aukele St., Lihue* ☎ *808/246–8777* ⊕ *www.twofrogs-hugging.com.*

SHOPPING CENTERS

Hokulei Village

SHOPPING CENTER | Just down the highway between Kauai Community College and the Lihue town center, this newer retail plaza has a bank and Verde New Mexican restaurant, plus a Safeway, Petco, Verizon store, Walgreens, and Domino's. It's got California vibes, and it is fresher and more inviting than some of Kauai's older malls. ⊠ *4454 Nuhou St., Lihue* ☎ *808/742–9003.*

Kilohana Plantation Shops

SHOPPING CENTER | With shops and art galleries tucked into the 16,000-square-foot Tudor mansion and restored outbuildings, Kilohana Plantation offers quality clothing, jewelry, candy, handmade pottery, Hawaiian collectibles, and train memorabilia. The grounds are home to Koloa Rum Company, Luau Kalamaku, and a restaurant, while the historic mansion is filled with antiques from the previous owner. Train rides on a restored railroad are available, with knowledgeable guides recounting the history of sugar on Kauai. ⊠ *3–2087 Kaumualii Hwy., Lihue* ☎ *808/245–5608* ⊕ *www.kilohanakauai.com.*

Kukui Grove Center

SHOPPING CENTER | This is Kauai's only true mall. Anchor tenants are Longs Drugs, Macy's, Ross, Kukui Grove Cinemas, and Times Supermarket. The mall's stores offer women's clothing, surf wear, art, toys, athletic shoes, jewelry, a hair salon, and locally made crafts. Restaurants range from fast food and sandwiches to sushi and Korean, with a popular Starbucks and Jamba Juice. The center stage often has entertainment, especially on Friday night, and there is a farmers' market on Monday afternoon. ⊠ *3–2600 Kaumualii Hwy., Lihue* ☎ *808/245–7784* ⊕ *www.kukuigrovecenter.com.*

MARKETS

★ Kauai Community Market

MARKET | FAMILY | This is the biggest and best farmers' market on Kauai, sponsored by the Kauai Farm Bureau and Kauai Community College and held 9:30 am to 1 pm Saturday in the college's parking lot in Lihue. You'll find fresh produce and flowers, as well as packaged products like breads, goat cheese, pasta, honey, coffee, soaps, lotions, and more, all made locally. The market also offers educational displays and cooking tips. Seating areas are convenient if you want to grab a tasty snack or lunch from the food booths and lunch wagons that set up here. ⊠ *3–1901 Kaumualii Hwy., Lihue* ☎ *808/855–5429* ⊕ *www.kauaicommunitymarket.com.*

🏃 Activities

SPAS

Alexander Day Spa & Salon at the Royal Sonesta Kauai Resort Lihue

SPAS | This sunny, pleasant spa focuses on body care rather than exercise, so don't expect any fitness equipment or exercise classes, just pampering and beauty treatments. Massages are available in treatment rooms, your room, and on the beach, although the beach locale isn't as private as you might imagine. Wedding-day and custom spa packages can be arranged. ⊠ *Royal Sonesta Kauai Resort Lihue, 3610 Rice St., Suite 9A, Lihue* ☎ *808/246–4918* ⊕ *www.alexanderspa.com* 🍽 *Massages from $145.*

THE SOUTH SHORE

Updated by
Mary F. Williamson

⊙ Sights
★★★★★

🍴 Restaurants
★★★★★

🛏 Hotels
★★★★★

🛍 Shopping
★★★★★

🍸 Nightlife
★★★☆☆

WELCOME TO THE SOUTH SHORE

TOP REASONS TO GO

★ **Natural wonders.** Whether it's a stop at Spouting Horn blowhole, a hike along wild sea cliffs, or a stroll through lush tropical gardens, you'll have lots of opportunity to unplug and marvel at nature.

★ **Beautiful beaches.** Sunny and swimmable most of the year, South Shore beaches are perfect for snorkeling or taking a surf lesson. Poipu Beach is one of the best on Kauai.

★ **Farming heritage.** Koloa was the birthplace of the sugar industry in Hawaii, and the monument at the center of town is worth a look. The crop shaped the demographics, food, and language of today.

★ **Active adventure.** Besides beach fun, you can try zip-lining, ATV-ing, and exploring miles of trails by horseback or on foot.

★ **All the food.** With choices of everything from picnic fare to casual fine dining, you'll have a good selection of Hawaii cuisine classics.

The sunny South Shore is one of Kauai's primary resort areas, thanks to its pleasant climate year-round, popular beaches, and natural wonders and sights like Spouting Horn, the Tree Tunnel, and the National Tropical Botanical Garden. Hotels and condos stretch along the shoreline in Poipu and serve as a good, fairly central base for exploring the rest of the island. Slightly inland, delightful Koloa Town is a hub for shops and services, including the area's only gas station. A 12-minute drive west of Poipu passes through rolling pastureland to Lawai, gateway to the West Side.

1 **Koloa.** Home to Hawaii's first sugar plantation, Koloa Town is the South Shore's commercial hub, with shops, eateries, grocery and hardware stores, a post office, and a bank.

2 **Poipu.** Resorts hug the sunny coast of Kauai's most popular yet still low-key area. The beaches are well worth a day or two of downtime.

3 **Lawai.** You'll pass through this former pineapple town when you head west from the South Shore. Trendy shops and food trucks here are worth a stop.

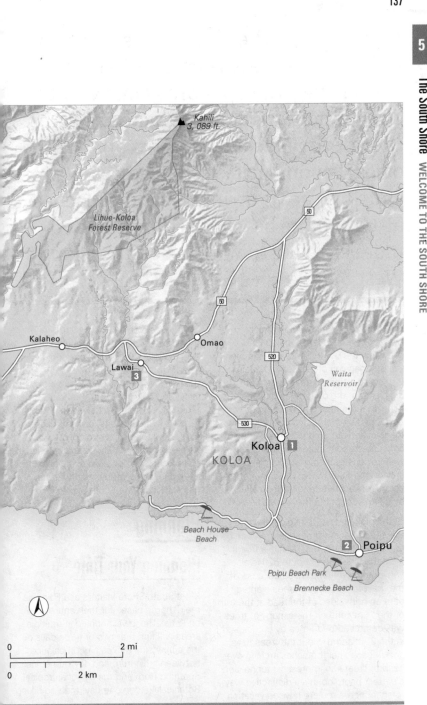

As you follow the main road south from Lihue, the landscape becomes lush and densely vegetated before giving way to drier conditions that characterize Poipu, the South Side's major resort area. Poipu owes its popularity to a steady supply of sunshine and a string of sandy beaches, although the beaches are smaller and more covelike than those on the island's West Side.

With its extensive selection of accommodations, services, shopping, and activities, the South Shore attracts more visitors than any other area of Kauai. It has also attracted developers with big plans for the onetime sugarcane fields that are nestled in this region and enveloped by mountains. There are few roads in and out, and local residents are concerned about increased traffic as well as construction. If you're planning to stay on the South Side, ask if your hotel, condo, or vacation rental will be affected by development during your visit.

Both Poipu and nearby Koloa, the latter the site of Kauai's first sugar mill, can be reached via Route 520 (Maluhia Road) from the Lihue area. Route 520 is also known as Tree Tunnel Road because of the graceful eucalyptus trees planted here on both sides of the road at the turn of the 20th century. The canopy of trees was destroyed two times by hurricanes in the 20th century, but the trees have grown back, their branches arching overhead to create an impressive tunnel and a perfect photo op. It's a distinctive way to announce, "You are now on vacation,"

and there's a definite feel of leisure in the air here. There's still plenty to do—snorkel, bike, walk, horseback ride, take an ATV tour, surf, scuba dive, shop, and dine—everything you'd want on a tropical vacation. From the west, Route 530 (Koloa Road) starts in Lawai—a good stop for a coffee, quick bite, or handmade gifts—and then slips into downtown Koloa, a row of fun shops and eateries in historical plantation buildings well worth exploring, at an intersection with the only gas station on the South Shore.

Planning

Planning Your Time

Most South Shore visitors use Poipu as their "home base" for their entire stay on Kauai. Those vacationing in multiple areas will find that two or three days on the sunny side strikes a good balance between adventure and downtime. Visit Spouting Horn and the National Tropical Botanical Garden one day; then go hiking, horseback riding, zip-lining, or fishing the next. In the afternoons, fit in some world-class golf, wander Koloa's quaint shops, and, of course, get sand between your toes before taking in an epic sunset.

Getting Here and Around

Lihue Airport serves all areas of Kauai, and it's about a half-hour drive from there to the South Shore, depending on traffic. The South Shore's primary access road is Route 520, a tree-lined, two-lane road. As you drive along it, there's a sense of tunneling down a rabbit hole into another world, à la Alice in Wonderland—and the South Shore is certainly a wonderland. On average, it rains only 30 inches per year, so if you're looking for fun in the sun, this is a good place to start. Taxis and ride-sharing services are limited on this rural island; a car still is essential.

Beaches

The South Shore's beaches, with their powdery-fine sand, are consistently good year-round except during high surf, which, if it hits at all, will be in summer. If you want solitude, this isn't it; if you want excitement—well, as much excitement as quiet Kauai offers—this is the place for you. ■TIP→ **Poipu's beaches are among the best on the island for families, with sandy shores, shallow waters, and grassy lawns down to the sand.**

Hotels

Sunseekers usually head south to the condo-studded shores of Poipu, where three- and four-story complexes line the coast and the sea is generally ideal for swimming. As the island's primary resort community, Poipu has the bulk of the island's accommodations, and more condos than hotels, with prices in the moderate to expensive range. Although it accommodates many visitors, Poipu's

extensive, colorful landscaping and low-rise buildings save it from feeling dense and overcrowded, and it has a delightful coastal promenade perfect for sunset strolls.

Hotel and restaurant reviews have been shortened. For full information, see Fodors.com. Hotel prices in the reviews are the lowest cost of a standard double room in high season. Restaurant prices are the average cost of a main course at dinner, or if dinner is not served, at lunch.

WHAT IT COSTS in U.S. Dollars			
$	$$	$$$	$$$$
RESTAURANTS			
under $17	$17–$26	$27–$35	over $35
HOTELS			
under $180	$180–$260	$261–$340	over $340

Restaurants

Most South Shore restaurants are fairly upscale and located within resorts and shopping centers. If you're looking for a gourmet meal in a classy setting, the South Shore is where you'll find it. Poipu has a number of excellent restaurants in dreamy settings and fewer family-style, lower-price eateries. As with most of the island, there's not much nightlife once restaurants close after dinner.

Safety

It's wise to get in the water only at beaches with lifeguards, especially if you are trying snorkeling or bodyboarding for the first time. Kauai currents are strong and surf conditions change, sometimes unpredictably, from season to season. Taking a surf lesson or adventuring with a guided group is a good idea. Always watch conditions for a while before going in, and never turn your back on the sea.

Visitor Information

CONTACTS Poipu Beach Foundation.
✉ *Poipu* ⊕ *poipubeach.org.*

Koloa

11 miles southwest of Lihue.

Hawaii's lucrative foray into sugar was born in this sleepy town, where the first cane was milled in 1836. You still can see the mill's old stone smokestack, though little else remains, save for the vintage plantation-style buildings that have kept Koloa from becoming a tacky tourist trap for Poipu-bound visitors. The original small-town character has been preserved by converting historic structures along the main street into boutiques, restaurants, and outlets for edible gifts. Placards describe the original tenants and life in the old mill town. Places to look for include Koloa Fish Market (now at 3390 Poipu Road), Crazy Shirts, and Billabong surf shop.

GETTING HERE AND AROUND

The classic approach to Koloa from Lihue is through the Tree Tunnel, the eucalyptus-lined section of Route 520, off Route 50. Once you find a parking spot, Koloa is a highly walkable town where some sidewalks are raised and mature monkeypod trees provide shade.

◉ Sights

Koloa Heritage Trail

TRAIL | Throughout the South Shore, you'll find brass plaques with details of historical stops along the 10-mile Koloa Heritage Trail. Start at Spouting Horn in Poipu and bike it, hike it, or drive it, your choice. You'll learn about Koloa's whaling history, sugar industry, ancient Hawaiian cultural sites, the island's volcanic formation, and more. Pick up a free self-guided trail map at shops in Koloa Town or

South Shore Festivals

Each July, **Koloa Plantation Days** enlivens the area, with a parade, craft fair, concerts, historical tours, and a rodeo. ⊕ *www.koloaplantationdays.com.*

In September, treat your tastebuds to the three-day **Poipu Food & Wine Festival.** It celebrates Kauai's diverse resources and talents, while supporting the culinary program at Kauai Community College. ⊕ *www.poipufoodandwinefestival.com.*

download a PDF from ⊕ *poipubeach. org.* ✉ *Koloa* ⊕ *poipubeach.org/business/ koloa-heritage-trail.*

★ Old Koloa Town

TOWN | Koloa's first sugar plantation opened in 1835, ushering in an era of sugar production throughout the islands, with more than 100 plantations established by 1885. Many of the workers came from the Philippines, Japan, China, Korea, and Portugal, creating Hawaii's multiethnic mélange. Today, many of Koloa's historic buildings, beneath the shade of stately old monkeypod trees, have been converted into fun shops, galleries, and places to eat. Even the newer developments mimic quaint plantation camp architecture. You'll just want to stroll and take it all in. Try a sweet treat from The Fresh Shave, Kauai Gourmet Nuts, or Koloa Mill Ice Cream after a food truck lunch taken to nearby Knudsen Park. ■ TIP→ Be sure to approach Old Koloa Town via the Tree Tunnel, a romantic canopy of eucalyptus trees planted more than a century ago along a stretch of Maluhia Road. ✉ *Koloa Rd., Koloa* ⊕ *www. oldkoloa.com.*

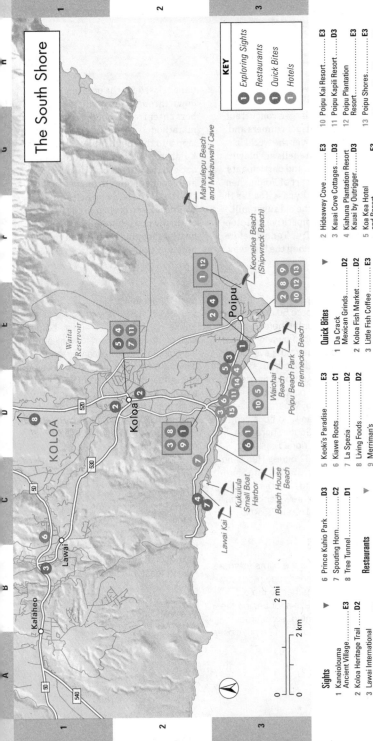

The South Shore

KEY

- ① Exploring Sights
- ① Restaurants
- ① Quick Bites
- ① Hotels

Sights ▶

1 Kaneiolouma
  Ancient Village............**E3**
2 Koloa Heritage Trail....**D2**
3 Lawai International
  Center..........................**B1**
4 National Tropical
  Botanical Garden........**C2**
5 Old Koloa Town..........**D2**
6 Prince Kuhio Park.......**D3**
7 Spouting Horn.............**C2**
8 Tree Tunnel.................**D1**

Restaurants ▶

1 Beach House................**D3**
2 Brennecke's
  Beach Broiler...............**E3**
3 Eating House 1849.......**D2**
4 Kenji Burger Koloa......**D2**
5 Keoki's Paradise..........**E3**
6 Kiawe Roots.................**C1**
7 La Spezia.....................**D2**
8 Living Foods................**D2**
9 Merriman's
  Fish House...................**D2**
10 Red Salt.....................**E3**
11 The Tasting Room.......**D2**
12 Tidepools....................**E3**

Quick Bites ▶

1 Da Crack
  Mexican Grinds............**D2**
2 Koloa Fish Market.........**D2**
3 Little Fish Coffee..........**E3**
4 Puka Dog......................**E3**

Hotels ▶

1 Grand Hyatt Kauai
  Resort and Spa............**E3**
2 Hideaway Cove............**E3**
3 Kauai Cove Cottages....**D3**
4 Kiahuna Plantation Resort
  Kauai by Outrigger.......**D3**
5 Koa Kea Hotel
  and Resort...................**E3**
6 Koloa Landing..............**D3**
7 The Lodge at Kukuiula...**C2**
8 Makahuena at Poipu......**E3**
9 Poipu Crater Resort.......**E3**
10 Poipu Kai Resort..........**E3**
11 Poipu Kapili Resort......**D3**
12 Poipu Plantation
   Resort........................**E3**
13 Poipu Shores...............**E3**
14 Sheraton Kauai Resort...**D3**
15 Whalers Cove Resort....**D3**

0 ___ 2 mi
0 ___ 2 km

Kalaheo
Lawai
KOLOA
Koloa
Poipu

Waita Reservoir

Lawai Kai
Kukuiula Small Boat Harbor
Beach House Beach
Waiohai Beach
Poipu Beach Park
Brennecke Beach
Keoneloa Beach (Shipwreck Beach)
Mahaulepu Beach and Makauwahi Cave

The Kauai Marathon

Heading into its second decade, the Kauai Marathon (⊕ *thekauaimarathon.com*) and its larger, concurrent Half Marathon attract runners and walkers from all over the world in September. Conch shells are blown to signal the start, and participants set off from the heart of Poipu, then turn up the Koloa Bypass Road as the sun rises behind the old sugar mill. Even the most competitive will stop for a selfie in the Tree Tunnel before continuing west along the highway (lanes closed for the occasion) and down through Omao, where neighbors cheer from front porches. Full marathoners then turn right for a long loop into the tough hills of Lawai and Kalaheo; "halfers" turn left to head back to the waterfront. Hula dancers and Japanese *taiko* drummers pepper the route. The large free Health & Wellness Expo is open to the public, as are many marathon-related events at nearby shopping centers and sponsor hotels.

Tree Tunnel

NATURE SIGHT | Off Route 50 as you head from Lihue to the South Shore, Route 520 (Maluhia Road) is known locally as Tree Tunnel Road, due to the avenue of tall eucalyptus trees lining both sides. A drive here is a lovely introduction to the area. The trees were planted at the turn of the 20th century by Walter Duncan McBryde, a Scotsman who began cattle ranching on Kauai's South Shore. The canopy of trees was ripped to literal shreds twice—in 1982 during Hurricane Iwa and then again in 1992 during Hurricane Iniki. And, true to Kauai's resilience, both times the trees grew back into an impressive tunnel. ✉ *Rte. 520, Koloa*.

🍴 Restaurants

Most eateries in Koloa are come-as-you-are casual, family-friendly, and modestly priced. Food trucks gather by the old sugar monument and in a lot behind the main street. Finer dining, sometimes with a view, can be found in Poipu, closer to the sea.

Kenji Burger Koloa

$ | **ASIAN FUSION** | New to Koloa, this is Erik Tanigawa's third Asian-flair burger joint on the island, named Kenji after his grandfather. American fare with Japanese flavors is served on covered decks that have plenty of TVs for catching a game. **Known for:** burgers with a twist; large sushi-ritos; later hours. ⑤ *Average main: $13* ✉ *5404 Koloa Rd., Koloa* ☎ *808/431–4770* ⊕ *www.kenjiburger.com*.

La Spezia

$$ | **ITALIAN** | Homestyle Italian cuisine including house-made pasta is served in a small, lively dining room and bar area at this main street restaurant. Choose from the cellar list or bring your own bottle, perhaps from the wine shop next door. **Known for:** Brie and bacon French toast; organic ingredients; good weekend brunch. ⑤ *Average main: $25* ✉ *5492 Koloa Rd., Koloa* ☎ *808/742–8824* ⊕ *www.laspeziakauai.com* ⊘ *Closed Mon. No lunch.*

Continued on page 146

BIRTH OF THE ISLANDS

How did the volcanoes of the Hawaiian Islands come to be here, in the middle of the Pacific Ocean? The ancient Hawaiians believed that the volcano goddess Pele's hot temper was the key to the mystery; modern scientists contend that it's all about plate tectonics and one very hot spot.

Plate Tectonics and the Hawaiian Question: The theory of plate tectonics says that the Earth's surface is comprised of plates that float around slowly over the planet's hot interior. The vast majority of earthquakes and volcanic eruptions occur near plate boundaries—the San Francisco earthquakes in 1906 and 1989, for example, were the result of activity along the nearby San Andreas Fault, where the Pacific and North American plates meet. Hawaii, more than 1,988 miles from the nearest plate boundary, is a giant exception. For years scientists struggled to explain the island chain's existence—if not a fault line, what caused the earthquakes and volcanic eruptions that formed these islands?

What's a hot spot? In 1963, J. Tuzo Wilson, a Canadian geophysicist, argued that the Hawaiian volcanoes must have been created by small concentrated areas of extreme heat beneath the Pacific Plate. Wilson hypothesized that there is a hot spot beneath the present-day position of Hawaii Island (the "Big Island") and its heat produced a persistent source of magma. Magma is produced by rising-but-solid mantle rock that melts when it reaches about 100 km. At that depth, the lower pressure can no longer stop the rock from melting, and the magma rises to erupt onto the sea floor, forming an active seamount. Each flow caused the seamount to grow until it finally emerged above sea level as an island volcano. Plausible so far, but why then, is there not one giant Hawaiian island?

THE JOURNEY OF PELE

Holo Mai Pele, often told through hula, is the Hawaiian story of how volcano goddess Pele sends her sister Hiiaka on an epic quest from the Big Island to fetch her lover Lohiau, living on Kauai. Overcoming many obstacles, Hiiaka reaches full goddess status and falls in love with Lohiau herself. When Pele finds out, she destroys everything dear to her sister, killing Lohiau and burning her sister's ohia groves. Each time lava flows from a volcano, ohia trees sprout shortly after, in a constant cycle of destruction and renewal.

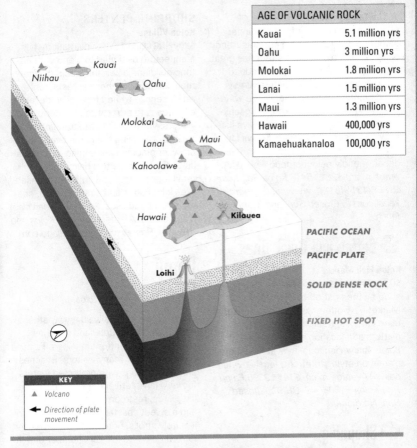

AGE OF VOLCANIC ROCK	
Kauai	5.1 million yrs
Oahu	3 million yrs
Molokai	1.8 million yrs
Lanai	1.5 million yrs
Maui	1.3 million yrs
Hawaii	400,000 yrs
Kamaehuakanaloa	100,000 yrs

PACIFIC OCEAN

PACIFIC PLATE

SOLID DENSE ROCK

FIXED HOT SPOT

KEY
▲ Volcano
◄ Direction of plate movement

Volcanoes on the Move: Wilson further suggested that the movement of the Pacific Plate itself eventually carries the island volcano beyond the hot spot. Cut off from its magma source, the island volcano becomes dormant. As the plate slowly moved to the northwest, one island volcano would become extinct just as another would develop over the hot spot. After several million years, there is a long volcanic trail of islands and seamounts across the ocean floor. The oldest islands are those farthest from the hot spot. The exposed rocks of Kauai, for example, are about 5.1 million years old, but those on the Big Island are less than half a million years old, with new volcanic rock still being formed.

An Island on the Way: Off the coast of the Big Island of Hawaii, another volcano is still submerged but erupting. Geologists long believed it to be a retired seamount volcano, but in the 1970s they discovered both old and new lava on its flanks, and in 1996 it erupted with a vengeance. It is believed that thousands of generations from now, it will be the newest addition to the Hawaiian archipelago, so in July 2021 was given the name Kamaehuakanaloa, "the red child of Kanaloa."

★ The Tasting Room

$$ | AMERICAN | Popular for a predinner gathering or a full evening out, this trendy wine bar on Koloa's main street has great flights and small bites, and has added a few larger entrées. A venture run by the daughters of the owner of the wine shop next door, it offers knowledgeable, nonsnooty service and an extensive list of wines, beers, and spirits. **Known for:** charcuterie and small plates; farmhouse decor; friendly neighborhood vibe. ⑤ *Average main: $26* ✉ *5476 Koloa Rd., Koloa* ☎ *808/431–4311* ⊕ *www.tastingroom-kauai.com* ⊙ *Closed Sun. and Mon. No lunch.*

☕ Coffee and Quick Bites

Koloa Fish Market

$ | SEAFOOD | Having outgrown its tiny shop by the post office, Koloa Fish Market now offers tasty take-out poke, plate lunches, fresh fish, and party platters at a location along the road to Poipu. **Known for:** long lines at lunchtime; plantation-style storefront; family-owned deli. ⑤ *Average main: $14* ✉ *3390 Poipu Rd., Koloa* ☎ *808/742–6199* ⊙ *Closed Sun. No dinner.*

👜 Shopping

FOOD AND DRINK
★ The Wine Shop

WINE/SPIRITS | As you browse shelves stocked with international wines, gourmet nibbles, local rum, and etched glassware, you may notice romance in the air. The Wine Shop is where couples can obtain a state marriage license, gather charcuterie supplies for a honeymoon beach picnic, or order a gift basket for a milestone anniversary. Want a particular vintage for an upcoming family trip? They will bring in special orders and hold them for your arrival. ✉ *5470 Koloa Rd., Koloa* ✛ *Across from Koloa Post Office* ☎ *808/742–7305* ⊕ *www.thewineshop-kauai.com.*

SHOPPING CENTERS
Koloa Village

SHOPPING CENTER | With plantation-style architecture designed to blend with historic buildings down the block, this new multiuse complex houses restaurants, retail, services, and offices. The developer's idea is to attract both residents and visitors, whether they're attending yoga classes, watching the game over a local brew, or grabbing something from Kauai Juice Co. en route to a haircut. Most retail tenants are local small businesses like Hoku Foods and a ramen shop, not mainland franchises. ✉ *5460 Koloa Village Rd., Koloa* ✛ *At intersection of Koloa and Weliweli Rds.* ⊕ *www.koloavillage.com.*

Poipu

2 miles southeast of Koloa.

Thanks to its generally sunny weather and a string of golden-sand beaches dotted with oceanfront lodgings, Poipu is a top choice for many visitors. Beaches are user-friendly, with protected waters for *keiki* (children) and novice snorkelers, lifeguards, restrooms, covered pavilions, and a sweet coastal promenade ideal for leisurely strolls. Some experts have even ranked Poipu Beach Park number one in the nation. It depends on your preferences, of course, though it certainly does warrant high accolades.

GETTING HERE AND AROUND

Poipu is the one area on Kauai where you could get by without a car, though that might mean an expensive taxi ride from the airport and limited access to other parts of the island. To reach Poipu by car, follow Poipu Road south from Koloa. After the traffic circle, the roads curve to follow the coast, leading to some of the popular South Shore beaches.

Seal-Spotting on the South Shore

When strolling on one of Kauai's lovely beaches, don't be surprised if you find yourself in the rare company of a Hawaiian monk seal. These seals are among the most endangered of all marine mammals, with perhaps fewer than 1,400 remaining. They primarily inhabit the Northwestern Hawaiian Islands, although more are showing their sweet faces on the main Hawaiian Islands, especially Kauai. They're fond of hauling out on the beach for a long snooze in the sun, particularly after a night of gorging on fish. They need this time to rest and digest, safe from predators.

Female seals regularly birth their young on the beaches around Kauai, where they stay to nurse their pups for upward of six weeks. It seems the seals enjoy particular beaches for the same reasons we do: the shallow, protected waters.

If you're lucky enough to see a monk seal, keep your distance and let it be. Although they may haul out near people, they still want and need their space. Stay several hundred feet away, and forget photos unless you have a zoom lens. It's illegal to do anything that causes a monk seal to change its behavior, with penalties that include big fines and even jail time. In the water, seals may appear to want to play. It's their curious nature. Don't try to play with them. They are wild animals—mammals, in fact, with teeth.

If you have concerns about the health or safety of a seal, or just want more information, contact the **Hawaiian Monk Seal Conservation Hui** (☎ *808/651–7668*).

◉ Sights

Kaneiolouma Ancient Village

HISTORIC SIGHT | Stone masons are rebuilding the walls of this largely intact 13-acre Hawaiian village dating back to the mid-1400s. Fishponds, taro patches, a temple, and a festival arena eventually will be restored, serving as a cultural learning center for residents and visitors. You can walk around the outside and check out the statues and signage; the interior is set to open in 2024. ⊠ *2000 Poipu Rd., Koloa ✛ Intersection of Poipu Rd. and Hoowili Rd.* ⊕ *www.kaneiolouma.org* ⊠ *Free.*

★ National Tropical Botanical Garden (NTBG)

GARDEN | FAMILY | Tucked away in Lawai Valley, this collection of gardens includes lands and a cottage once used by Hawaii's Queen Emma (1836–85) for a summer retreat. Trams depart frequently to transport people from the visitor center to the gardens. The rambling 252-acre McBryde Garden has exhibits and easy trails to help visitors learn about biodiversity and plants collected throughout the tropics, including a Canoe Garden that features plants introduced to Hawaii by early Polynesian voyagers. ■ **TIP→ The biodiversity path in McBryde is accessible for people with mobility issues.** The 100-acre Allerton Garden, which can be visited only on a guided tour, artfully displays statues and water features originally developed as part of a private estate. A famous scene in *Jurassic Park* was filmed here.

Reservations and closed-toe shoes are required for all tours. The visitor center has a high-quality gift shop and grab-and-go refreshments. Besides propagating rare and endangered plants from Hawaii and elsewhere, NTBG functions as a scientific research and education center. The organization also operates gardens in Limahuli, on Kauai's North Shore; in Hana, on Maui's east shore; and in Florida. ⊠ *4425 Lawai Rd., Poipu* ☎ *808/742–2623* ⊕ *www.ntbg.org* ✉ *McBryde self-guided tour $30, Allerton guided tour $60.*

Prince Kuhio Park

CITY PARK | A field next to Prince Kuhio Condominiums honors the birthplace of Kauai's beloved Prince Jonah Kuhio Kalanianaole. Known for his kind nature and tireless work on behalf of the Hawaiian people, he lost his chance at the throne when Americans staged an illegal overthrow of Queen Liliuokalani in 1893 and toppled Hawaii's constitutional monarchy. He served as a delegate to the U.S. Congress for 19 years after Hawaii became a territory in 1900. An annual commemoration is held around his March birthday, a state holiday. This is a great place to watch wave riders surfing a popular break known as PKs, or to see the sun sink into the Pacific. ⊠ *Lawai Rd., Poipu.*

★ Spouting Horn

NATURE SIGHT | When conditions are right, a natural blowhole in the rocky shoreline behaves like Old Faithful, shooting salt water high into the air and making a hollow, echoing sound. It's most dramatic during big summer swells, which jam large quantities of water through an ancient lava tube with great force. Most sidewalk vendors hawk inexpensive souvenirs, but a few carry locally set South Sea pearls or rare Niihau-shell creations, with prices ranging from affordable to several thousand dollars. Look for green sea turtles bobbing in the adjacent cove. ⊠ *End of Lawai Rd., Poipu* ⊕ *www.gohawaii.com.*

⚓ Beaches

Beach House Beach

BEACH | Don't pack the beach umbrella, beach mats, and cooler for this one—just your snorkel gear, when the seas are calm. The beach, named after neighboring restaurant The Beach House and located on the road to Spouting Horn, is a small slip of sand during low tide and a rocky shoreline when it's high; however, it is conveniently located by the road's edge, and its rocky edge and bottom make it great for snorkeling. (As a rule, sandy-bottom beaches are not great for snorkeling. Rocks provide safe hiding places and grow the food that fish and other marine life like to eat.)

A sidewalk along the coastline on the restaurant side of the beach makes a great vantage point from which to peer into the water and look for *honu*, the Hawaiian green sea turtles. It's also a very popular gathering spot to watch the sun set. You can park in the public lot across from the beach. ■ **TIP→** **Make reservations for dinner at The Beach House in advance, and time it around sunset. Amenities:** parking (free); showers; toilets. **Best for:** snorkeling; sunset; surfing. ⊠ *Lawai Rd., off Poipu Rd., Poipu* ⊹ *Across from Lawai Beach Resort* ✉ *Free.*

Brennecke Beach

BEACH | FAMILY | This beach is synonymous on Kauai with board surfing and bodysurfing, thanks to its shallow sandbar and reliable shore break. Because the beach is small and often congested, surfboards are prohibited near shore. The water on the rocky eastern edge of the beach is a good place to see the endangered green sea turtles noshing on plants growing on the rocks. Monk seals sometimes haul out here; please allow them to rest. Playground equipment is available here, and there's free street parking. **Amenities:** food and drink. **Best for:** sunset; surfing. ⊠ *Hoone Rd., off Poipu Rd., Poipu* ✉ *Free.*

Did You Know?

Spouting Horn on Kauai's South Shore is a blowhole that shoots water through a lava tube up to 50 feet in the air. This impressive natural feature is a great photo op.

Sun Safety on Kauai

Hawaii's weather—seemingly never-ending warm, sunny days with gentle trade winds—can be enjoyed year-round with good sun sense. Because of Hawaii's subtropical location, the length of daylight here changes little throughout the year. The sun is particularly strong, with a daily UV average of 14. Visitors should take extra precaution to avoid sunburns and long-term cancer risks due to sun exposure.

While protecting your skin, protect Hawaii's reefs, too. Hawaii has banned the sale of sunscreens containing oxybenzone and octinoxate, ingredients that can harm coral reefs and marine ecosystems. Pack a reef-safe alternative, such as TropicSport.

The Hawaii Dermatological Society recommends these sun safety tips:

■ Plan your beach, golf, hiking, and other outdoor activities for the early morning or late afternoon, avoiding the sun between 10 am and 4 pm, when it's the strongest.

■ Apply a broad-spectrum, reef-safe sunscreen with a sun protection factor (SPF) of at least 15. Cover areas that are most prone to burning, like your nose, shoulders, tops of feet, and ears. And don't forget your lips.

■ Apply sunscreen at least 30 minutes before you plan to be outdoors and reapply every two hours, even on cloudy days. Clouds scatter sunlight, so you can still burn on an overcast day.

■ Wear light, protective clothing, such as a long-sleeve shirt and pants, broad-brimmed hat, and sunglasses.

■ Stay in the shade whenever possible—especially on the beach—by using an umbrella. Remember that sand and water can reflect up to 85% of the sun's damaging rays.

■ Children need extra protection from the sun. Apply sunscreen frequently and liberally on children over six months of age and minimize their time in the sun. Sunscreen is not recommended for children under six months.

Keoneloa Beach (*Shipwreck Beach*)
BEACH | The Hawaiian name for this stretch of beach, Keoneloa, means "long sand," but many refer to this beach fronting the Grand Hyatt Kauai Resort & Spa as Shipwreck Beach. Both make sense. It is a long stretch of crescent beach punctuated by stunning sea cliffs on both ends, and, yes, a ship once wrecked here. With its rough onshore break, the waters off "Shippies" are best for bodyboarding and bodysurfing experts; however, the beach itself is plenty big for sunbathing, sandcastle building, Frisbee throwing, and other beach-related fun. The eastern edge of the beach

is the start of an interpretive cliff and dune walk (complimentary) held by the hotel staff; check with the concierge for days and times, and keep an eye out for snoozing monk seals below. Parking is limited. **Amenities:** food and drink; parking (free); showers; toilets. **Best for:** walking, photography, surfing. ⊠ *Ainako Rd., Poipu* ✛ *Continue on Poipu Rd. past Grand Hyatt Kauai, turn makai (toward the ocean) on Ainako Rd.* ⌷ *Free.*

Kukuiula Small Boat Harbor
BEACH | **FAMILY** | This is a great beach to sit and people-watch as diving and fishing boats, kayakers, and canoe paddlers head out to sea. Shore and throw-net

South Shore beaches have good surf breaks. Head to Poipu Beach for board rentals or lessons.

fishermen frequent this harbor as well. It's not a particularly large harbor, so it retains a quaint sense of charm, unlike Nawiliwili Harbor or Port Allen. The lawn is a good picnic and ball-tossing spot, and the bay is a nice, protected area for limited swimming, but with all the boat traffic kicking up sand and clouding the water, it's not good for snorkeling. Outside the breakwater, there is a decent surf spot. **Amenities:** parking (free); showers; toilets. **Best for:** picnics; sunset; swimming. ✉ La-wai Rd., off Poipu Rd., Poipu 🖾 Free.

Lawai Kai

BEACH | One of the most spectacular beaches on the South Shore is inaccessible by land unless you tour the National Tropical Botanical Garden's Allerton Garden, which we highly recommend. On the tour, you'll see the beach, but you won't step on the sand. The only way to legally access the beach on your own is by paddling a kayak 1 mile from Kukuiula Harbor. However, you have to rent the kayaks elsewhere and haul them on top of your car to the harbor. Also, the

wind and waves usually run westward, making the in-trip a breeze but the return trip a workout against Mother Nature. ■TIP➔ **Do not attempt this beach in any manner during a south swell; do not trespass. Amenities:** none. **Best for:** solitude; sunset. ✉ 4425 Lawai Rd., off Poipu Rd. 🖀 808/742–2623 for tour information at the National Tropical Botanical Garden ⊕ www.ntbg.org 🖾 NTBG tour $60.

★ Mahaulepu Beach and Makauwahi Cave

BEACH | This 2-mile stretch of coast, with its sand dunes, limestone hills, sinkholes, and the Makauwahi Cave, is unlike any other on Kauai. Remains of a large, ancient settlement, evidence of great battles, and the discovery of a now-underwater petroglyph field indicate that Hawaiians lived in this area as early as AD 700. Mahaulepu's coastline is unprotected and rocky, which makes venturing into the ocean hazardous. There are three beach areas with bits of sandy-bottom swimming; however, the best way to experience Mahaulepu is simply to roam, on foot or horseback, along the sand or

trails. Pack water and sun protection.
■TIP→ **Access to this beach is via private property. Before driving or hiking here, check current gate hours and conditions as the unpaved road can be closed due to weather, grading, or movie filming. Access is during daylight hours only, so be sure to depart before sunset or risk getting locked in for the night. Amenities:** parking (free). **Best for:** solitude; sunrise; walking. ⊠ *Poipu Rd., Poipu* ⊕ *Past Grand Hyatt Kauai and CJM Stables* ⊕ *www.cavere-serve.org* ⊡ *Free.*

★ Poipu Beach Park

BEACH | FAMILY | At the most popular beach on the South Shore, the snorkeling and swimming are good during calm seas, and when the surf's up, the bodyboarding and surfing are good, too. Frequent sunshine, grassy lawns, play equipment, and easy access add to the appeal, especially with families. The beach is frequently crowded and great for people-watching. Even the endangered Hawaiian monk seal often makes an appearance. Take a walk west on a path fronting numerous resorts. Note that at time of writing, this beach is one of a few on Kauai that may institute a parking fee for nonresidents. **Amenities:** food and drink; lifeguards; parking (free); showers; toilets. **Best for:** partiers; snorkeling; sunbathing; swimming. ⊠ *Hoone Rd., off Poipu Rd., Poipu* ☎ *808/742–7444* ⊡ *Free.*

Waiohai Beach

BEACH | FAMILY | The first hotel built in Poipu in 1962 overlooked this beach, adjacent to Poipu Beach Park. Actually, there's little to distinguish where this one ends and the other begins, other than a crescent reef at the eastern end of Waiohai Beach. That crescent, however, is important. It creates a small, protected bay—good for snorkeling and beginning surfers. However, when a summer swell kicks up, the near-shore conditions become dangerous; offshore, there's a splendid surf break for experienced surfers. The beach itself is narrow and, like its neighbor, gets very crowded in summer. **Amenities:** parking (free). **Best for:** snorkeling; sunset; surfing; swimming. ⊠ *Hoone Rd., off Poipu Rd., Poipu* ⊡ *Free.*

🍴 Restaurants

The Beach House

$$$$ | MODERN HAWAIIAN | This busy restaurant has a dreamy ocean view, making it one of the best settings on Kauai for a special dinner or a cocktail and appetizer while the sun sinks into the glassy blue Pacific and surfers slice the waves. The prices have gone up, but you can still find satisfaction in the pork potsticker appetizer or fresh catch of the day served with *lilikoi* (passion fruit) lemongrass beurre blanc. **Known for:** indoor-outdoor dining; gluten-free and vegan entrées; small bar with a big view. ⑤ *Average main: $45* ⊠ *5022 Lawai Rd., Poipu* ☎ *808/742–1424* ⊕ *www.the-beach-house.com* ⊘ *No lunch.*

Brennecke's Beach Broiler

$$$ | AMERICAN | FAMILY | Casual and fun, with a busy mai tai bar and windows overlooking the beach, Brennecke's specializes in big portions in a wide range of offerings including rib-eye steak, burgers, fish tacos, pasta, and shrimp. You can create your own combination meal if you can't pick only one. **Known for:** take-out deli with shave ice; good-value happy hours; fresh catch of the day. ⑤ *Average main: $27* ⊠ *2100 Hoone Rd., Poipu* ☎ *808/742–7588* ⊕ *www.brenneckes.com.*

★ Eating House 1849

$$$ | ASIAN FUSION | Hawaii's culinary superstar, Roy Yamaguchi, runs his signature Hawaiian-fusion-cuisine restaurant on Kauai's South Shore in a shopping village that suits the name and creative fare. Though billed as "plantation cuisine," the hot pot rice bowl, spicy ramen, and burger that's half wild boar are about the

The Plate-Lunch Tradition

To experience island history first-hand, step up to the counter at one of Hawaii's ubiquitous "plate lunch" eateries and order a segmented plate piled with beef, chicken, two scoops of rice, macaroni salad, and maybe a pickled vegetable condiment. On the sugar plantations, Native Hawaiians and immigrant workers from many different countries ate together in the fields, sharing food from their "kaukau tins," the utilitarian version of the Japanese *bento* lunchbox. From this mix of cultures came the vibrant pidgin language and its equivalent in food: the plate lunch.

Along roadsides and at beaches and events, you will see food trucks, another excellent venue for sampling plate lunches. These portable

restaurants are descendants of "lunch wagons" that began selling food to plantation workers in the 1930s. Try deep-fried chicken *katsu* (rolled in Japanese panko bread crumbs and spices). Marinated beef teriyaki is another good choice, as is miso butterfish. The noodle soup, saimin, with its Japanese fish stock and Chinese red-tinted barbecue pork, is a distinctly local medley. Koreans have contributed spicy barbecue *kalbi* ribs, often served with chili-laden kimchi (pickled cabbage). Portuguese bean soup and tangy Filipino adobo stew are also favorites. The most popular Hawaiian contribution to the plate lunch is the laulau, a mix of meat and fish and young taro leaves, wrapped in more taro leaves and steamed.

only items that might have their roots in the days when sugar was king; otherwise, the menu is classic Asian fusion. **Known for:** lively atmosphere; molten chocolate soufflé; use of local ingredients. ⑤ *Average main: $35* ✉ *Shops at Kukuiula, 2829 Ala Kalanikaumaka Rd., No. A-201, Poipu* ☎ *808/742–5000* ⊕ *www.eatinghouse1849.com* ⊘ *Closed Mon. and Tues. No lunch.*

Keoki's Paradise

$$$ | ASIAN FUSION | FAMILY | Built to resemble a dockside boathouse, this active, semi-outdoor place fills up quickly for dinner thanks to a busy lounge and frequent live music. The day's fresh catch is available in various styles and sauces, and other favorites include coconut shrimp, seafood risotto, and roasted pork ribs that are cooked in a traditional Hawaiian *imu* (an underground oven). **Known for:** Hawaiian atmosphere, with hula; weekend brunch and theme nights; children's menu. ⑤ *Average main: $35*

✉ *Poipu Shopping Village, 2360 Kiahuna Plantation Dr., Poipu* ☎ *808/742–7534* ⊕ *www.keokisparadise.com* ⊘ *No lunch weekends. No brunch weekdays.*

Living Foods

$$ | AMERICAN | FAMILY | A range of light fare is served from lunchtime through evening on the covered lanai attached to Living Foods general store at The Shops at Kukuiula. Locally sourced starters, sandwiches, fish preparations, entrée salads, and desserts can be ordered via the café's website, which speeds up table service. **Known for:** weekend breakfast, with cocktails; all-day menu; grab-and-go bakery. ⑤ *Average main: $17* ✉ *The Shops at Kukuiula, 2829 Ala Kalanikaumaka St., Suite D124, Poipu* ☎ *808/320–7642* ⊕ *www.livingfoodshawaii.com.*

Merriman's

$$$$ | MODERN HAWAIIAN | The Hawaii Regional Cuisine served up at chef Peter Merriman's namesake restaurant is

enhanced by a sophisticated setting and lovely views from a pretty second-floor dining veranda. Start at the bar, where fine wines are offered by the glass, and then continue to the dinner menu, which states the origins of the fish, shrimp, lamb, beef, chicken, and veggies: 90% is locally grown or caught. **Known for:** upscale, plantation-home atmosphere; partnerships with local fishers and farmers; sunset views. $ *Average main: $46* ⊠ *2829 Ala Kalanikaumaka St., G-149, Poipu* ☎ *808/742–8385* ⊕ *www. merrimanshawaii.com.*

★ Red Salt

$$$$ | **ECLECTIC** | Smart, sophisticated decor, attentive and skilled service, and an exceptional menu that highlights Hawaiian seafood make Red Salt a great choice for leisurely fine dining. A daily breakfast also is served, featuring lobster Benedict and lemon-pineapple soufflé pancakes. **Known for:** sushi and sake; dramatic presentation; perfectly grilled meats. $ *Average main: $51* ⊠ *Koa Kea Resort, 2251 Poipu Rd., Poipu* ☎ *808/742–4200* ⊕ *meritagecollection. com/koa-kea* ☽ *No dinner Sun. and Mon. No lunch.*

Tidepools

$$$$ | **SEAFOOD** | Of the Grand Hyatt's restaurants, this is definitely the most tropical and campy, with grass-thatch huts that seem to float on a koi-filled pond beneath starry skies while torches flicker in the lushly landscaped grounds nearby. The equally distinctive food has an island flavor that comes from the chef's advocacy of Hawaii Regional Cuisine and extensive use of island-grown products, including fresh herbs from the resort's organic garden. **Known for:** excellent service; reservations needed weeks in advance; macadamia nut–crusted mahimahi. $ *Average main: $50* ⊠ *Grand Hyatt Kauai Resort and Spa, 1571 Poipu Rd., Poipu* ☎ *808/742–1234* ⊕ *grandhyattkauai.com* ☽ *No lunch.*

☕ Coffee and Quick Bites

Da Crack Mexican Grinds

$ | **MEXICAN** | **FAMILY** | Fresh, fast, and affordable, Da Crack is everything you could ask for when refueling between outdoor activities. Fill your burrito, bowl, or taco with locally caught fish, traditional beans, homemade salsa, and local avocado guacamole—or many other choices made from scratch—then head back out to eat and explore more of the island. **Known for:** children's menu; vegan friendly; no MSG or trans fat oils. $ *Average main: $13* ⊠ *2827 Poipu Rd., by Kukuiula Market, Poipu* ☎ *808/742–9505* ⊕ *www. dacrackkauai.com.*

Little Fish Coffee

$ | **AMERICAN** | A perfect beach day starts with coffee and an acai bowl or bagel sandwich from Little Fish, a popular snack shack along the main road in Poipu. Spreads are house-made, bakery treats are mom's recipes, and the flavor-packed smoothies will have you back tomorrow for another. **Known for:** healthy breakfast bowls named for surf spots; full espresso menu; homemade cookies, bars, and scones. $ *Average main: $11* ⊠ *Next to Poipu Beach Athletic Club, 2294 Poipu Rd., Poipu* ☎ *808/742–2113* ⊕ *littlefishcoffee.com* ☽ *No dinner.*

Puka Dog

$ | **AMERICAN** | **FAMILY** | It takes four steps to customize a Hawaiian-style hot dog here, so your crew may want to study the menu in advance. Choose a Polish sausage or veggie dog, top it with a house-made sauce and one of six intriguing tropical fruit relishes, then add mustard (*lilikoi*—passion fruit —is best.) All this deliciousness won't fall out on your bathing suit because the bun is baked with a *puka*, a hole, rather than sliced. **Known for:** secret garlic lemon sauce with four heat levels; Hawaiian sweet bread bun; Kauai Special with mango relish. $ *Average main: $10* ⊠ *Poipu Beach Park, 2100 Hoone Rd.,*

below Brennecke's restaurant, Poipu
☎ 808/742–6044 ⊕ www.pukadog.com
⊗ No dinner.

🛏 Hotels

★ Grand Hyatt Kauai Resort & Spa

$$$$ | RESORT | FAMILY | Dramatically hand-
some, Kauai's best megaresort is this
classic Hawaiian low-rise built into the
cliffs overlooking an unspoiled coastline;
it boasts mouthwatering restaurants and
also has taken great strides to reduce its
carbon footprint. **Pros:** elegant Hawaiian
ambience; fabulous pool and spa; cultural
activities. **Cons:** the large size may not
appeal to all tastes; small balconies;
dangerous swimming beach during
summer swells. ⑤ Rooms from: $424
⊠ 1571 Poipu Rd., Poipu ☎ 808/742–1234
⊕ www.grandhyattkauai.com ⇨ 604
rooms ⦿ No Meals.

Hideaway Cove

$$$ | APARTMENT | Set back from the
ocean's edge on a quiet road in the heart
of Poipu, Hideaway Cove is a boutique
vacation rental with units ranging from
studios to two bedrooms, each appoint-
ed with tropical-style furniture and
original artwork. **Pros:** rates drop with a
weeklong stay; high-quality furnishings;
private lanai. **Cons:** no pool; better for
couples than families; not on the ocean.
⑤ Rooms from: $275 ⊠ 2315 Nalo Rd.,
Poipu ☎ 310/502–5023 ⊕ www.hideaway-
cove.com ⇨ 3 units ⦿ No Meals.

Kauai Cove Cottages

$$ | APARTMENT | Located in a residential neighborhood, this vacation rental
includes quaint studio units near the
mouth of Waikomo Stream, about two
blocks from a nice snorkeling cove,
and the Pool Cottage in central Poipu.
Pros: quiet neighborhood; walk to
shops and restaurants; great snorkeling
nearby. **Cons:** better for couples than
families; $105–$125 cleaning fee upon
departure; not on beach. ⑤ Rooms
from: $180 ⊠ 2672 Puuholo Rd., Poipu

☎ 808/631–9313 ⊕ www.kauaicove.com
⇨ 3 units ⦿ No Meals.

Kiahuna Plantation Resort Kauai by Outrigger

$$$ | APARTMENT | FAMILY | This longtime
Kauai condo project consists of 42 plan-
tation-style, low-rise buildings with indi-
vidually owned one- and two-bedroom
units set on grassy fields leading to a
lovely beach. **Pros:** swimmable beach and
lawn for picnics and games; great sunset
and ocean views are bonuses in some
units; convenient to restaurants, shops,
athletic club. **Cons:** housekeeping is extra;
be prepared for stairs; no air-conditioning.
⑤ Rooms from: $289 ⊠ 2253 Poipu Rd.,
Poipu ☎ 808/742–6411, 866/994–1588
reservations ⊕ www.outrigger.com
⇨ 100 units ⦿ No Meals ☞ Additional
units managed by Castle Resorts.

★ Koa Kea Hotel & Resort

$$$$ | RESORT | This boutique property
offers a stylish, high-end experience
without the bustle of many larger resorts,
making it a great place to forget it all
while relaxing at the spa or lounging by
the pool on a honeymoon or babymoon.
Pros: perfect romantic getaway; incredibly
comfortable beds; friendly service. **Cons:**
very busy area; all parking is valet; not
much for children. ⑤ Rooms from: $599
⊠ 2251 Poipu Rd., Poipu ☎ 808/742–4200
general information, 808/742–4271
reservations ⊕ www.koakea.com ⇨ 121
rooms ⦿ No Meals.

Koloa Landing

$$$$ | RESORT | FAMILY | A family-friendly
option, this resort has incredible pools,
an on-site spa, plenty of play space, and
rooms the size of apartments. **Pros:** large
units; easy walk to dining and shopping;
350,000-gallon pool with waterslides.
Cons: restaurant is poolside, not much
view; better for families than couples;
beach not good for swimming. ⑤ Rooms
from: $450 ⊠ 2641 Poipu Rd., Koloa
☎ 866/476–2964 ⊕ koloalandingresort.
com ⇨ 306 units ⦿ No Meals.

The Lodge at Kukuiula

$$$$ | RESORT | The private Kukuiula development rents one- to four-bedroom luxury cottages and villas to nonmembers; all homes have spacious lanai with expansive views, high-end kitchens, and both indoor and outdoor showers. **Pros:** cultural activities; top-tier luxury; golf, tennis, bikes, and a 32-foot boat. **Cons:** set apart from local scene; must drive to beach, shops, and restaurants; high price point. ⑤ *Rooms from: $1279* ⊠ *2700 Ke Alaula St., Koloa* ☎ *866/901–5204* ⊕ *www.lodgeatkukuiula.com, www.kukuiula.com* ⇨ *39 homes* ¶⊙¶ *Free Breakfast.*

Makahuena at Poipu

$$$ | APARTMENT | Situated on the southernmost point of Kauai, the large, individually owned one-, two-, and three-bedroom condos have dramatic oceanfront views of both sunrises and sunsets. **Pros:** right on the ocean; tennis court; scenic walking path. **Cons:** individually owned condos means the decor and upkeep vary; no air-conditioning; no-swimming beach. ⑤ *Rooms from: $325* ⊠ *1661 Pee Rd., Poipu* ☎ *877/367–1912 Castle Resorts* ⊕ *www.castleresorts.com/kauai* ⇨ *78 units* ¶⊙¶ *No Meals.*

Poipu Crater

$$ | APARTMENT | FAMILY | Set down within an extinct volcanic crater known as Piha ke Akua, or "Place of the Gods," these two-bedroom condominium units in South Pacific–style townhomes are fairly spacious, with large windows, high ceilings, and full kitchens. **Pros:** family-friendly, with table tennis, pool, and clubhouse; attractive and generally well-kept; jungle-in-crater setting. **Cons:** individually owned units means upkeep and decor vary; few resort amenities; beach isn't good for swimming. ⑤ *Rooms from: $249* ⊠ *2330 Hoohu Rd., Poipu* ☎ *808/742–7260* ⊕ *VRBO.com, Suite-Paradise.com, Parrish.Kauai.com* ⇨ *30 units* ¶⊙¶ *No Meals.*

Poipu Kai Resort

$ | APARTMENT | FAMILY | The condos here, many with cathedral ceilings and all with large, furnished lanai and big windows overlooking the lawns, give the 85-acre development the feeling of a quiet retreat inside and out. **Pros:** good rates for the location; close to ocean; tennis club. **Cons:** minimum stays usually required; closest beaches not ideal for swimming; some units don't have air-conditioning. ⑤ *Rooms from: $175* ⊠ *1941 Poipu Rd., Poipu* ☎ *844/860–6181 Suite Paradise, 808/377–4998 Villas, 855/945–4092 Aston* ⊕ *www.suite-paradise.com, www.aquaaston.com, villasatpoipukai.com* ⇨ *450 units* ¶⊙¶ *No Meals.*

Poipu Kapili Resort

$$$ | APARTMENT | FAMILY | White-frame exteriors and double-pitched roofs complement the tropical landscaping at this resort, which offers spacious one- and two-bedroom condo units—with full kitchens, bedroom air-conditioning, entertainment centers, and garden or ocean views—that are minutes from Poipu's restaurants and across the street from a nice beach. **Pros:** tennis and pickleball on-site; units are well-spaced; parking is close to the unit. **Cons:** minimal amenities; three-night minimum stay; units are ocean-view but not oceanfront. ⑤ *Rooms from: $325* ⊠ *2221 Kapili Rd., Poipu* ☎ *808/742–6449, 800/443–7714* ⊕ *www.poipukapili.com* ⇨ *60 units* ¶⊙¶ *No Meals.*

Poipu Plantation

$ | APARTMENT | Plumeria, ti, and other tropical foliage create a lush landscape for this resort, which rents a four-bedroom/four-bath plantation home and nine one- and two-bedroom cottage apartments. **Pros:** free Wi-Fi and parking; attractively furnished; air-conditioning. **Cons:** no resort amenities; not on the ocean; three-night minimum. ⑤ *Rooms from: $165* ⊠ *1792 Pee Rd., Poipu* ☎ *808/742–6757, 800/634–0263* ⊕ *www.poipubeach.com* ⇨ *13 units* ¶⊙¶ *No Meals.*

Poipu Shores

$$$$ | APARTMENT | FAMILY | Perched on a rocky point above pounding surf—perfect for whale- or turtle-watching—three low-rise buildings have individually owned condos with full kitchens, washer-dryers, and central air-conditioning. **Pros:** condos have lanai or share a sundeck; every unit faces the water; heated oceanfront pool. **Cons:** swimming beach is a 10-minute walk away; no resort amenities; units vary widely in style. $ Rooms from: $350 ⊠ 1775 Pee Rd., Poipu ☎ 800/325–5701 Parrish, 877/367–1912 Castle ⊕ www.castleresorts.com, www.parrishkauai.com, vrbo.com ⥲ 39 units ⦵ No Meals.

★ Sheraton Kauai Resort

$$$ | RESORT | The Sheraton is a sprawling resort with rooms that offer views of the ocean and lovely landscaped gardens; it's worth splurging on the ocean-wing accommodations, which are so close to the water you can practically feel the spray of the surf as it hits the rocks below. **Pros:** good facilities for meetings, events, reunions; ocean-view pool; restaurant with spectacular sunset views. **Cons:** basic gym and no spa; renovated rooms but some dated infrastructure; parking can be a ways from the room. $ Rooms from: $340 ⊠ 2440 Hoonani Rd., Poipu Beach, Koloa ☎ 808/742–1661, 888/627–8113 ⊕ www.sheraton-kauai.com ⥲ 188 rooms ⦵ No Meals.

Whalers Cove Resort

$$$$ | APARTMENT | Perched about as close to the water's edge as they can get, these one-, two-, and three-bedroom condos are the most luxurious on the South Shore. **Pros:** spacious, with full kitchens; on-site staff and housekeeping; outstanding setting. **Cons:** resort fee, but few amenities (curb-free parking, enhanced Wi-Fi); no air-conditioning; rocky beach not ideal for swimming. $ Rooms from: $430 ⊠ 2640 Puuholo Rd., Poipu ☎ 808/742–7571, 800/225–2683 ⊕ www.whalerscoveresort.com ⥲ 24 units ⦵ No Meals.

ⓨ Nightlife

BARS

Keoki's Paradise Bar

COCKTAIL LOUNGES | A young, energetic crowd makes this a lively spot on Friday and Saturday evenings. When the dining room clears out, there's a bit of a scene in the tropical lounge. Live music, Taco Tuesday, and Burger & Beer Wednesday keep the Bamboo Bar a happening place. Try the Poipu Piña to sip from a pineapple. ⊠ Poipu Shopping Village, 2360 Kiahuna Plantation Dr., Poipu ☎ 808/742–7534 ⊕ www.keokisparadise.com.

Lava's on Poipu Beach

BARS | This poolside bar and grill is a scenic place to be on the South Shore to celebrate sunset with a drink and casual meal because the ocean view is unsurpassed. On the nights Lava's is open, happy hour is from 3 to 5 pm, and there's live music. It's closed for dinner when Rum Fire restaurant is open. ⊠ Sheraton Kauai Resort, 2440 Hoonani Rd., Poipu ☎ 808/742–1661 ⊕ www.sheraton-kauai.com/dining.

COCKTAIL LOUNGES

Stevenson's Library

COCKTAIL LOUNGES | A 24-foot koa-wood bar anchors this sophisticated nightspot with a spectacular ocean view. Sushi, sashimi, spirits, and live music make for a memorable date night or celebration with friends (get a sitter for the kids). It's known for craft cocktails, an extensive wine and sake list, tasting flights, sustainable seafood, and "tiramisu-shi"—the familiar Italian mocha dessert served sushi style. Put on your resort attire when you go. ⊠ Grand Hyatt Kauai Resort and Spa, 1571 Poipu Rd., Poipu ☎ 808/240–6456 ⊕ www.hyatt.com.

🎭 Performing Arts

LUAU AND POLYNESIAN REVUES

Grand Hyatt Kauai Luau

CULTURAL FESTIVALS | FAMILY | Excellent unlimited buffet food, an open bar, and exciting music and dance performances characterize this traditional luau, held twice weekly (Wednesday and Saturday) in a garden setting near majestic Keoneloa Bay. ⊠ *Grand Hyatt Kauai Resort and Spa, 1571 Poipu Rd., Poipu* 🕾 *808/742–1234* ⊕ *www.grandhyattkauailuau.com* ✆ *From $175.*

🛍️ Shopping

Surprisingly, the South Shore doesn't have as many shops as one might expect for such a popular resort region. However, it does have convenient shopping clusters, including Poipu Shopping Village and the upscale The Shops at Kukuiula. There are many high-priced options, but some unique clothing and gift selections.

ART GALLERIES

Halelea Gallery

ART GALLERIES | In addition to offering original works by Hawaii artists, this stylish gallery in The Shops at Kukuiula doubles as a boutique that sells a unique sampling of clothing, jewelry, bags, and gifts by local designers. Its other location, The Black Pearl, focuses on fine art and fine jewelry. ⊠ *2829 Kalanikaumaka Rd., Suite K, Poipu* 🕾 *808/742–9525* ⊕ *www.haleleagallery.com.*

SHOPPING CENTERS

Poipu Shopping Village

SHOPPING CENTER | FAMILY | Convenient to hotels and condos along the shore, the two dozen shops at Poipu Shopping Village sell resort wear, gifts, souvenirs, jewelry, and art. This complex also has a number of food choices, from casual Thai and pizza sit-down restaurants to a gelato stand and Starbucks. Hula shows and farmers' markets in the open-air courtyard add to the ambience. ⊠ *2360*

Try a Lomilomi 🏃 Massage

Life in ancient Hawaii wasn't about sunbathing and lounging at the beach. Growing taro was hard work, and building canoes, fishing for dinner, and pounding tapa cloth for clothing, sails, and blankets were hard too. Enter lomilomi —a Hawaiian-style massage. It's often described as being more vigorous, more rhythmic, and faster than Swedish massage, and it incorporates more elbow and forearm work. It might even involve chanting, music, and four hands (in other words, two people).

Kiahuna Plantation Dr., Poipu 🕾 *808/742–2831* ⊕ *www.poipushoppingvillage.com.*

★ The Shops at Kukuiula

SHOPPING CENTER | The South Shore's upscale shopping center has boutiques, exclusive galleries, several great restaurants, a gourmet grocer, a large drugstore, and Kauai-made Lappert's Ice Cream. The flagship of the Malie Organics bath line, used by many top hotels and spas, is here. Check out the Kauai Culinary Market on Wednesday afternoon to see cooking demonstrations, listen to live music, and shop from local vendors. This attractive open-air, plantation-style center gets busy on Friday night. It's at the roundabout as you enter Poipu. ⊠ *2829 Kalanikaumaka St., Poipu* 🕾 *808/742–9545* ⊕ *www.theshopsatkukuiula.com.*

🏃 Activities

SPAS

Anara Spa

SPAS | The luxurious Anara Spa has all the equipment and services you expect from a top resort spa, along with a pleasant, professional staff. Best of all, it has indoor and outdoor areas that capitalize on the tropical locale and balmy weather, further distinguishing it from other hotel spas. Its 46,500 square feet of space includes the lovely Garden Treatment Village, an open-air courtyard with private thatched-roof huts, each featuring a relaxation area, misters, and an open-air shower in a tropical setting. Ancient Hawaiian remedies and local ingredients are featured in many treatments, such as a pineapple-papaya body hydration, a coffee body polish, and a traditional lomilomi massage. The open-air lava-rock showers are wonderful, introducing many guests to the delightful island practice of showering outdoors. The spa, which includes a full-service salon, adjoins the Grand Hyatt's legendary swimming pool. ✉ *Grand Hyatt Kauai Resort and Spa, 1571 Poipu Rd., Poipu* ☎ *808/742–1234* ⊕ *www.anaraspa.com* ✉ *Massages from $180.*

Lawai

4½ miles west of Poipu, 11 miles west of Lihue.

Lawai is becoming a trendy hub for artists' studios, food trucks, and independent shops. It's worth a stop, especially if you want a snack, when passing through between the West Side and South Shore. The terraced hills of the Lawai and Kalaheo Valleys once supplied golden pineapples to the Lawai Cannery. After closing in 1964, the cannery was ravaged by two hurricanes and eventually demolished.

GETTING HERE AND AROUND

Lawai Town has two separate retail areas: along Route 50, look for the post office, minimart, and Kiawe Roots restaurant. Heading toward the ocean on Route 530 (Koloa Road), pull into the parking lot of Warehouse 3540 and then explore on foot; Lawai Market is a few doors down.

Rainbow Capital ⊙ of the World

While folks in Western Europe and North America may catch a rainbow only a dozen times a year, these beautiful optical effects make a daily showing in Hawaii thanks to sunny days and frequent light, passing showers. Look for them in the afternoon, with the sun behind you. Also keep an eye out for double rainbows, which make a lovely photograph. Rainbows even appear on state license plates and University of Hawaii logo wear.

⊙ Sights

Lawai International Center

HISTORIC SIGHT | Spend a serene morning in Lawai Valley, a pastoral corridor that joins verdant hills to the beach where Queen Emma (1836–85) had a home. In 1904, Japanese plantation workers created a miniature version of the famed 88 temples of Shikoku so they could complete a sacred pilgrimage despite being far from home. This is the only replica of this temple route outside Japan and one of the country's oldest Buddhist sites. Ancient Hawaiians built a *heiau* (temple) in Lawai, and then each group of immigrants that followed—Chinese, Japanese, Portuguese, and Filipino—built their own places of worship in this area known for its healing waters.

Engulfed by vegetation for decades, this hillside dotted with knee-high shrines was excavated and restored by volunteers, who now offer bimonthly tours. After a welcome of tea and *manju* (Japanese cookies) and a short presentation, you can borrow a walking staff to wind your way up an orchid-lined path for a silent stroll, pausing to peek into each handmade shrine. Afterward, visitors may enter the 13th century–style Hall of Compassion, built without nails under the guidance of Japanese master carpenters. ■TIP→ **Reservations are required by phone, text, or email. Arrive 15 minutes early and wear comfortable shoes.** ✉ *3381 Wawae Rd.* ✛ *On open house days, look for small sign at driveway just west of the Koloa Rd. and Rte. 50 intersection* ☎ *808/639–1718* ⊕ *www.lawaicenter. org* ✉ *By donation* ☉ *Closed to visitors except for bimonthly tours.*

🍴 Restaurants

★ Kiawe Roots
$$ | MODERN HAWAIIAN | FAMILY | This place is back, with both dine-in and takeout, at a cozy storefront where family recipes bring a mix of local cultures to the table. Meats are grilled over *kiawe*, Hawaiian mesquite. **Known for:** tropical BBQ flavors; gluten-free choices; comfort food with a local twist. ⑤ *Average main: $22* ✉ *2–3687 Kaumualii Hwy.* ✛ *Next to Lawai post office* ☎ *808/855–5055* ⊕ *www.eatatkiawe.com* ☉ *Closed Sun. and Mon.*

🛍 Shopping

FOOD AND DRINK
Lawai Market
FOOD | The original Lawai General Store got a face-lift and now offers grab-and-go breakfast and lunch, groceries, sundries, a good selection of beer and wine, and a coffee/smoothie bar. At the gateway between the South Shore and the West Side, it's a fine spot to provision for adventures in the mountains or at the shore. Locals and condo renters alike stop by for farm produce, local beef, and house-baked bread, or to refuel with an acai bowl on the porch. ✉ *3586 Koloa Rd.* ☎ *808/332–7001* ⊕ *www.lawaimarket. com.*

Monkeypod Jam
FOOD | The storefront café has closed, but Monkeypod's award-winning preserves made from tropical fruits can be found at its "provisions cottage" tucked away in Lawai. In winery fashion, you can sign up for a tasting ($10; deducted from purchase) and then buy jars. At weekly classes, people cook jelly, jam, curd, chutney, salsa, or pickles, depending on what's in season. Or you can learn to make local favorites like Spam musubi, poke bowls, and coconut mochi. A six-week produce plan is perfect for folks staying on the Garden Island for a longer winter escape. At this writing, weekly tastings, shopping, and classes are by appointment, though this could change. ✉ *3540 Koloa Rd.* ✛ *Exact location provided after booking a tasting or class* ☎ *808/378–4208* ⊕ *www.monkeypod-jam.com.*

LOCAL SPECIALTIES
Warehouse 3540
OTHER SPECIALTY STORE | An old warehouse has new life as a marketplace for a dozen creative entrepreneurs and as a hub for food trucks. Hand-printed clothing, authentic lauhala hats, boho chic jewelry, letterpressed cards, specialty food products, and locally crafted soaps are offered at the oft-changing microshops. On Second Saturday evenings each month, craft vendors, farmers, take-out food cooks, and musicians join the shops. Locals and visitors mingle at picnic tables outside. ✉ *3540 Koloa Rd.* ⊕ *www.warehouse3540.com.*

Chapter 6

THE WEST SIDE

Updated by
Mary F. Williamson

◉ Sights	🍴 Restaurants	🛏 Hotels	🛍 Shopping	🍸 Nightlife
★★★★★	★★☆☆☆	★★☆☆☆	★☆☆☆☆	★☆☆☆☆

WELCOME TO THE WEST SIDE

TOP REASONS TO GO

★ **Waimea Canyon.** Witness how the dramatic erosional forces of wind, water, and rain have left their mark in this colorful, deep chasm that has been dubbed the Grand Canyon of the Pacific.

★ **Quiet beaches.** Seemingly endless beaches, including Kekaha Beach Park and Polihale State Park, make up the distinctive, remote West Side scenery.

★ **Wilderness trails.** With more than 45 miles of trails, Kokee State Park offers a chance to see native plants and sweeping views from the Kalalau Lookout.

★ **Old Hawaii.** With its historic towns and slower way of life, the West Side still feels like the old Hawaii. It's a great place to escape the resort scene and experience nature at its finest.

★ **The art scene.** Hanapepe is home to eclectic galleries, local crafts studios, and a lively street fair on Friday night.

Kauai's West Side is arid but offers some striking natural beauty, notably Waimea Canyon. Most of the towns and villages here sprang up from sugar camps, but not all. Cooler, hilly Kalaheo began with ranchers and homesteaders, and artsy Hanapepe was a freewheeling port town (Port Allen is the port) not subject to the rules of plantation life.

The farther west you travel on the West Side, the hotter the air and the redder the dirt, until you reach the town, river, and canyon named Waimea for the reddish water. Here, there's a choice: continue on past miles of white-sand beaches to Polihale State Park at road's end, or head up along the Waimea Canyon rim to the mountain forests of Kokee for spectacular hikes and postcard views.

1 Kalaheo. An upcountry community that retains its ranching roots, Kalaheo is a convenient stop for lunch, supplies, or even nine holes of golf before heading west.

2 Hanapepe. Brilliant bougainvillea blossoms cover the hillsides that mark the entry to Hanapepe, a cheerful little town with historical buildings and a burgeoning art scene.

3 Waimea and Waimea Canyon. Though Waimea is often billed as the gateway to the dramatic spectacle of Waimea Canyon, this pretty little town warrants its own visit. It's one of the few places in the Islands that still retains the look and lifestyle of old Hawaii.

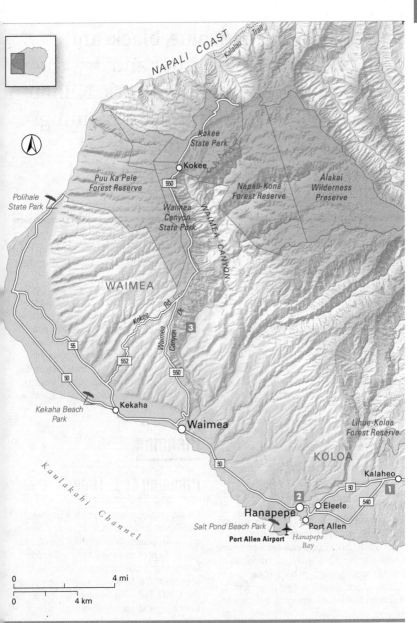

NAPALI COAST

Kalalau Trail

Kokee State Park

Kokee

550

Puu Ka Pele Forest Reserve

Napali-Kona Forest Reserve

Alakai Wilderness Preserve

Polihale State Park

Waimea Canyon State Park

WAIMEA CANYON

WAIMEA

Kokee Rd.

Waimea Canyon Dr.

3

55

552

550

50

Kekaha Beach Park

Kekaha

Waimea

Lihue-Koloa Forest Reserve

50

KOLOA

Kalaheo

1

50

Kaulakahi Channel

50

2

Eleele

540

Hanapepe

Salt Pond Beach Park

Port Allen Airport

Port Allen

Hanapepe Bay

0   4 mi

0   4 km

Exploring the West Side is akin to visiting an entirely different world. The landscape is dramatic and colorful—a patchwork of green, blue, black, and orange. The weather is hot and dry, the beaches long, and the sand dark. Niihau, a private island and the last remaining place in Hawaii where Hawaiian is spoken exclusively, can be glimpsed offshore.

This is rural Kauai, where sugar made its last stand and taro is still cultivated in the fertile river valleys. The lifestyle is slow, easy, and traditional, with many folks fishing and hunting to supplement their diets. Here and there modern industry has intruded into this pastoral scene: huge generators turn oil into electricity at Port Allen; seed companies cultivate experimental crops of genetically engineered plants in Kekaha and Waimea; the Navy launches rockets at Mana to test the "Star Wars" missile defense system; and NASA has a tracking station in the wilds of Kokee. It's a region of contrasts that simply shouldn't be missed.

Heading west from Lihue or Poipu, you pass through a string of tiny towns, plantation camps, and historic sites, each with a story to tell of centuries past. There's Kalaheo, with its ranching roots; Hanapepe, whose coastal salt ponds have been harvested since ancient times; Kaumakani and Makaweli, picturesque former sugar camps; and Waimea, where Captain Cook made his first landing in the Islands, forever changing the face of Hawaii.

From Waimea Town you can head up into the mountains, skirting the rim of magnificent Waimea Canyon and climbing higher still until you reach the cool, often-misty forests of Kokee State Park. From vantage points at the top of this gemlike island, 3,200 to 4,200 feet above sea level, you can gaze into the deep, verdant valleys of the North Shore and Napali Coast. This is where the "real" Kauai can still be found: the native plants, insects, and birds that are located nowhere else on Earth.

Planning

Planning Your Time

Cruise ship passengers check off the highlights of the West Side in less than a day, with coach stops at the Kauai Coffee Visitor Center and the Waimea Canyon lookout for a classic Hawaii vacation snapshot. The best way to experience the area's stunning beauty, though, is to unplug and spend several days or more. An open schedule creates time for watching birds, clouds, and sunsets; browsing shops and galleries in Hanapepe; and walking the seemingly endless sands of Kekaha and Polihale beaches. Avid hikers could spend a week exploring all the forest and canyon trails in Kokee State Park.

Getting Here and Around

Visitors typically fly into Lihue Airport and then drive about an hour to the West Side. Some flightseeing tours are offered from Burns Field (airstrip) in Hanapepe. Kauai County offers near-hourly bus service from Lihue to Kekaha, with stops in major towns along the way, from approximately 5 am to 9 pm.

Beaches

The West Side of the island receives hardly enough rainfall year-round to water a cactus, and because it's also the leeward side, there are few tropical breezes. That translates to sunny and hot conditions, with long, languorous, and practically deserted beaches. You'd think the leeward waters—less touched by wind—would be calm, but there's no reef system, so the beach drops off quickly and currents are common. Rivers often turn the ocean water murky. Big Save stores in Eleele and Waimea carry some beach gear and souvenirs; otherwise there's not much catering to visitors.

Hotels

To do a lot of hiking or immerse yourself in the island's history, get a room in Waimea or Kokee. You won't find many hotels, restaurants, or shops, but you will encounter quiet days, miles of largely deserted beach, and a rural environment.

Hotel and restaurant reviews have been shortened. For full information, see

Fodors.com. Hotel prices in the reviews are the lowest cost of a standard double room in high season. Restaurant prices are the average cost of a main course at dinner, or if dinner is not served, at lunch.

WHAT IT COSTS in U.S. Dollars			
$	$$	$$$	$$$$
RESTAURANTS			
under $17	$17–$26	$27–$35	over $35
HOTELS			
under $180	$180–$260	$261–$340	over $340

Restaurants

When it comes to dining on the West Side, pickings are slim, very casual, and changeable. Fortunately, the few eateries that are here are generally worth patronizing.

Shopping

The West Side is years behind the South Shore in development, offering minimal, simple shops with authentic local flavor. Food products and handmade items make good gifts.

Visitor Information

For information about hiking and camping permits, and rules and regulations for Napali Coast and other parks, visit the Division of State Parks section of ⊕ *hawaii.gov*. Once in Kokee State Park, the Kokee Natural History Museum (⊕ *www.kokee.org*) staff act in lieu of park rangers, providing trail and nature information. For information about Waimea Town, visit the West Kauai Heritage Center (⊕ *www.wsmmuseum.org*) in Waimea.

Kalaheo

6½ miles northwest of Poipu, 13 miles southwest of Lihue.

Cool, upcountry Kalaheo—"the proud day" in Hawaiian—offers worthy stops for visitors. The world-famous Kauai Coffee Company, the largest producer of export-quality Hawaiian coffee, is based here, along with the headquarters of the National Tropical Botanical Garden, which has operations throughout Hawaii and Florida. The hilltop Kukuiolono Park offers a friendly nine-hole golf course, minigolf, walking paths, and special gardens. You'll also find a gas station, notable eateries, and services that welcome visitors, like a yoga studio and nail salon. Kalaheo was never a plantation town; instead, Portuguese homesteaders and ranchers settled the area.

While many communities go crazy for their sports teams, Kauai fans feel intense pride in their Kalaheo-based hula *halau* (school)—a troupe of powerful, precise, elegant women that in 2022 swept the prestigious Merrie Monarch Festival competition on the Big Island of Hawaii. They perpetuate not only traditional dance but also the very soul of Hawaiian culture.

GETTING HERE AND AROUND

Route 50 heads west from Lihue to Kalaheo, where Kalaheo Town's shops and restaurants are strung along the highway, with easy parking and Kauai Bus stops. The highway bisects this bedroom community into a lower, sunnier, more suburban side with the golf course, and an upper, rainier, semirural side where it's not uncommon to see loose goats and folks riding horses on the back roads.

⊙ Sights

★ Kauai Coffee Estate Visitor Center

FARM/RANCH | **FAMILY** | Two restored camp houses, dating from the days when sugar was the main agricultural crop on the Islands, have been converted into a museum, visitor center, snack bar, and gift shop. About 3,100 acres of McBryde sugar land have become Hawaii's largest coffee plantation, with its 4 million trees producing more than half of the state's beans. You can walk among the trees, view old grinders and roasters, watch a video to learn how coffee is harvested and processed, sample various estate roasts, and check out the gift store.

The center offers free self-guided tours through a small coffee grove (about 20 minutes) and a personalized, one-hour "coffee on the brain" tour for a fee. From Kalaheo, take Route 50 in the direction of Waimea Canyon (west) and veer left onto Route 540. It's 2½ miles from the Route 50 turnoff. ⊠ *870 Halewili Rd.* ✛ *Between Kalaheo and Eleele on Rte. 540* ☎ *808/335–0813* ⊕ *www.kauaicoffee.com* 🎫 *Free; guided tour $25, $20 kids 8–16.*

Kukuiolono Park & Golf Course

CITY PARK | **FAMILY** | Translated as "Torchlight of the God Lono," Kukuiolono has serene Japanese gardens, a display of significant Hawaiian stones, a meditation pavilion, and spectacular panoramic views of the south and west shorelines. This quiet hilltop park is one of Kauai's most scenic areas and ideal for a picnic or easy hike through an ironwood grove. The nine-hole golf course has the island's least expensive fees, and there's a new minigolf activity. Nongolfers can explore walking paths with interpretive signage; just keep alert. ⊠ *Puu Rd.* ✛ *From Hwy. 50, turn south on Papalina Rd. and enter gates at Puu Rd.* ☎ *808/332–9151* ⊕ *www.kukuiolonogolf.com* 🎫 *Free.*

Restaurants

Kalaheo Café & Coffee Company

$$ | **AMERICAN** | **FAMILY** | Folks love this roadside café—especially at breakfast and lunch, though it's good for dinner, too—for its casual neighborhood feel and lengthy menu with omelets, sandwiches, burgers, and plenty more. Lots of Kauai products are used here, including Anahola Granola, fruit for smoothies, fresh-caught fish, and coffee, which you can also buy by the pound. **Known for:** hearty portions, like the Kahili Breakfast; fresh-baked pastries and bread; often busy, especially weekend mornings. $ *Average main: $22* ✉ *2–2560 Kaumualii Hwy. (Rte. 50)* ☎ *808/332–5858* ⊕ *www.kalaheo.com* ⊗ *No dinner Sun. and Mon.*

 ## Hotels

Kalaheo Inn

$ | **B&B/INN** | **FAMILY** | It isn't easy to find good budget lodgings on the southwest side of the island, but this old-fashioned neighborhood inn with studios and one-, two-, and three-bedroom suites does an adequate job in cooler upcountry Kalaheo Town. **Pros:** coin-operated laundry on-site; free Wi-Fi; walking distance to café and takeout. **Cons:** dated furnishings; no air-conditioning; three-night minimum stay. $ *Rooms from: $83* ✉ *4444 Papalina Rd.* ☎ *808/332–6023, 888/332–6023* ⊕ *www.kalaheoinn.com* ⟳ *15 units* ⊙ *No Meals.*

Shopping

Aloha Exchange

SPORTING GOODS | The best-known brands in camp, beach, surf, and skate gear can be found at this flagship of Aloha Exchange, along with a good selection of locally designed graphic T-shirts and caps available exclusively here. Personalize your water flask with a couple of their stickers as island souvenirs. It's popular with locals, especially younger beachgoers. ✉ *2–2535 Kaumualii Hwy.* ☎ *808/332–5900* ⊕ *www.alohaxchng.com.*

Kauai Coffee Estate Visitor Center Shop

FOOD | Kauai produces more coffee than any other Island, and this is the largest

coffee farm in the United States. The 100% local product can be purchased from grocery stores or here at the plantation, where you can sample nearly two dozen coffees before or after a self-guided tour. Be sure to try some of the exclusive estate-roasted varieties. Coffee is available online, too. Fun fact: The factory, quaint old camp houses, and visitor center are located in a settlement called Numila, which is a Hawaiian way to say "new mill." ✉ *870 Halewili Rd., off Rte. 50* ☎ *808/335–0813* ⊕ *www.kauaicoffee.com.*

The Right Slice

FOOD | Blueberry-piña colada, *lilikoi* (passion fruit) cheesecake, coconut or banana cream: these are among the mouthwatering tropical pies offered at the full-service main location of this bakery. It also delivers desserts and savory pot pies to several points around the island and sells at farmers' markets—check the website for a schedule. Seating and parking are very limited, so get pies to go. ✉ *2–2459 Kaumualii Hwy.* ✛ *Near the stoplight* ☎ *808/212–5798* ⊕ *www.rightslice.com.*

Hanapepe

6 miles west of Kalaheo, 15 miles west of Poipu.

Kauai's "biggest little town" is now an art colony with galleries, craft studios, cafés, a bookshop, and a lively street fair on Friday night. The main street has a new vibrancy enhanced by the restoration of several historic buildings where entrepreneurs have set up shop.

Once a bustling "free town" not tied to a plantation, Hanapepe was the center of West Side commerce, home to pool halls, a movie theater, and multiple brothels. By the 1980s, though, it was fast becoming a ghost town, its farm-based economy mirroring the decline of agriculture on the island. The emergence of Kauai coffee as a major West Side crop, a

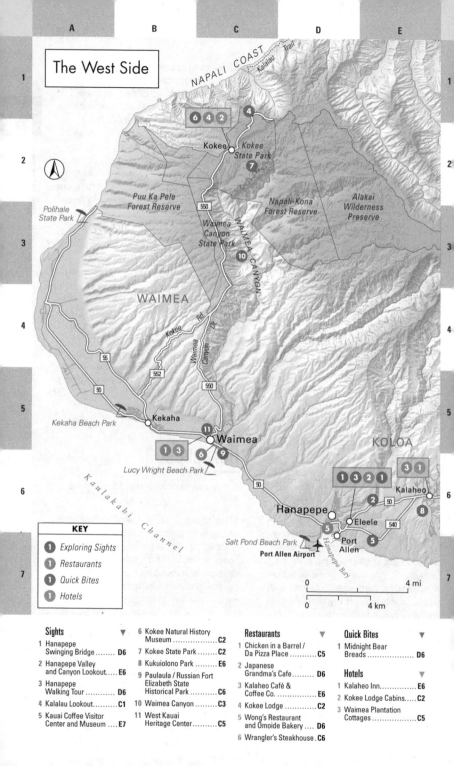

The West Side

Polihale State Park

NAPALI COAST

Kalalau Trail

Puu Ka Pele Forest Reserve

Kokee State Park

Napali-Kona Forest Reserve

Alakai Wilderness Preserve

Waimea Canyon State Park

WAIMEA CANYON

WAIMEA

Kekaha Beach Park

Kekaha

Waimea

Lucy Wright Beach Park

KOLOA

Kaulakahi Channel

KEY
- **1** Exploring Sights
- **1** Restaurants
- **1** Quick Bites
- **1** Hotels

Hanapepe

Salt Pond Beach Park

Port Allen Airport

Eleele

Port Allen

Hanapepe Bay

Kalaheo

0   4 mi
0   4 km

housing boom, and expanded activities at Port Allen—now the main departure point for tour boats—have given the town's economy a boost.

GETTING HERE AND AROUND

Hanapepe is just past the Eleele Shopping Center on the main highway (Route 50) as you head west. A sign leads you to the town center, where street parking is easy and there's an enjoyable walking tour. Don't miss the swinging bridge.

Sights

Hanapepe Swinging Bridge

BRIDGE | FAMILY | This narrow, pedestrian-only bridge may not be the biggest adventure on Kauai, but it's enough to make your heart hop. What is interesting is that it's not just for show; it actually provides the only access to taro fields across the Hanapepe River. Considered a historic suspension bridge even though it was rebuilt in 1996 after the early 1900s original was destroyed—like so much of the island—by Hurricane Iniki, the bridge was also repaired following flood damage in 2019. If you're in the neighborhood, it's worth a stroll. ⊠ *Off Hanapepe Rd., next to Banana Patch Studios parking lot, Hanapepe.*

Hanapepe Valley and Canyon Lookout

VIEWPOINT | From the roadside lookout, you can take in the farms on the valley floor with the majestic mountains and misty valley as a backdrop. This dramatic divide and fertile river valley once housed a thriving Hawaiian community of taro farmers, with some of the ancient fields still in cultivation. ⊠ *Rte. 50, Hanapepe.*

Hanapepe Walking Tour

HISTORIC DISTRICT | The 1½-mile self-guided walking tour takes you to 14 plaques with historic photos and stories mounted on buildings throughout Hanapepe Town. This little main street had a colorful past—it was a portside "free town," not governed by sugar plantation company rules or decorum, and a deadly labor battle known as the "Hanapepe Massacre" happened here in 1924. ⊠ *Hanapepe Town, Hanapepe* ⊕ *www.hanapepe.org/history* ⊠ *Free.*

Beaches

Salt Pond Beach Park

BEACH | FAMILY | A great family spot, Salt Pond Beach Park features a naturally made, shallow swimming pond behind a curling finger of rock where *keiki* (children) splash and snorkel. This pool is generally safe except during a large south summer swell. The center and western edge of the beach are popular with bodyboarders and bodysurfers. The beach is also an easy spot to see stilts, tattlers, shearwaters, and other seabirds. Pavilions with picnic tables offer shade, and there's a campground that tends to attract a rowdy bunch at the eastern end. On a cultural note, the mudflat behind the beach is the last spot in Hawaii where salt is harvested in the dry heat of summer, using pans passed down within families. The park is popular with locals, and it can get crowded on weekends and holidays. **Amenities:** lifeguard; parking (free); showers; toilets. **Best for:** sunset; swimming; walking. ⊠ *Lolokai Rd., off Rte. 50, Hanapepe* ⊠ *Free.*

Restaurants

★ Japanese Grandma's Cafe

$$ | JAPANESE | Traditional methods for sushi, tempura, bento, and bowls meet fresh local ingredients to create delicious food in this intimate modern café at the center of old Hanapepe. One of the few sit-down dinner options in the area, Grandma's also brings in chefs for monthly tasting menus. **Known for:** trendy atmosphere; build-your-own bento bowl; ume-tini (plum wine martini). ⑤ *Average main: $22* ⊠ *3871 Hanapepe Rd., Hanapepe* ☎ *808/855–5016* ⊕ *www.japanesegrandma.com* ⊘ *Closed Tues.*

Wong's Restaurant & Bakery

$ | **CHINESE** | Wong's family-run, family-style restaurant has been serving up hearty portions of local favorites for decades. Specials change, but plate lunches are always available to go, complete with rice and mac salad (which Hawaii practically considers a "vegetable"). **Known for:** classic diner decor; original home of *lilikoi* (passion fruit) pie; Asian and Hawaiian food. $ *Average main: $15* ⊠ *13516 Kaumualii Hwy., Hanapepe* ☎ *808/335–5066* ⊗ *Closed Mon.*

☕ Coffee and Quick Bites

Midnight Bear Breads

$ | **BAKERY** | Organic, non-GMO flour is transformed into breads and pastries available at the bakery or at farmers' markets and health food stores around the island. Hot panini, tartines (open-faced sandwiches), pizza, and deli favorites use island-grown produce and make for a satisfying, quick breakfast or lunch, for here or to go. **Known for:** good bread selection; local fruit Danish pastries; European-style buns and croissants. $ *Average main: $11* ⊠ *3830 Hanapepe Rd., Hanapepe* ☎ *808/335–2893* ⊕ *www.midnightbearbreads.com* ⊗ *Closed Sun.–Tues. No dinner.*

▼ Nightlife

Port Allen Sunset Grill & Bar

GATHERING PLACES | One of the few places for evening life on the West Side, this casual eatery overlooks the harbor at Port Allen in Eleele and has a friendly bar, with sports on TV, that stays open until 10:30 pm. The patio is a popular spot for locals to *pau hana* on Friday (decompress at the end of a workweek). It's open for lunch and dinner. ⊠ *4353 Waialo Rd., Eleele* ☎ *808/335–3188.*

Lappert's Hawaii Ice Cream

It's not ice cream on Kauai if it's not handmade fresh, super-premium Lappert's Hawaii Ice Cream (⊕ *lapperts.com*). Guava, mac nut, pineapple, coffee, coconut, banana—Lappert's is the island's ice cream king. The factory in Port Allen roasts coffee, bakes cones and pastries, and churns out ice cream to ship statewide. Try Kauai Pie: coffee ice cream with chocolate fudge, coconut flakes, and macadamia nuts. Cheat your diet at ice cream shops in Poipu and Princeville; at this writing, the Hanapepe shop was closed temporarily.

⊖ Shopping

Banana Patch Studio

CERAMICS | What started as a one-woman operation in 1991 now employs more than 20 artists, who hand-paint ceramic tiles, tableware, ornaments, and fun signs at this factory store in a 1926 former pool hall. Glazes are lead-free and kilns are powered by solar panels, which feed back to the power grid when they're not firing. The studio's "Mahalo for Removing your Slippers" plaques are a classic island souvenir. Custom orders are available. ⊠ *3865 Hanapepe Rd., Hanapepe* ☎ *808/335–5944* ⊕ *www.bananapatchstudio.com.*

Eleele Shopping Center

SHOPPING CENTER | Kauai's West Side has a scattering of stores, including those at this no-frills strip mall. It has a post office, several banks, a hardware store around back, a pharmacy, a laundromat, and a hair salon, and you'll rub elbows with local folks at the Big Save grocery store. Also here are a McDonald's, a Subway, and a few little local eateries. ✉ *4469 Waialo Rd., Eleele* ☎ *808/245–7238* ⊕ *www.eleeleshoppingcenter.com.*

★ **Kauai Chocolate Company**

CHOCOLATE | The signature treat here, the chocolate opihi, is made with a dash of culinary humor: layers of crispy cookie, gooey caramel, crunchy macadamia nut, and chocolate shell form a little cone ... a lot like the shape and texture of limpets found clinging to shoreline rocks and also considered a delicacy. Fear not: no seafood is involved in this decadent candy. Fudge, bars, and chocolate-covered pretzels make good gifts, and the gelato is *ono* (delicious). ✉ *4353 Waialo Rd., Suite 1B, Eleele* ⊹ *In Port Allen Marina* ☎ *808/335–0448* ⊕ *kauaichocolate.com.*

Salty Wahine

FOOD | Hanapepe has been a salt-making center for centuries, so it's only appropriate to pick up some gourmet ingredients at this family-run factory store. Salt is blended with herbs and spices or infused with tropical fruits, and staff readily share recipes that use favorites like Passion Fruit Chili Pepper, Java Steak Rub, and Guava Garlic Salt. Impress guests at your next cocktail hour by rimming mai tai glasses with coconut cane sugar. ✉ *1–3529 Kaumualii Hwy., Unit 2B, Hanapepe* ☎ *808/378–4089* ⊕ *www. saltywahine.com.*

Talk Story Bookstore

BOOKS | Located in a historic building in quiet Hanapepe Town, this is the only bookstore on Kauai, with some 25,000 titles and a resident cat named Celeste. When Friday Art Nights are on, local authors sign their books while live music and food trucks entertain meandering crowds outside. New, used, rare, and out-of-print books are sold here, as well as vinyl records, comics, vintage video games, and Celeste's own cute sticker line. ✉ *3785 Hanapepe Rd., Hanapepe* ☎ *808/335–6469* ⊕ *www.talkstorybookstore.com.*

West Side Festivals

Various festivals celebrating Kauai crops like coffee and chocolate (October) or orchids (spring) dot the West Side event calendar and are an insider's way to experience local culture. The **Waimea Town Celebration** is a 10-day extravaganza in February with an outrigger canoe regatta, a rodeo, a 5K/10K race, a food and craft fair at the old sugar mill site, a film festival, a live music stage, lei-making and ukulele contests, and a luau honoring King Kaumualii (⊕ *waimeatowncelebration.com*).

Waimea and Waimea Canyon

Waimea is 7 miles northwest of Hanapepe; Waimea Canyon is approximately 10 miles northeast of Waimea.

An ideal place for a refreshment break while sightseeing on the West Side, Waimea is a serene, pretty town that has the look of the Old West and the feel of old Hawaii, with a lifestyle that's decidedly laid-back. The town has played a major role in Hawaiian history since 1778, when Captain James Cook became the first European to set foot on the Hawaiian Islands. Waimea was also the place where Kauai's King Kaumualii acquiesced to King Kamehameha's island unification drive in 1810, averting a bloody war. The town hosted the first Christian missionaries, who hauled in massive timbers and coral-stone blocks to build the sturdy Waimea Foreign Church in 1846. It's one of many lovely historic buildings preserved by residents who take great pride

Birds of Kauai

Kauai offers some of the best birding in the state, due in part to the absence of the mongoose. Many nene (the endangered Hawaiian state bird) reared in captivity have been successfully released here, along with an endangered forest bird called the puaiohi. The island is also home to multiple species of migratory nesting seabirds and has three refuges protecting endangered Hawaiian waterbirds and seabirds. The Kokee Natural History Museum and Kilauea Lighthouse have informative displays.

Kauai's most noticeable fowl, however, is the wild chicken. A cross between jungle fowl (*moa*) brought by the Polynesians and domestic chickens and fighting cocks that escaped during the last two hurricanes, they are everywhere, and the roosters crow when they feel like it, not only at dawn. Consider yourself warned.

in their heritage and history. The Historic Waimea Theater, which opened in 1938 with the first electric marquee lights on the island, still shows movies.

North of Waimea town, via Route 550, you'll find vast, gorgeous Waimea Canyon, also known as the Grand Canyon of the Pacific. The spectacular vistas from the lookouts along the road culminate in two overviews of Kalalau Valley, and various hiking trails lead to the inner heart of Kauai. A camera is a necessity in this region.

GETTING HERE AND AROUND

Route 50 continues northwest to Waimea and Kekaha from Hanapepe. You can reach Waimea Canyon and Kokee State Park from either town—the way is clearly marked. Some pull-off areas on Route 550 are fine for a quick view of the canyon, but the designated lookouts have bathrooms and parking.

TOURS

Waimea Historic Tour

DRIVING TOURS | FAMILY | Tuesday through Thursday, the West Kauai Heritage Center offers private, car-based tours of historic Waimea Town by reservation, led by a local *kupuna* (elder). You can also get their map and take a self-guided walking tour. ⊠ *9565 Kaumualii Hwy., Waimea (Kauai County)* ☎ *808/338–1332* ⊕ *www. wsmmuseum.org* ✉ *Suggested tour donation $10.*

◉ Sights

Kalalau Lookout

VIEWPOINT | At the end of the road, high above Waimea Canyon, the Kalalau Lookout marks the start of a 1-mile (one-way) walk along the road to the Puu o Kila Lookout. On a clear day at either spot, you can see a dreamy landscape of gaping valleys, sawtooth ridges, waterfalls, and turquoise seas, where whales can be seen spouting and breaching during the winter months. If clouds block the view, don't despair—they tend to blow through fast, giving you time to snap that photo of a lifetime. You may spot wild goats clambering on the sheer rocky cliffs and white-tailed tropicbirds. If it's very clear to the northwest, drink in the shining sands of Kalalau Beach, gleaming like golden threads against the deep blue of the Pacific. ⊠ *Kokee State Park, Waimea Canyon Dr.* ✛ *4 miles beyond Kokee Museum* ⊕ *dlnr.hawaii.gov/dsp/ parks* ✉ *$10 parking and $5 per person admission fee for nonresidents.*

Did You Know?

It's possible to see vast stretches of the Kalalau Valley from Kokee State Park, which is about 4,000 feet above sea level.

Kokee Natural History Museum

SCIENCE MUSEUM | FAMILY | A great place to start your visit in Kokee State Park, the museum has friendly staff who are knowledgeable about trail conditions and weather, as well as informative displays and a good selection of books about the area's unique native flora and fauna and social history. You may also find that special memento or gift you've been looking for. ■ TIP➔ **Note that the park has no cell service, but a pay phone is outside the museum.** ☒ *Rte. 550, Kokee* ✛ *In Kanaloahuluhulu Meadow, after mile marker 15 mile* ☎ *808/335–9975* ⊕ *kokee.org* ☜ *Donations welcome.*

Kokee State Park

STATE/PROVINCIAL PARK | FAMILY | This 4,345-acre wilderness park is 4,000 feet above sea level, an elevation that affords you breathtaking views and a cooler, wetter climate that's in marked contrast to the beach. You can gain a deeper appreciation of the island's rugged terrain and dramatic beauty from this vantage point. Large tracts of native ohia and koa forest cover much of the land, along with many varieties of exotic plants. Hikers can follow a 45-mile network of trails through diverse landscapes that feel wonderfully remote—until the tour helicopters pass overhead. The small nonprofit museum provides park information, and the lodge offers hearty lunches. ■ TIP➔ **Note that there's no cell phone service in the park.** ☒ *Rte. 550, Kekaha* ✛ *15 miles north of Kekaha* ⊕ *kokee.org, dlnr.hawaii.gov/dsp* ☜ *$10 parking and $5 per person fee for nonresidents.*

Pauluala State Historic Park State Historical Park

RUINS | The ruins of this stone fort, built in 1816 by an agent of the imperial Russian government named Georg Anton Schäffer, are a reminder of the days when he tried to conquer the island for his homeland, or so one story goes. Another claims that Schäffer's allegiance lay with King Kaumualii, who was attempting to keep leadership of his island nation from the grasp of Kamehameha the Great. The crumbling walls of the fort, a National Historic Landmark, are not particularly interesting, but the signs loaded with historical information are. A bronze statue of King Kaumualii was installed in 2021, marking 200 years since the king was kidnapped to Oahu aboard the ship *Haaheo o Hawaii* in July 1821, during a reception aboard. ☒ *Rte. 50, Waimea (Kauai County)* ✛ *Just above Waimea River bridge* ⊕ *dlnr.hawaii. gov/dsp, www.kauaikingkaumualii.org* ☜ *Free.*

★ Waimea Canyon

CANYON | Carved over countless centuries by the Waimea River and the forces of wind and rain, Waimea Canyon is a dramatic gorge nicknamed the "Grand Canyon of the Pacific"—but not by Mark Twain, as many people mistakenly think. Hiking and hunting trails wind through the canyon, which is more than 3,600 feet deep, 1 mile wide, and about 14 miles long. The cliff sides have been sharply eroded, exposing swatches of colorful soil. The deep red, brown, and green hues are constantly changing in the sun, and frequent rainbows and waterfalls enhance the natural beauty. This is one of Kauai's prettiest spots, and it's worth stopping at both the Puu ka Pele and Puu Hinahina lookouts within the state park.

Clean public restrooms and parking are at both lookouts, and the main lookout has ramps for strollers and wheelchairs. If you stop at small pullouts, park completely off the highway and be alert to cyclists. ☒ *Waimea Canyon State Park, Rte. 550 (Kokee Rd.), Waimea (Kauai County)* ☎ *808/274–3444* ⊕ *dlnr.hawaii. gov/dsp* ☜ *$10 parking and $5 per person daily fee for nonresidents at main park lookouts.*

West Kauai Heritage Center

VISITOR CENTER | FAMILY | Cultural information and local exhibits about sugar, weaving, shells, and poi-making highlight this small, museum-style resource center in Waimea Town. Shop counters offer island-made items, Niihau-shell jewelry, photographs of Kauai, children's books, and snacks. Lei-making and music sessions happen regularly on the patio. ⊠ *9565 Kaumualii Hwy. (Rte. 50), Waimea (Kauai County)* ☎ *808/338–1332* ⊕ *www.wsmmuseum.org* ⊠ *Donations welcome* ⊗ *Closed weekends and Mon.*

🏖 Beaches

Kekaha Beach Park

BEACH | This is one of the premier spots on Kauai for sunset walks and the start of the state's longest beach. We don't recommend much water activity here without first talking to a lifeguard. The beach is exposed to open ocean and has an onshore break that can be hazardous any time of year. However, there are some excellent surf breaks for experienced surfers. If you'd like to run or stroll on a beach, this is the one—the hard-packed sand goes on for miles, all the way to Napali Coast, but you won't get past the Pacific Missile Range Facility and its access restrictions. Another bonus for this beach is its relatively dry weather year-round. If it's raining where you are, try Kekaha Beach Park. Toilets at the west MacArthur Park section are the portable kind. **Amenities:** lifeguards; parking (free); showers; toilets. **Best for:** sunset; surfing; walking. ⊠ *Rte. 50, near mile marker 27, Kekaha* ⊠ *Free.* ·

Lucy Wright Beach Park

BEACH | Named in honor of the first Native Hawaiian schoolteacher, this beach is on the western bank of the Waimea River. It is also where Captain James Cook first came ashore in the Hawaiian Islands in 1778. If that's not interesting enough, the sand here is not the white, powdery kind you see along the South Shore. It's a salt-and-pepper combination of pulverized, black lava rock and lighter-color reef. Unfortunately, the intrigue of the beach doesn't extend to the waters, which are reddish and murky (thanks to river runoff) and choppy (thanks to an onshore break). Don't swim here after heavy rains. Instead, watch the local outrigger canoe club head out, or stroll the Waimea State Recreational Pier, from which fishers drop their lines, about 100 yards west of the river mouth. **Amenities:** parking (free); showers; toilets. **Best for:** sunset; walking. ⊠ *Pokile Rd., off Rte. 50, Waimea (Kauai County)* ⊠ *Free.*

★ Polihale State Park

BEACH | The longest stretch of beach in Hawaii starts in Kekaha and ends west about 15 miles away at the start of Napali Coast. On the far west end is the 5-mile-long, 140-acre Polihale State Park, a remote beach accessed via a rough, rutted, potholed, 5-mile road at the end of Route 50 in Mana. (Four-wheel drive is recommended, and rental car companies may prohibit use of their vehicles here.) In addition to being long, this beach is 300 feet wide in places and backed by sand dunes 50 to 100 feet tall. Cultural sites, including burials, are located within the sensitive dune system. It is frequently very hot, with almost no shade and scorching sand. Start the day with a full tank of gas and a cooler filled with food and drink. ⚠ **Though it's a popular beach, the ocean here has dangerous currents and is not recommended for recreation.** No driving is allowed on the beach. The U.S. Navy's Pacific Missile Range Facility is adjacent, so access to the coastline in front of the base is monitored and restricted. Note that the park is open for day use only; camping permits are required when overnight use is allowed. **Amenities:** parking (free); showers; toilets. **Best for:** solitude; sunset; walking. ⊠ *Dirt road at end of Rte. 50, Kekaha* ☎ *808/587–0300* ⊕ *dlnr.hawaii.gov/dsp.*

Did You Know?

Waimea Canyon's rugged cliffs, valley gorges, and waterfalls can be spotted from three lookout points: Waimea Canyon, Puu ka Pele, and Puu Hinahina.

🍴 Restaurants

Chicken in a Barrel / Da Pizza Place

$ | **AMERICAN** | **FAMILY** | Located in the laid-back Waimea Plantation Cottages hotel, this equally casual eatery has a veranda that's a great place to sit with a beer and watch the sunset while the kids run around on the lawn. The fare is simple and hearty: barrel-smoked barbecue chicken, pork, brisket, or ribs; plus salads, tacos, burgers, and pizza. **Known for:** great selection of sides; large portions; good breakfast options. ⑤ *Average main: $15 ⊠ 9400 Kaumualii Hwy., Waimea (Kauai County)* ☎ *808/320–8379* ⊕ *www.chickeninabarrel.com.*

Kokee Lodge

$ | **AMERICAN** | Talk about "farm to table"—Kokee Lodge grows much of its own produce, and the tables are handmade from local lumber. Makaweli beef is used for *loco mocos* (white rice topped with a hamburger patty, brown gravy, and fried egg) and burgers, which can be served on fresh greens with homemade dressings; a veggie strata or a kalua pork plate, with Kokee plum barbecue sauce, is a perfect hot lunch on chilly days. **Known for:** pie and specialty coffee; Portuguese bean soup; live music on weekends. ⑤ *Average main: $12 ⊠ Kokee State Park, 3600 Kokee Rd., mile marker 15, Kokee* ☎ *808/335–6061* ⊕ *kokeelodge.com* ☾ *No dinner.*

Wrangler's Steakhouse

$$$ | **STEAKHOUSE** | **FAMILY** | Steaks are grilled over kiawe wood and ribs are succulent here, although Wrangler's could be called "Anglers" instead, as they do a nice job with fresh fish, too; a trip to a small salad bar, soup, and sides are included with entrées. Local folks love the *kaukau* tin special: rice, chicken teriyaki, and vegetable tempura with kimchi served in a three-tier *kaukau* tin, a lunch pail just like the ones sugar-plantation workers once carried. **Known for:** sushi nights (reservations required); local,

grass-fed beef; Western decor. ⑤ *Average main: $32 ⊠ 9852 Kaumualii Hwy., Waimea (Kauai County)* ☎ *808/338–1218* ☾ *Closed Sun. and Mon. No lunch.*

🛏 Hotels

The Cabins at Kokee

$ | **HOUSE** | If you're an outdoors enthusiast, you can appreciate Kauai's mountain wilderness from the dozen rustic cabins—of varying age and quality—that make up this lodge. **Pros:** cooking facilities; outstanding setting; more refined than camping. **Cons:** $45 cleaning fee; no Wi-Fi or cell service; wood-burning stove is the only heat. ⑤ *Rooms from: $89 ⊠ Kokee State Park, 3600 Kokee Rd., at mile marker 15, Kokee* ☎ *808/652–6852* ⊕ *www.westkauailodging.com* ⬭ *12 cabins* ☾ *No Meals.*

★ Waimea Plantation Cottages

$$ | **RESORT** | Originally built in the early 1900s, these relocated and refurbished one- to five-bedroom sugar-plantation workers' cottages are tucked in a coconut grove along a lovely, walkable stretch of beach on the sunny West Side. **Pros:** lovely grounds; unique lodging experience; quiet and low-key. **Cons:** cottages can be hot in summer; rooms are simple; not a good swimming beach. ⑤ *Rooms from: $250 ⊠ 9400 Kaumualii Hwy., Waimea (Kauai County)* ☎ *808/338–1923, 800/716–6199* ⊕ *www.coasthotels.com* ⬭ *56 cottages* ☾ *No Meals.*

🛍 Shopping

Menehune Food Mart

CONVENIENCE STORE | Besides the grocery stores in Waimea Town two miles away, this locally owned minimart in Kekaha is the last stop for snacks, beverages, ice, sunscreen, and limited grocery items before folks head up to Waimea Canyon or out to Polihale Beach. ⊠ *8171 Kekaha Rd., at Rte. 50, Kekaha* ☎ *808/337–1335.*

Chapter 7

ACTIVITIES AND TOURS

Updated by
Joan Conrow

Kauai's outdoor recreation options extend well beyond the sand and surf, with plenty of activities to keep you busy on the ground and even in the air. You can hike the island's many trails, or consider taking your vacation into flight with a treetop zip line. You can have a backcountry adventure in a four-wheel drive, or relax in an inner tube floating down old cane-field irrigation canals.

Before booking tours, check with your concierge to find out what the forecast is for water and weather conditions. If you check online weather sources, be sure you search for Kauai-specific weather. There's plenty of variation around the Islands. If you happen to arrive during a lull in the North Shore surf, you'll want to plan to be on the ocean in a kayak or snorkeling on the reef. If it's raining, ATV tours are the activity of choice.

Golfers should be aware that Kauai's spectacular courses are rated among the most scenic, as well as the most technical, in the country. Princeville Makai Golf Course has garnered accolades from numerous national publications, and Poipu Bay Golf Course hosted the prestigious season-end PGA Grand Slam of Golf for 13 years.

One of the most popular, though pricey, Kauai experiences is to tour the island from the air. In an hour or so, you can see waterfalls, craters, and other places that are inaccessible even by hiking trails (some say that 70% or more of the island is inaccessible). The majority of flights

depart from the Lihue airport and follow a clockwise pattern around the island. Be prepared to relive your flight in dreams for the rest of your life. The most popular flight is 60 minutes long. ■ TIP→ **If you plan to take an aerial tour, it's a good idea to fly when you first arrive, rather than saving it for the end of your trip. It will help you visualize what's where on the island, and it may help you decide what you want to see from a closer vantage point during your stay.**

Ancient Hawaiians were water-sports fanatics—they invented surfing, after all—and that propensity hasn't strayed far from today's mindset. Even if you're not into water sports or sports in general, there's only a slim chance that you'll leave this island without getting out on the ocean, because Kauai's top attraction—Napali Coast—is not to be missed.

For those who can't pack enough snorkeling, fishing, bodyboarding, or surfing time into a vacation, Kauai has it all—everything except parasailing, that is, as it's illegal to do it here (though not on Maui, the Big Island, or Oahu). If you need to rent gear for any of these activities, you'll find plenty of places with large selections at reasonable prices. And no matter what part of the island you're staying on, you'll have several options for choice spots to enjoy playing in the water.

One thing to note, and we can't say this enough—the waters off the coast of Kauai have strong currents and can be unpredictable, so always err on the side of caution and know your limits. Follow the tagline repeated by the island's lifeguards—"When in doubt, don't go out."

Aerial Tours

If you only drive around Kauai in your rental car, you will not see *all* of Kauai. There is truly only one way to see it all, and that's by air. Helicopter tours are the favorite way to get a bird's-eye view of Kauai—they fly at lower altitudes, hover above waterfalls, and wiggle their way into areas that a fixed-wing aircraft cannot. That said, if you've already tried the helitour, how about flying in the open cockpit of a biplane, à la the Red Baron?

Air Tour Kauai

AIR EXCURSIONS | This company can hold up to six people in its Cessna 206 plane, where every seat has a big window. The flights take off from less crowded Port Allen Airport on the West Side and last 65 to 70 minutes. ☒ *Port Allen Airport, 3441 Kuiloko Rd., Hanapepe* ☎ *808/335–5859* ⊕ *www.airtourkauai.com* 🎟 *$99.*

Blue Hawaiian Helicopters

AIR EXCURSIONS | This multi-island operator flies the latest in helicopter technology, the spacious Eco-Star. It boasts 23% more interior space for its six passengers, as well as unparalleled viewing and a few extra safety features. As the name implies, the helicopter is also a bit more environmentally friendly, with a 50% noise-reduction rate. A DVD of your tour is available for an additional $25. Charters can be arranged. ☒ *3651 Ahukini Rd.,*

Heliport 8, Lihue ☎ *808/245–5800, 800/745–2583* ⊕ *www.bluehawaiian.com* 🎟 *$339.*

★ Jack Harter Helicopters

AIR EXCURSIONS | The first company to offer helicopter tours on Kauai flies the six-passenger ASTAR helicopter with floor-to-ceiling windows, as well as the four-person Hughes 500, which is flown with no doors. The exciting doorless ride can get windy, but it's the best bet for taking reflection-free photos. Pilots provide information on the Garden Island's history and geography through two-way intercoms. The company flies out of Lihue. Tours are longer than the average at 60 to 65 minutes and 90 to 95 minutes. ☒ *4231 Ahukini Rd., Lihue* ☎ *808/245–3774, 888/245–2001* ⊕ *www. helicopters-kauai.com* 🎟 *From $339.*

Sunshine Helicopters

AIR EXCURSIONS | If the name of this company sounds familiar, it may be because its pilots fly on all the main Hawaiian Islands except Oahu. On Kauai, Sunshine Helicopters flies the six-passenger FX STAR or the super-roomy six-passenger WhisperSTAR birds. Flights are from Lihue and last 50 to 55 minutes. ■ **TIP→ Discounts can be substantial by booking online and taking advantage of the "early bird" seating during off-hours.** ☒ *3730 Ahukini Rd., #2, Lihue* ☎ *808/270–3999, 866/501–7738* ⊕ *www. sunshinehelicopters.com* 🎟 *From $230.*

ATV Tours

Although all the beaches on the island are public, much of the low-elevation interior land—once sugar and pineapple plantations—is privately owned. This is really a shame, because the valleys and mountains that make up the vast interior of the island easily rival the beaches in sheer beauty. The good news: some tour operators have agreements with landowners that make exploration possible, albeit a bit bumpy—and unless you have back troubles, that's half the fun. ■TIP→ **If it looks like rain, book an ATV tour ASAP. That's the thing about these tours: the muddier, the better.**

★ Kauai ATV

FOUR-WHEELING | This is *the* thing to do when it rains on Kauai—if you're into an extreme mud bath. Kauai ATV in Koloa is the originator of the island's all-terrain-vehicle tours and has upgraded with a brand-new fleet of UTVs (utility task vehicles). The three-hour Koloa tour takes you on 18 miles of trails through a private sugar plantation and historic haul-cane tunnel. It includes visits to movie filming sites and Waita Reservoir for catch-and-release fishing. You must be 18 or older to operate your own vehicle, but Kauai ATV also offers its four-passenger "Ohana Bug" and two-passenger "Mud Bugs" to accommodate families with kids ages 5 and older. You must be 25 or older to drive minors under age 18. ⊠ *3477A Weliweli Rd., Koloa* ☎ *808/742–2734* ⊕ *www.kauaiatv.com* ✉ *From $253 for 2 people.*

Kipu Ranch Adventures

FOUR-WHEELING | This 3,000-acre property extends from the Huleia River to the top of Mt. Haupu. *Jurassic Park* and *Indiana Jones* were filmed here, and you'll see the locations for them on either of the three-hour tours. The Ranch Tour covers a lot of territory so you'll see a range of landscapes, from pastures to rain forest. The Waterfall Tour includes waterfall views and a swim. Once a sugar plantation, Kipu Ranch today is a working cattle ranch, so you'll be in the company of bovines as well as pheasants, wild boars, and peacocks. If you're not an experienced ATV driver, they also offer guide-driven tour options. ⊠ *235 Kipu Rd., off Hwy. 50, Lihue* ☎ *808/246–9288* ⊕ *www.kiputours.com* ✉ *From $187.*

Biking

Kauai is a labyrinth of cane-haul roads, which are fun for exploring on two wheels. The challenge is finding roads where biking is allowed and then not getting lost in the maze. Maybe that explains why Kauai is not a hub for the sport—yet. Still, there are some epic rides for those who are interested, both the adrenaline-rush and the mellower beach-cruiser kind. If you want to grind out some mileage, you could take the main highway that skirts the coastal area, but be careful: there are only a few designated bike lanes, the shoulders are often crowded with invasive guinea grass, and the terrain is hilly. You may find that keeping your eyes on the road rather than the scenery is your biggest challenge. "Cruisers" should head to Kapaa, where Ke Ala Hele Makalae, a pedestrian and bicycle trail, runs along the East Side of Kauai for miles.

You can rent bikes (with helmets) from the activities desks of certain hotels, but these are not the best quality. You're better off renting from Hele On Kauai in Kapaa, Outfitters Kauai in Poipu, or Pedal 'n' Paddle in Hanalei. Ask for the "Go Green Kauai" map for a full description of Kauai biking options.

BEST SPOTS
★ Ke Ala Hele Makalae

BIKING | FAMILY | This county beach park multi-use path follows the coastline on Kauai's East Side and is perfect for cruisers. Eventually, the path is projected to run some 20 miles, but an existing 8-mile-long stretch already offers scenic views, picnic pavilions, and restroom facilities along the way—all in compliance with the Americans with Disabilities Act. The path runs from Lydgate Beach Park north to secluded Kuna Bay (aka Donkey Beach).

Bikers who prefer a leisurely cruise can pedal along Ke Ala Hele Makalae, an 8-mile path in Kapaa on the East Side.

An easy way to access the longest completed section of the path is from Kealia Beach. Park here and head north into rural lands with spectacular coastline vistas, or head south into Kapaa for a more immersive experience. ⊠ *Kealia Beach, Kapaa* ⚓ *Trailhead: 1 mile north of Kapaa; park at north end of Kealia Beach* ⊕ *www.kauaipath.org.*

Kokee Road

BIKING | Those wanting a challenging workout can climb this road, also known as Route 550. After a 3,000-foot climb, Kokee Road levels out somewhat and continues for several miles past the Kokee Natural History Museum, ending at the spectacular Kalalau Lookout. It's uphill 100% and curvy, and the ride down can be a bit wild. Cyclists should exercise extreme caution on this road. Though it is paved the entire way, expect potholes and consistent vehicular traffic, including tour buses. Some cyclists use Waimea Canyon Road for the ascent,

but it is steeper and narrower, with more potholes and an extremely precarious descent. ■ **TIP**→ **There's not much of a shoulder on either road—sometimes none—so be extra careful.** Both roads get busier as the day wears on, so you may want to consider a sunrise ride.

Bicycles aren't allowed on the hiking trails in and around Waimea Canyon and Kokee State Park, but there are miles of wonderful four-wheel-drive roads perfect for mountain biking. Check at the Kokee Museum for a map and conditions. ⊠ *Off Rte. 50, near grocery store, Waimea (Kauai County).*

Moalepe Trail

BIKING | Intermediate to advanced trail-bike riders can tackle this trail on the East Side. The first 2 miles of the 5-mile narrow dirt road wind through pastureland, but the real challenge begins when you reach the steep and rutted switchbacks. A rainy spell can make the mud slick and hazardous. Moalepe intersects the Kuilau

Trail, which you can follow to its end at the Keahua Arboretum stream, though the riding is more challenging on this section. ✉ *Wailua (Kauai County)* ✛ *From Kuhio Hwy. in Kapaa drive mauka (toward mountains) on Kuamoo Rd. for 3 miles and turn right on Kamalu Rd., which dead-ends at Olohena Rd. Turn left and follow until road veers sharply right.*

Powerline Trail

BIKING | Even advanced riders are challenged by this trail, which is actually an abandoned electric-company service road that splits the island. It's 13 miles long; the first 5 miles go from 620 feet in elevation to almost 2,000. The remaining 8 miles descend gradually over a variety of terrain, some technical. You'll have to carry your bike through some sections, but the views will stay with you forever. It offers little shade, so be prepared for the heat. ■ **TIP**➜ **When it's wet—in summer or winter—this trail is a mess. Check with a knowledgeable bike shop for trail conditions first and be prepared to improvise.** ✉ *Powerline Rd., Kilauea* ✛ *The trailhead is mauka (toward the mountains), just past stream crossing at Keahua Arboretum, or at end of Powerline Rd. in Princeville, past Princeville Ranch Stables.*

Spalding Monument

BIKING | A good option for the novice rider, this ride offers a workout and a summit ocean view that's not overly strenuous to reach. If you pick up a bike at Kauai Cycle in Kapaa, you can pedal a mile up Ke Ala Hele Makalae to reach the start of the ride. From near the end of Kealia Beach, ride up a gradual incline 2 miles through horse pastures to Spalding Monument, named for a former plantation owner. Palms circle the lava-rock wall, where you can picnic while enjoying a 180-degree ocean view. Behind you is the glorious mountain backdrop of Kalalea. Coasting back down the road offers an almost continual ocean view along with a peek into rural Kauai most visitors miss. ✉ *Kealia* ✛ *The loop begins at the end of Kealia Beach, past mile marker 10 on mauka (mountain) side of road.*

Wailua Forest Management Road

BIKING | For the novice mountain biker, this is an easy ride, and it's also easy to find. From Route 56 in Wailua, turn *mauka* (toward the mountains) on Kuamoo Road and continue 6 miles to the picnic area known as Keahua Arboretum; park here. After crossing the stream on a bridge, you'll be biking along a potholed four-wheel-drive road through lush vegetation—stay away during heavy rains because the streams flood—that continues for 2 miles to a T-stop, where you should turn right. Stay on the road for about 3 miles until you reach a gate; this is the spot where the gates in the movie *Jurassic Park* were filmed, though it looks nothing like the movie. Go around the gate and down the road for another mile to a confluence of streams at the base of Mt. Waialeale. Be sure to bring your camera. ✉ *Kuamoo Rd., Kapaa.*

EQUIPMENT

Hele On Kauai

BIKING | In a location offering easy access to the Ke Ala Hele Makalae bike trail, this shop has a range of rental options, including beach cruisers, hybrids, mountain bikes, road bikes, and even electric bikes, by the hour and day. They also service bikes and sell bikes and riding gear. You can even arrange to have bikes delivered to a riding location for a fee. Rental hours are 11 am to 2 pm, Tuesday through Sunday. ✉ *4–1302 Kuhio Hwy., Kapaa* ☎ *808/822–4628* ⊕ *www.kauaibeachbikerentals.com* 🖃 *Rentals from $15 per hr.*

Kauai Cycle

BIKING | This reliable, full-service bike shop sells and repairs bikes and has a wide range of cycling gear. The Ke Ala Hele Makalae coastal path is right out the back door. ✉ *4–934 Kuhio Hwy., Kapaa* ✛ *Across from Taco Bell* ☎ *808/821–2115* ⊕ *www.kauaicycle.com.*

Pedal 'n' Paddle

BIKING | Located in the heart of Hanalei, this company rents old-fashioned, single-speed beach cruisers. This is a great way to cruise the town. It's not recommended to venture out of town because there are no bike lanes on the twisting-and-turning road. ✉ *Ching Young Village, 5–5190 Kuhio Hwy., Hanalei* ☎ *808/826–9069* ⊕ *www.pedalnpaddle. com* ✉ *Rentals from $15 per day and $60 per wk.*

Boat Tours

Deciding to see Napali Coast by boat is an easy decision, but choosing the outfitter to go with is not. There are numerous boat-tour operators to choose from, and, quite frankly, they all do a good job. Before you even start thinking about whom to go out with, answer these three questions: What kind of boat do I prefer? Where am I staying? Do I want to go in the morning or afternoon? Once you settle on these three, you can easily zero in on the tour outfitter.

First, the boat. The most important thing is to match your personality and that of your group with the personality of the boat. If you like thrills and adventure, the rubber inflatable rafts—often Zodiacs, which Jacques Cousteau made famous and which the U.S. Coast Guard uses— will entice you. They're fast, likely to leave you drenched and windswept, and quite bouncy. If you prefer a smoother, more leisurely ride, then the large catamarans are the way to go.

The next boat choice is size. Both the rafts and catamarans come in small and large. Again—think smaller, more adventurous, and a rougher ride or larger, more leisurely, and comfortable. ■ TIP→ **Do not choose a smaller boat simply because you think there will be fewer people. There might be fewer people, but you'll be jammed together sitting close to strangers.** If you

Boat Tour Checklist

- Swimsuit
- Reef-safe sunscreen
- Hat
- Sunglasses
- Beach towel
- Light jacket
- Camera (in waterproof bag, just in case)
- Motion sickness meds (take well before departure)
- Change of clothes (post-cruise)

prefer privacy over socializing, go with a larger boat, so you'll have more room to spread out. The smaller boats will take you along the coast at a higher rate of speed, making photo opportunities a bit more challenging. One advantage to smaller boats, however, is that—depending on ocean conditions—some may slip into a sea cave or two. If that sounds interesting to you, call the outfitter and ask their policy on entering sea caves. Some won't, no matter the conditions, because they consider such actions inappropriate or because they don't want to cause any environmental damage.

Boats leave from three points around the island (Hanalei, Port Allen, and Waimea), and all head to the same spot: Napali Coast. If you're staying on the North Shore, choose to depart out of the North Shore, except in wintertime when the boats sometimes can't navigate the big surf. If you're staying anywhere else, depart out of the West Side. It's that easy. Sure, the North Shore is closer to Napali Coast; however, you'll pay more for less overall time. The West Side boat operators may spend more time getting to Napali Coast, but they'll spend about the same amount of time along Napali, plus you'll pay less.

Finally, you'll also have to decide whether you want to go on a morning tour, which includes a deli lunch and a stop for snorkeling, or an afternoon tour, which does not always stop to snorkel but does include a sunset over the ocean. The morning tours with snorkeling are more popular with families and those who love dolphins, as the animals enjoy the "waves" created by the front of the catamarans and might just escort you down the coast. Hawaiian spinner dolphins are so plentiful in the mornings that some tour companies guarantee you'll see them, though you won't get in the water and swim with them. The winter months will also be a good chance to spot some whales breaching, though surf is much rougher along Napali. You don't have to be an expert snorkeler or even have any prior experience, but if it is your first time, note that although there will be some snorkeling instruction, there might not be much and you'll be in deep water in the open ocean. The afternoon tours are more popular with nonsnorkelers—obviously—and photographers interested in capturing the setting sunlight on the coast. Another factor to consider is that the winds often pick up in the afternoons, making the water rougher.
■ TIP→ **No matter which tour you select, book it online whenever possible to ensure a spot.**

CATAMARAN TOURS
★ Blue Dolphin Charters
BOATING | Offering the largest selection of tours, Blue Dolphin operates 65-foot sailing (rarely raised and always motoring) catamarans designed with three decks of spacious seating with great visibility, as well as motorized rafts. ■ TIP→ **The lower deck is best for shade seekers.** The most popular is a daylong tour of Napali Coast, which includes snorkeling and diving.

Best Boat Tours ⊙

Best for snorkeling: Z-Tourz

Best for romance: Capt. Andy's Star Dinner Sunset Sail

Best for thrill seekers: Napali Riders

Best for mai tais: Blue Dolphin Charters

Best for pregnant women: Capt. Andy's

Best for charters: Blue Dolphin Charters

Best for price: Catamaran Kahanu

Morning snorkel tours of Napali include a deli lunch. Sunset sightseeing tours include a Hawaiian-style buffet. North Shore and South Shore rafting tours are also available, as are daily sportfishing charters of four to eight hours for no more than six guests. Blue Dolphin promises dolphin sightings and the best mai tais "off the island." Book online in at least ten days advance for a $10 discount. ⊠ 4353 Waialo Rd., #7B, Eleele ☎ 808/335–5553 ⊕ www.kauaiboats.com ⊠ From $180; 2-hr whale-watching/sunset tours, winter only, $110.

★ Capt. Andy's Sailing Adventures
BOATING | FAMILY | Departing from Port Allen on the West Side and running 55- and 60-foot sailing catamarans, as well as 24-foot inflatables out of Kikiaola Harbor in Kekaha, Capt. Andy's offers something for every taste, from raft expeditions to yachting. They have several lunch and snorkeling packages and four-hour sunset tours along Napali Coast. The Zodiac rafts have hydrophones to hear whales and other underwater sounds. The longtime Kauai company also operates a snorkel

If you choose to sail by yourself in Kauai, be prepared for strong currents and know your limits.

barbecue sail and a dinner sunset sail aboard its *Southern Star* yacht, originally built for private charters, for an upgraded feel. ■**TIP→ If the winds and swells are up on the North Shore, this company is usually a good choice—especially if you're prone to seasickness.** ⊠ *4353 Waiola Rd., Suite 1A–2A, Eleele* ☏ *808/335–6833* ⊕ *www. napali.com* ⌁ *From $99.*

Catamaran Kahanu

BOATING | Hawaiian-owned and-operated, Catamaran Kahanu has been in business since 1985 and runs a 40-foot power catamaran with 18-passenger seating. It offers seasonal whale-watching and snorkeling cruises, ranging from two to five hours, and departs from Port Allen. The five-hour, year-round Napali Coast tour includes snorkeling at Nualolo Kai, plus a deli lunch and soft drinks. No alcohol is allowed. Check-in is at 7 am, and the boat returns at approximately 1 pm. The tour feels more personal than some operations, with a laid-back, *ohana* (family) style, and information is shared about Hawaiian culture and the natural environment. The two-hour whale-watching tour is available from late December through March and begins at 1 and 3:30 pm. ⊠ *4353 Waialo Rd., near Port Allen Marina Center, Eleele* ☏ *808/645–6176* ⊕ *www.catamarankahanu.com* ⌁ *From $90.*

Holo Holo Charters

BOATING | Choose between the 50-foot catamaran called *Leila* for a morning snorkel sail to Napali Coast or the 65-foot *Holo Holo* for a seven-hour catamaran trip to the "forbidden island" of Niihau. Both boats have large cabins and little outside seating. Holo Holo also offers a four-hour seasonal voyage along Napali from Hanalei Bay on its rigid-hull inflatable rafts, specifically for diving and snorkeling. Originators of the Niihau tour, Holo Holo Charters built their 65-foot powered catamaran with a wide beam to reduce side-to-side motion and twin 425 HP turbo diesel engines specifically for the 17-mile channel crossing to Niihau.

Boat Tour Weather Cancellations ◉

If it's raining where you're staying, that doesn't mean it's raining over the water, so don't shy away from a boat tour. Besides, it's not the rain that should concern you—it's the wind and waves. Especially from due north and south, wind creates surface chop and makes for rough riding. Larger craft are designed to handle winter's ocean swells, however, so unless monster waves are out there, your tour should depart without a hitch. If the water is too rough, your boat captain may reroute to calmer waters. It's a tough call to make, but your comfort and safety are always the foremost factor.

In winter months, North Shore departures are cancelled much more often than those departing the West Side. This is because the waves are often too big for the boats to leave Hanalei Bay, and as a result, some operators only work the summer season. If you want the closest thing to a guarantee of seeing Napali Coast in winter, choose a West Side outfitter. Oh, and even if your tour boat says it cruises the "entire Napali," keep in mind that "ocean conditions permitting" is always implied.

It's the only outfitter running daily Niihau tours. The *Holo Holo* also embarks on a daily sunset and sightseeing tour of Napali Coast. *Leila* can hold 37 passengers, while her big sister can take a maximum of 47. Check-in is at Port Allen Marina Center. ⊠ *4353 Waialo Rd., Suite 5A, Eleele* ☎ *808/335-0815* ⊕ *www.holoholocharters.com* ⌨ *From $159.*

Kauai Sea Tours

BOATING | Sailing from Port Allen, this company operates the *Lucky Lady*, a 60-foot sailing catamaran with spacious seating, and the sleeker, faster *Imiloa*, a 40-foot express catamaran. Snorkeling tours anchor near Makole (based on the captain's discretion). If snorkeling isn't your thing, try the two-hour, seasonal whale-watching cruise or the four-hour sunset tour with beer, wine, mai tais, *pupu* (appetizers), and a hot buffet dinner. Tours of Napali, one with a beach landing in a remote valley, are offered on inflatable rafts. ⊠ *4353 Waialo Rd., 2B–3B, Eleele* ☎ *808/335-5309, 800/733-7997* ⊕ *www.kauaiseatours.com* ⌨ *From $125.*

Liko Kauai Cruises

BOATING | There are many things to like about Liko Kauai Cruises, including the choice of a 49-foot smooth-riding powered catamaran that carries a maximum of 32 passengers or the 32-foot custom-built lightning catamaran that accommodates 12. Sometimes, Captain Liko himself—a Native Hawaiian—still takes the helm. The larger vessel, with its 360-degree walk-around, is perfect for photography. Both boats have a freshwater shower on board and offer five-hour morning and afternoon tours of Napali that include snorkeling, food, and soft drinks. Trips usually depart out of Kikiaola Harbor in Waimea, a bit closer to Napali Coast than those leaving from Port Allen. ⊠ *4516 Alawai Rd., Waimea (Kauai County)* ☎ *808/338-0333* ⊕ *www.liko-kauai.com* ⌨ *From $169.*

Na Pali Catamaran

BOATING | One of the few tour companies departing from Hanalei on the North Shore has been around since 1973. Once on board, it takes about 15 minutes before you're witnessing the magnificence of Napali Coast. It operates two 35-foot powered catamarans, each with a maximum of 16 passengers, that are small enough—and with no mast, short enough—to dip into sea caves. Between March and October, they run two four-hour snorkeling tours per day, stopping at Nualolo Kai, the best snorkeling site along Napali. The rates are a bit pricey, but the four-hour tour includes a deli-style lunch. ⊠ *Ching Young Village, 5–5190 Kuhio Hwy., Hanalei* ☎ *808/826–6853, 866/255–6853* ⊕ *www.napalicatamaran.com* ✉ *From $300.*

RAFT TOURS

Blue Ocean Adventure Tours

BOATING | This West Side–based company focuses on Napali Coast tours using either rafts or a super-fast and comfortable 48-foot catamaran. The five-hour morning and afternoon tours cover the entire 17-mile coast, with snorkeling, snacks, and photography stops. A six-hour tour option also includes landing at Nualolo Kai for a Hawaiian-style buffet picnic on the beach and 30-minute nature walk. The tours are lively and informative. Private adventures can be arranged. ⊠ *Kikiaola Small Boat Harbor, 8932 Kekaha Rd., Kekaha* ☎ *800/451–6133* ⊕ *goblueadventure.com* ✉ *From $169.*

Capt. Andy's Raft Expeditions

BOATING | Departing out of Kikiaola Harbor in Kekaha, Capt. Andy's Raft Expeditions offers both snorkeling and beach-landing excursions. The Zodiac rafts are on the smaller side—24 feet with a maximum of 14 passengers—and all seating is on the rubber hulls, so hang on. They operate three rafts, so there's a good chance of availability. Tours include snorkeling at Nualolo Kai (ocean conditions permitting), sea caves, and sightseeing along Napali Coast; the full-day trip also offers a hiking tour through an ancient Hawaiian fishing village and a picnic lunch on the beach. You're closer to the water on the Zodiacs, so you'll have great views of humpbacks,

spinner dolphins, sea turtles, and other wildlife. ⊠ *Kikiaola Small Boat Harbor, Kaumualii Hwy., Kekaha* ☎ *808/335–6833* ⊕ *www.napali.com* ✉ *From $99.*

Kauai Sea Tours

BOATING | The company holds a special permit from the state to land at Nualolo Kai along Napali Coast, ocean conditions permitting. Here, you'll enjoy a picnic lunch, as well as an archaeological tour of an ancient Hawaiian fishing village, ocean conditions permitting. Kauai Sea Tours operates four 24-foot inflatable rafts—maximum occupancy 14. These are small enough for checking out the insides of sea caves and the undersides of waterfalls. Four different tours are available, with morning and afternoon departures. ⊠ *Port Allen Marina Center, 4353 Waialo Rd., 2B–3B, Eleele* ☎ *808/335–5309, 800/733–7997* ⊕ *www.kauaiseatours.com* ✉ *From $180.*

Na Pali Riders

BOATING | This tour-boat outfitter distinguishes itself by cruising the entire 17-mile Napali Coast, clear to Kee Beach and back. It's a no-frills tour—no lunch provided, just beverages and snacks. The company runs morning and afternoon four-hour snorkeling, sightseeing, and whale-watching trips out of Kikiaola Harbor in Waimea on a 30-foot inflatable raft with a 28-passenger maximum, which can feel a bit cramped. ⊠ *9600 Kaumualii Hwy., Waimea (Kauai County)* ☎ *808/742–6331* ⊕ *www.napaliriders.com* ✉ *$169.*

Z-Tourz

BOATING | **FAMILY** | What we like about Z-Tourz is that it's a boat company that makes safety and snorkeling its priority. Its two- and three-hour guided tours focus solely on the South Shore's abundant offshore reefs. If you're new to snorkeling, or want someone to actually identify the tropical reef fish you're seeing, this is your company. Turtle sightings are pretty much guaranteed. The craft is a 26-foot rigid-hull inflatable (think Zodiac) with a maximum of 16 passengers. Rates include snacks and snorkel gear. Snorkeling tours that depart from the shore (no boats) are also available. ✉ *3417 Poipu Rd., #105, Poipu* ☎ *808/742–7422* ⊕ *www.kauaiztours.com* ⌨ *From $125.*

RIVERBOAT TOURS TO FERN GROTTO

Smith's Motor Boat Service

BOATING | The 2-mile trip up the lush and lovely Wailua River, the only navigable waterway in Hawaii, culminates at the Fern Grotto, a yawning lava tube that is covered with fishtail ferns. During the boat ride, guitar and ukulele players serenade you with Hawaiian melodies and tell the history of the river. It's a kitschy, but fun, bit of Hawaiiana, and the river scenery is beautiful. Flat-bottom, 150-passenger riverboats (they rarely fill up) depart from Wailua Marina at the mouth of the Wailua River. ■ **TIP→ It's extremely rare, but occasionally after heavy rains the tour doesn't disembark at the grotto; if you're traveling in winter, ask beforehand.** Round-trip excursions take 1½ hours, including time to walk around the grotto and environs; check the website for times and days. ✉ *5971 Kuhio Hwy., Kapaa* ☎ *808/821–6895* ⊕ *www.smithskauai. com/fern-grotto* ⌨ *$30.*

Bodyboarding and Bodysurfing

The most natural form of wave riding is bodysurfing, a popular sport on Kauai because there are many shore breaks around the island. Wave riders of this style stand waist deep in the water, facing shore, and swim madly as a wave picks them up and breaks. It's great fun and requires no special skills and absolutely no equipment other than a swimsuit. The next step up is bodyboarding,

also called boogie boarding. In this case, wave riders lie with their upper body on a foam board about half the length of a traditional surfboard and kick as the wave propels them toward shore. Again, this is easy to pick up, and there are many places around Kauai to practice.

The locals wear short-finned flippers to help them catch waves, which is a good idea to enhance safety in the water. It's worth spending a few minutes watching these experts as they spin, twirl, and flip—that's right—while they slip down the face of the wave. ■ **TIP→ Of course, all beach-safety precautions apply, and just because you see wave riders of any kind in the water doesn't mean the water is safe for everyone. Be especially cautious when there's a strong shore break.** Most snorkeling-gear outfitters also rent bodyboards.

Some of our favorite bodysurfing and bodyboarding beaches are **Brennecke, Wailua, Kealia, Kalihiwai,** and **Hanalei Bay.**

Deep-Sea Fishing

Simply step aboard and cast your line for mahimahi, ahi, ono, and marlin. That's about how quickly the fishing—mostly trolling with lures—begins on Kauai. The water gets deep quickly here, so there's less cruising time to fishing grounds, which is nice, since Hawaii's seas are notoriously rough. Of course, your captain may elect to cruise to a hot location where they've had good luck lately.

There are oodles of charter fishers around; most depart from Nawiliwili Harbor in Lihue, and most use lures instead of live bait. Inquire about each boat's "fish policy"; that is, what happens to the fish if any are caught. Some boats keep all; others will give you enough for a meal or two, even doing the cleaning themselves. On shared charters, ask about the maximum passenger count

The Makai course at Princeville Makai Golf Club has consistently been ranked a top course in the United States.

and about the fishing rotation. You'll want to make sure everyone gets a fair shot at reeling in the big one. Another option is to book a private charter. Shared and private charters run four, six, and eight hours in length.

FISHING BOATS AND CHARTERS
Captain Don's Sportfishing
FISHING | Captain Don is very flexible and treats everyone like family—he'll stop to snorkel or whale-watch if that's what the group (four to six) wants. Saltwater fly fishers (bring your own gear) are welcome. He'll even fish for bait and let you keep part of whatever you catch, as long as the fish is less than 25 pounds. On a shared trip, everyone gets part of the catch. His *Happy Ryder,* a 39-foot Hatteras boat, sails out of Nawiliwili, near Lihue. ⊠ *Nawiliwili Small Boat Harbor, 2494 Niumalu Rd., Nawiliwili* ☎ *808/639–3012* ⊕ *www.captaindons-fishing.com* ✉ *From $175 (shared); from $750 (private).*

Kai Bear
FISHING | What's particularly nice about this company is its roomy, 38-foot Bertram, *Kai Bear.* It docks in Nawiliwili Small Boat Harbor near Lihue, which is convenient for those staying on the East Side. The prices are reasonable ($180 per person for the four-hour shared charter or $1,375 for the eight-hour private charter), and they share the catch. ⊠ *Nawiliwili Small Boat Harbor, 2900 Nawiliwili Rd., Nawiliwili* ☎ *808/652–4556* ⊕ *www.kai-bear.com* ✉ *From $180; private charters from $900.*

Golf

For golfers, the Garden Isle might as well be known as the Robert Trent Jones Jr. Isle. Four of the island's eight courses, including Poipu Bay—onetime home of the PGA Grand Slam of Golf—are the work of Jones, who previously lived at Princeville. Combine these four courses with those from Jack Nicklaus, Robin Nelson, and local legend Toyo Shirai, and you'll see that golf sets Kauai apart from the other Islands as much as the Pacific Ocean does. ■TIP➔ **Afternoon tee times at most courses can save you big bucks.**

Kiahuna Golf Club

GOLF | A meandering creek, lava outcrops, and thickets of trees give Kiahuna its character. Robert Trent Jones Jr. was given a smallish piece of land just inland at Poipu, and defends par with smaller targets, awkward stances, and optical illusions. In 2003 a group of homeowners bought the club and brought Jones back to renovate the course (it was originally built in 1983), adding tees and revamping bunkers. The pro here boasts his course has the best putting greens on the island. This is the only course on Kauai with a complete set of tee boxes for juniors. ✉ *2545 Kiahuna Plantation Dr., Koloa* ☎ *808/742–9595* ⊕ *www.kiahunagolf. com* ✎ *$115, including cart* ⅄ *18 holes, 6787 yards, par 70.*

The Ocean Course at Hokuala

GOLF | The Jack Nicklaus–designed Ocean Course at Hokuala offers a beautiful and distinctly Hawaiian golf experience. With an assortment of plants and tropical birds adding to the atmosphere, this course winds through dark ravines and over picturesque landscape. The fifth hole is particularly striking, as it requires a drive over a valley populated by mango and guava trees. The final holes feature unmatched views of Nawiliwili Bay, including the harbor, a lighthouse, and secluded beaches. This course also offers footgolf, played with a soccer ball, on a nine-hole loop. ■TIP➔ **Get the lowest rates by booking online.** ✉ *3351 Hoolaulea Way, Lihue* ☎ *808/241–6000* ⊕ *www. golfhokuala.com* ✎ *From $260* ⅄ *18 holes, 7156 yards, par 72.*

Poipu Bay Golf Course

GOLF | Poipu Bay on the South Shore has been called the Pebble Beach of Hawaii,

and the comparison is apt. Like Pebble Beach, Poipu is a links course built on headlands, not true links land. There's wildlife galore. It's not unusual for golfers to see monk seals sunning on the beach below, sea turtles bobbing outside the shore break, and humpback whales leaping offshore. From 1994 to 2006, the course (designed by Robert Trent Jones Jr.) hosted the annual PGA Grand Slam of Golf. Tiger Woods was a frequent winner here. Prices are slightly higher in the winter high season. The course is adjacent to the Grand Hyatt Kauai Resort & Spa. ✉ *2250 Ainako St., Koloa* ☎ *808/742–8711* ⊕ *www.poipubaygolf.com* ✎ *$219 before noon, $195 after noon* ⅄ *18 holes, 6127 yards, par 72.*

★ Princeville Makai Golf Club

GOLF | The 27-hole Princeville Makai Golf Club on the North Shore was named for its five ocean-hugging front holes. Designed by golf-course architect Robert Trent Jones Jr. in 1971, the 18-hole championship Makai Course has consistently been ranked a top golf course in the United States. ■TIP➔ **Check the website for varying rates as well as other nongolf activities at the facility, including disc golf or the Sunset Golf Cart Tour, where you ride the course, sans clubs, and take in the spectacular ocean views.** ✉ *4080 Lei O Papa Rd., Princeville* ☎ *808/826–1912* ⊕ *www.makaigolf.com* ✎ *$315* ⅄ *Makai Course: 18 holes, 7223 yards, par 72; Woods Course: 9 holes, 3445 yards, par 36.*

Wailua Municipal Golf Course

GOLF | Considered by many to be one of Hawaii's best public golf courses, this seaside course provides an affordable game with minimal water hazards, but it is challenging enough to have been chosen to host three USGA Amateur Public Links Championships. It was first built as a nine-holer in the 1930s, and the second nine holes were added in 1961. Course designer Toyo Shirai created a course

Requiring a permit, the very strenuous 11-mile (one-way) Kalalau Trail will lead you from Kee Beach to Kalalau Beach on Napali Coast.

that is fun but not punishing. The trade winds blow steadily on the East Side of the island, adding a challenge to play. An ocean view and affordability make this one of the most popular courses on the island with locals and visitors alike. Tee times are accepted up to seven days in advance and can be paid in cash and some credit cards. ✉ *3–5350 Kuhio Hwy., Lihue* ☎ *808/241–6666* ⊕ *www.kauai. gov/golf* ⛳ *$48 weekdays, $60 weekends; cart rental $20* ⛳ *18 holes, 6585 yards, par 72.*

Hiking

The best way to experience the *aina*— the land—on Kauai is to step off the beach and hike in the hills and valleys of the island's interior. You'll find waterfalls so tall you'll strain your neck looking, pools of crystal-clear water for swimming, tropical forests teeming with plant life, and ocean vistas that will make you wish you could stay forever.

All hiking trails on Kauai are free. Hikers are reminded to leave no trace and pay attention to weather conditions, especially flash flood warnings, that could leave them stranded. Backcountry hikers anywhere in Hawaii should also clean their shoes, gear, and clothing thoroughly before and after a hike to prevent the spread of ohia rust, a deadly fungal disease that is killing the beautiful ohia trees that dominate Hawaii forests. ■**TIP➔ For your safety, wear sturdy shoes, preferably water-resistant ones.**

BEST SPOTS
Hoopii Falls

HIKING & WALKING | Tucked among the winding roads and grassy pastures of Kapahi, 3 miles inland from Kapaa Town, is a moderate, 2.4-mile out-and-back hike that leads to two waterfalls. A 10-minute walk will deliver you to the creek. Follow it around to see the first set of falls. The more impressive second falls are another mile on, and the swimming hole alone is worth the journey. Just climb the rooted path next to the first falls and turn left on the trail above. Turn left on the very next trail to descend back into the canyon and follow the leafy path that zigzags along the creek—the falls and the swimming hole lie below. ✉ *Kapaa* ✛ *On north end of Kapaa, ¼ mile past last lookout, is side road called Kawaihau. Follow road up 3 miles, then turn right on Kapahi Rd. into residential neighborhood. Kapahi Rd. dead-ends near trailhead. Look for yellow gate on your left.*

★ Kalalau Trail

HIKING & WALKING | Of all the hikes on Kauai, the Kalalau Trail (11 miles one-way; permit and reservation required) is by far the most famous and the most strenuous, and one to be undertaken only by well-prepared hikers. A moderate hiker can handle the 2-mile trek to Hanakapiai Beach. This steep, often muddy trail is best approached with a walking stick. If there has been any steady rain, wait for drier days for a more enjoyable trek. A hardy outdoorsperson may wish to hike an additional 2 miles up to the falls. But be prepared to rock-hop along a creek and ford waters that can get waist high and dangerous during the rain. Round-trip to Hanakapiai Falls is 8 miles.

The narrow Kalalau Trail delivers one startling ocean view after another along a path that is alternately shady and sunny. Wear hiking shoes or water sandals, and bring drinking water since natural sources are not potable. Plenty of food is always encouraged on a strenuous hike such as this one. You must make a reservation at ⊕ *gohaena.com* to get into Haena State Park, where you'll find the trailhead, and hike to Hanakapiai.

If you plan to hike beyond Hanakapiai Valley or stay overnight, you must acquire a camping permit, either online or at the State Building in Lihue, for $35 per person per night. Hikers with camping permits do not need a reservation to enter Haena State Park. Trail and campground capacity beyond Hanakapiai is limited to 60 hikers/campers, and permits, issued

Lilikoi Alert 👁

If you're hiking in May and June, you may come across *lilikoi*—often referred to as passion fruit—scattered like yellow eggs among the ferns. The fruit tastes as sweet and floral as it smells—bite the tip of the rind off and you'll see speckled jelly with tiny black seeds; then slurp it right out of the skin. If you miss *lilikoi* season, scout out delicious *lilikoi* mustards and jams sold by local grocers. *Lilikoi* pie is also served at a few eateries.

90 days out, are snapped up quickly. Hikers and campers may want to make reservations to catch the Go Haena shuttle at Waipa, just west of Hanalei. ✛ *Drive north past Hanalei to end of road. Trailhead is directly across from Kee Beach* ⊕ *dlnr.hawaii.gov/dsp/hiking/kauai* 🎟 *$35 per person per night for camping permit.*

Mahaulepu Heritage Trail

HIKING & WALKING | This trail offers the novice hiker an accessible way to appreciate the rugged southern coast of Kauai. A 2-mile trail wends its way along the water, high above the ocean, through a lava field, and past a sacred *heiau* (stone structure). Walk north to Mahaulepu for a two-hour, 4-mile round-trip. If conditions and the season are right, you should be able to see dolphins, *honu* (green sea turtles), and whales. ✛ *Drive north on Poipu Rd., turn right at Poipu Bay Golf Course sign. The street name is Ainako, but sign is hard to see. Drive down to beach and park in lot.*

Okolehao Trail

HIKING & WALKING | *Okolehao* basically translates to "moonshine" in Hawaiian: this steep, challenging, and often muddy trail follows the Hihimanu Ridge and was established in the days of Prohibition, when this backyard liquor was distilled from the roots of ti plants. The 2-mile hike climbs 1,200 feet and offers a 360-degree view of Hanalei Bay and Waioli Valley. Your ascent begins at the China Ditch off the Hanalei River. Follow the trail through a lightly forested grove and then climb up a steep embankment. From here the trail is well marked. Most of the climb is lined with hala, ti, wild orchid, and eucalyptus. You'll get your first of many ocean views at mile marker 1. ⊠ *Hanalei* ♦ *Follow Ohiki Rd. (north of Hanalei Bridge) 5 miles to U.S. Fish and Wildlife Service parking area. Directly across street is small bridge that marks trailhead.*

Sleeping Giant (Nounou Mountain) Trail
HIKING & WALKING | An easily accessible trail practically in the heart of Kapaa, the moderately strenuous Sleeping Giant Trail—or simply Sleeping Giant—gains 1,000 feet over 2 miles for a 4-mile round trip. We prefer an early-morning—say, sunrise—hike up from the East Side trailhead, with sparkling blue-water vistas, but there are other backside approaches. At the top is a grassy plot with a picnic table. The trail is a local favorite, with many East Siders meeting here to exercise. ⊠ *Haleilio Rd., off Rte. 56, Wailua (Kauai County).*

Waimea Canyon and Kokee State Park
HIKING & WALKING | This park contains a 50-mile network of hiking trails of varying difficulty that take you through acres of native forests, across the highest-elevation swamp in the world, to the river at the base of the canyon, and onto pinnacles of land sticking out over Napali Coast. All hikers are encouraged to register at the Kokee Natural History Museum, which has trail maps, current trail information, and specific directions. Camping permits ($30 per night per campsite) can be obtained 90 days ahead of the date.

The steep **Kukui Trail** descends 2,200 feet over 2½ miles into Waimea Canyon

Waterfall Warning 👁

The many waterfalls on Kauai can be quite alluring; however, it's important to:

■ Evaluate water conditions before entering—do not enter a waterfall pool during or after heavy rains.

■ Never dive into the pool.

■ Remember that the leptospirosis bacteria may be present in freshwater streams and pools.

■ Wear water-friendly shoes as the rocks can be quite slippery on entering and exiting the pool.

7

Activities and Tours HIKING

to the edge of the Waimea River. The **Awaawapuhi Trail,** with 1,600 feet of elevation gains and losses over 3¼ miles, feels more gentle than the Kukui Trail, but it offers its own huffing-and-puffing sections in its descent along a spiny ridge to a perch overlooking the ocean.

The 3½-mile **Alakai Swamp Trail** is accessed via the **Pihea Trail** or a four-wheel-drive road. There's one strenuous valley section, but otherwise it's a pretty level trail—once you access it. This trail is a bird-watcher's delight and includes a painterly view of Wainiha and Hanalei Valleys at the trail's end. The trail traverses the purported highest-elevation swamp in the world via a boardwalk so as not to disturb the fragile plant and wildlife. It is typically the coolest of the hikes due to the tree canopy, elevation, and cloud coverage.

The **Canyon Trail** offers much in its short trek: spectacular vistas of the canyon and its only dependable waterfall. This easy 2-mile hike is especially lovely when the late-afternoon sun sets the canyon walls ablaze in color. (All distances are one-way.) ✉ *Kokee Natural History Museum, 3600 Kokee Rd., Kekaha* ☎ *808/335–9975 for trail conditions* ⊕ *dlnr.hawaii.gov/dsp/parks/kauai* ⚄ *$5 entrance fee for nonresidents; $10 parking fee for nonresidents.*

EQUIPMENT AND TOURS

Kauai Hiking Tours

GUIDED TOURS | Based in Koloa, this company offers six guided hikes for small groups that traverse both mountain and coastal areas around the island. Options vary from easy two-hour coastal and trail hikes to challenging full-day treks in Waimea Canyon and Kokee State Park. Hikes are customized to the abilities and interests of the group. Knowledgeable guides offer information about the flora and fauna and provide transportation to more remote trailheads. Private hikes are available. The company is certified as a Sustainable Tour Operator by the Sustainable Tourism Association of Hawaii. ✉ *Koloa Rd., Koloa* ☎ *808/212–9928* ⊕ *www.kauaihikingtours.com* ⚄ *From $300 for up to 4 people.*

★ Kauai Nature Tours

SPECIAL-INTEREST TOURS | Scientist Chuck Blay started this hiking tour business and continues to lead informative excursions to coastal and mountain localities, such as the Kokee State Park area, Mahaulepu, and other areas upon request, aside from the Kalalau Trail. His emphasis is on exploring and discussing the natural history of each place, including its geology, botany, fauna, and cultural aspects. While he will lead small groups, personal tours are encouraged so he can tailor the location and duration of hikes to the interests and physical condition of participants. ■TIP➔ **If you have a desire to see a specific location, just ask. He will do custom hikes to spots he doesn't normally hit if there is interest.** Hikes range from easy to strenuous. ✉ *5162 Lawai Rd., Koloa* ☎ *888/233–8365* ⊕ *www.kauainaturetours.com* ⚄ *From $175 per participant.*

Horseback Riding

Most of the horseback-riding tours on Kauai are primarily walking tours with little trotting and no cantering or galloping, so no experience is required. Zip. Zilch. Nada. If you're interested, most of the stables offer private lessons. The most popular tours are the ones including a picnic lunch by the water. Your only dilemma may be deciding what kind of water you want—waterfalls or ocean. You may want to make your decision based on where you're staying. The "waterfall picnic" tours are on the wetter North Shore, and the "beach picnic" tours take place on the South Shore.

CJM Country Stables

HORSEBACK RIDING | FAMILY | Just past the Grand Hyatt Kauai Resort & Spa in Poipu, CJM Stables offers a three-hour picnic ride with noshing on the beach, as well as their more popular two-hour trail ride without the picnic break. Private rides last 90 minutes. The landscape here is rugged and beautiful, featuring sand dunes and limestone bluffs. CJM can get you as close as anyone to secluded Mahaulepu Bay. The company sponsors seasonal rodeos that are free and open to the public, and participate in other popular community events. ✉ *Poipu Rd., Koloa* ✛ *1½ miles from Grand Hyatt Kauai Resort & Spa* ☎ *808/742–6096* ⊕ *www.cjmstables.com* ⚄ *From $169.*

Princeville Ranch

HORSEBACK RIDING | A longtime *kamaaina* (local resident) family operates Princeville Ranch, and their tour focuses on culture, history, and the local flora and fauna while also offering guidance on horsemanship. The two-hour rides are limited to four to six people, and they'll take out as few as two riders. The tour offers some splendid views of the mountains and the sea. They also offer riding lessons in their arena. ✉ *Kuhio Hwy., off Kapaka Rd., between mile markers*

27 and 28, Princeville ☎ 808/855–0064 ⊕ www.princevilleranch.com ✉ $199; private tours from $189.

Kayaking

Kauai is the only Hawaiian island with navigable rivers. As the oldest inhabited island in the chain, Kauai has had more time for wind and water erosion to deepen and widen cracks into streams and streams into rivers. Because this is a small island, the rivers aren't long, and there are no rapids, which makes them generally safe for kayakers of all levels, even beginners, except when rivers are flowing fast from heavy rains.

For more advanced paddlers, there aren't many places in the world more beautiful for sea kayaking than Napali Coast. If this is your draw to Kauai, plan your vacation for the summer months, when the seas are at their calmest. ■ TIP➔ **Tour and kayak-rental reservations are recommended at least two weeks in advance during peak summer and holiday seasons.**

In general, tours and rentals are available year-round, Monday through Saturday. Pack a swimsuit, sunscreen, a hat, rash guard, bug repellent, water shoes (sport sandals, aqua socks, old tennis shoes), and water and motion sickness medication (take in advance) if you're planning on sea kayaking.

RIVER KAYAKING
Tour outfitters operate on the Huleia, Wailua, and Hanalei Rivers with guided tours that combine kayaking with hiking to waterfalls, in the case of the first two rivers, and snorkeling, in the case of the third. Another option is renting kayaks and heading out on your own. Each river has its advantages and disadvantages, but it boils down as follows.

If you want to swim at the base of a remote, 100-foot-tall waterfall, sign up for a five-hour kayak (4-mile round-trip)

and hiking (2-mile round-trip) tour of the **Wailua River.** It includes a dramatic waterfall that is best accessed with the aid of a guide, so you don't get lost. ■ TIP➔ **Remember—it's dangerous to swim under waterfalls no matter how good a water massage may sound. Rocks and logs are known to plunge down, especially after heavy rains.**

If you want to kayak on your own, choose the **Hanalei River.** It's most scenic from the kayak itself; there are no trails to hike to hidden waterfalls. And better yet, a rental company is right on the river—no hauling kayaks on top of your car.

If you're not sure of your kayaking abilities, head to the **Huleia River**; a 3½-hour tour includes easy paddling upriver, a nature walk through a rain forest with a cascading waterfall, a rope swing for playing Tarzan and Jane, and a ride back downriver—into the wind—on a motorized, double-hull canoe.

As for the kayaks themselves, most companies use the two-person sit-on-top style that is quite buoyant—no Eskimo rolls required. The only possible danger comes in the form of communication. The kayaks seat two people, which means you'll share the work with a guide (good), or with your spouse, child, parent, or friend (the potentially dangerous part). On the river, the two-person kayaks are jokingly known as "divorce boats," so be patient with your partner. Counseling is not included in the tour price.

SEA KAYAKING
Kayaking Napali Coast has long been a thrill-seeker's dream, ranking right up there with rafting the Colorado River through the Grand Canyon. It's the adventure of a lifetime in one day, involving eight hours of paddling beneath the tropical sun or overnight camping in remote valleys. Although it's good to have some kayaking experience, feel comfortable on the water, and be reasonably fit, it doesn't require the preparation,

Wailua River, Hanalei River, and Huleia River are Kauai's most scenic spots for river kayaking.

stamina, or fortitude of, say, climbing Mt. Everest. Tours run May through September, ocean conditions permitting. In the winter months, sea-kayaking tours operate on the South Shore—a beautiful area, though not as dramatic as Napali.

EQUIPMENT AND TOURS
Kayak Kauai

KAYAKING | The company that pioneered kayaking on Kauai offers guided tours on the Wailua River and sea kayak tours departing out of Hanalei Bay, Haena, and Polihale. Adventure seekers can take multiday escorted summer sea kayak tours and camping trips on Napali Coast. From its convenient location in the Wailua Marina, Kayak Kauai can launch kayaks right into the Wailua River for its five-hour Secret Falls hike-paddle tour and three-hour paddle to a swimming hole. Sea-kayak whale-watching tours round out the aquatic repertoire. The company will shuttle kayakers as needed, and, for rentals, it provides the hauling gear necessary for your rental car. Snorkel gear, bodyboards, and stand-up paddleboards also can be rented, but note that it is closed weekends. ✉ *Wailua Marina, 3–5971 Kuhio Hwy., Wailua (Kauai County)* ☎ *808/826–9844, 888/596–3853* ⊕ *www.kayakkauai.com* ✉ *From $85 (river tours) and $240 (sea tours); kayak rentals from $110 per day.*

Kayak Wailua

KAYAKING | We can't quite figure out how this family-run business offers pretty much the same Wailua River kayaking tour as everyone else—except for lunch and beverages, which are BYO—for the lowest price, but it does. They say it's because they don't discount and don't offer commissions to activities and concierge desks. Their trip, a 4½-hour kayak, hike, and waterfall swim, is offered six times a day, with the last at 1 pm. With the number of kayaks going out, large groups can be accommodated. No tours are allowed on the Wailua River on Sunday. ✉ *4565 Haleilio Rd., Kapaa* ✛ *Behind old Coco Palms hotel* ☎ *808/822–3388* ⊕ *www.kayakwailua.com* ✉ *$75.*

Leptospirosis in Kauai

Before you go wading into a stream or river in Kauai, take note: leptospirosis, a bacterial disease that is transmitted from animals to humans, may be present. It can survive for long periods of time in freshwater and mud contaminated by the urine of infected animals, such as pigs, rats, and goats.

The bacteria enter the body through the eyes, ears, nose, mouth, and broken skin. To avoid infection, don't drink untreated water from streams, and don't wade in brown water or submerge skin with cuts and abrasions in streams or rivers.

Symptoms are often mild and resemble the flu—fever, diarrhea, chills, nausea, headache, vomiting, and body pains—and may occur 2 to 20 days after exposure. If you have these symptoms and think you could have been exposed to the disease, see a doctor right away. Treatment is with antibiotics.

★ Napali Kayak

KAYAKING | A couple of longtime guides ventured out on their own to create this company, which focuses solely on sea-kayaking paddles and multiday camping voyages along Napali Coast. These guys are highly experienced and still highly enthusiastic about their livelihood. They operate from April to October, offering full-day Napali Coast tours departing from Haena and five-hour tours out of Polihale; both tours stop for a lunch break at Miloli'i. They also rent river and ocean kayaks, camping equipment, and first-aid kits. Reservations well in advance are suggested. ⊠ 5–5075 Kuhio Hwy., next to Postcards Café, Hanalei ☎ 808/826–6900 ⊕ www.napalikayak. com ⊠ From $235.

Outfitters Kauai

KAYAKING | **FAMILY** | This well-established tour outfitter operates year-round river-kayak tours that go through some lovely scenery on the Huleia and Wailua rivers. Their specialty (though they have other tours) is the Kipu Safari, an all-day adventure that starts with an easy paddle up the Huleia River and includes swinging on a rope over a swimming hole, a wagon ride through a working cattle ranch, a picnic lunch by a private waterfall, hiking, and two "zips" across the rain-forest canopy (strap on a harness, clip into a cable, and zip over a quarter of a mile). They then offer a one-of-a-kind Waterzip Zip Line at their mountain stream–fed blue pool. The day ends with a leisurely ride on a motorized double-hull canoe. It's a great tour for the family, because no one ever gets bored. ⊠ 230 Kipu Rd., Lihue ☎ 808/742–9667, 888/742–9887 ⊕ www.outfitterskauai. com ⊠ Kipu Safari $219, $179 kids under 15.

Wailua Kayak & Canoe

KAYAKING | This purveyor of kayak rentals is right on the Wailua River, which means no hauling your kayak on top of your car (a definite plus). Morning and afternoon five-hour guided kayak tours are also offered, with a short hike to a waterfall and refreshments. The company is closed on weekends. ⊠ 162 Wailua Rd., Kapaa ☎ 808/821–1188 ⊕ www.wailua-riverkayaking.com ⊠ $65 per day for a single kayak, $125 per day for a double; guided tours from $115.

Mountain Tubing

Hawaii's sugarcane plantations have steadily closed one by one. In 2009, Gay & Robinson announced the closure of Kauai's last plantation; in 2016, HC&S ended the last operation in the state, on Maui. However, the sugarcane irrigation ditches remain, striating these Islands like spokes in a wheel. Inspired by the Hawaiian *auwai,* which diverted water from streams to taro fields, these engineering feats also diverted streams, often from many miles away. One ingenious tour company on Kauai has figured out a way to make exploring them an adventure: float inflatable tubes down the route.

TOURS

Kauai Backcountry Adventures

LOCAL SPORTS | FAMILY | Both zip-lining and tubing tours are offered by this company. Popular with all ages, the tubing adventure can book up two weeks in advance in busy summer months. Here's how it works: you recline in an inner tube and float down fern-lined irrigation ditches that were built more than a century ago—the engineering is impressive—to divert water from Mt. Waialeale to sugar and pineapple fields around the island. You are even given a headlamp so you can see as you float through five covered tunnels. The scenery from the island's interior at the base of Mt. Waialeale on Lihue Plantation land is superb. Ages five and up are welcome. The tour takes about three hours and includes a picnic lunch and a dip in a swimming hole. ■ TIP➔ **You'll definitely want to pack water-friendly shoes (or rent some from the outfitter), sunscreen, a hat, bug repellent, and a beach towel.** Thirteen tours are offered daily on the half hour. ✉ *3–4131 Kuhio Hwy., across from gas station, Hanamaulu* ☎ *808/245–2506, 855/846–0092* ⊕ *www.kauaibackcountry. com* ✈ *$136.*

Scuba Diving

The majority of scuba diving on Kauai occurs on the South Shore. Boat and shore dives are available, although boat sites surpass the shore sites for a couple of reasons. First, they're deeper and exhibit the complete symbiotic relationship of a reef system, and second, the visibility is better a little farther offshore. You'll also visit more than one site on a boat dive.

The dive operators on Kauai offer a full range of services, including certification dives, referral dives, boat dives, shore dives, night dives, and drift dives. Be sure to inquire about a company's safety record and precautions if you are new to the activity. ■ TIP➔ **As for certification, we recommend completing your confined-water training and classroom testing before arriving on the island.** That way, you'll spend less time training and more time diving.

BEST SPOTS

The closest and safest scuba-diving sites are accessed by boat on the South Shore of the island, right off the shores of Poipu. The captain selects the actual site based on ocean conditions of the day. Beginners may prefer shore dives, which are best at **Koloa Landing** on the South Shore year-round.

For the advanced and adventuresome diver, the island of **Niihau**—across an open ocean channel in deep and crystal-clear waters—beckons and rewards, usually with some big fish. Seasport Divers, Fathom Five, and Bubbles Below venture the 17 miles across the channel in summer when the crossing is smoothest. Divers can expect deep dives, walls, and strong currents at Niihau, where conditions can change rapidly. To make the long journey worthwhile, three dives and Nitrox are included.

Scuba Q&A

Q: Do I have to be certified to go scuba diving?

A: No. You can try Discover Scuba, which allows you to dive up to 40 feet after an introductory lesson in a pool. Most dive outfitters on Kauai offer this introductory program.

Q: Can I dive if I have asthma?

A: Only if your doctor signs a medical release—the original of which you must present to your dive outfitter.

Q: Can I get certified on Kauai?

A: Yes. Start to finish, it'll take three days. Or, you can complete your classroom and confined-water training at home and just do your check-out dives on Kauai.

Q: How old do you have to be to learn how to dive?

A: Most certifying agencies require that you be at least 12 years old (with PADI it's 10) when you start your scuba-diving course. Young divers will normally receive a junior certification, which can be upgraded to a full certification when the diver is 15 years old.

Q: Can I wear contact lenses or glasses while diving?

A: You can either wear contact lenses with a regular mask or opt for a prescription mask—just let your dive outfitter know in advance.

Q: What if I forget my certification card?

A: Let your dive outfitter know immediately; with advance notice, they can usually dig up your certification information online.

EQUIPMENT, LESSONS, AND TOURS

Bubbles Below

SCUBA DIVING | Marine ecology is the emphasis here aboard the 36-foot, eight-passenger *Kai Manu*. This longtime Kauai company discovered some pristine and adventuresome dive sites on the West Side of the island where white-tip reef sharks are common—and other divers are not. Thanks to the addition of a 32-foot powered catamaran—the six-passenger *Dive Rocket*—the group also runs Niihau, Napali, and North Shore dives year-round (depending on ocean conditions, of course). They're also known for their South Side trips, including a shore dive. A bonus on these tours is the wide variety of food served between dives. Open-water certification dives, check-out dives, and intro shore dives are available upon request. ✉ *Port Allen Small Boat Harbor, 4353 Waialo Rd., Eleele* ☎ *808/332–7333* ⊕ *www.bubblesbelowkauai.com* ✉ *$160 for 2-tank boat dive; Niihau charter $400.*

Dive Kauai

SCUBA DIVING | This company offers boat dives but specializes in shore diving for beginners, typically at Koloa Landing (year-round) on the South Shore. They're not only geared toward beginning divers and those who haven't been diving in a while—for whom they provide a gentle introductory/refresher dive—but they also offer scooter (think James Bond) dives for certified divers. Their main emphasis is a detailed review of marine biology, such as pointing out rare dragon eels and harlequin shrimp tucked away in pockets of coral. ■TIP➔ **Hands down, we recommend Dive Kauai for beginners, certification (all levels), and refresher dives.** One reason is that their instructor-to-student ratio does not exceed 1:4 for beginners; for certified divers the ratio can be 1:6. All dive gear is included. ✉ *Sheraton Kauai Resort, 2440 Hoonani Rd., Koloa* ☎ *808/321–9900* ⊕ *divekauai. com* ✉ *$156 for a 2-tank certified shore dive; $196 for a 2-tank boat dive.*

★ Fathom Five

SCUBA DIVING | This operator offers it all: boat dives, shore dives, night dives, Niihau-Lehua dives, certification dives. They pretty much do what everyone else does with a few twists. First, they offer a three-tank premium charter for those really serious about diving. Second, they operate a Nitrox continuous-flow mixing system, so you can decide the mix rate. Third, they add on a twilight dive to the standard, one-tank night dive, making the outing worth the effort. Fourth, their shore diving isn't an afterthought. Fifth, they don't mix advanced and rusty divers on their fleet of six-passenger boats. Finally, we think their dive masters are pretty darn good, too. Book well in advance. ✉ *3450 Poipu Rd., Koloa* ☎ *808/742–6991, 800/972–3078* ⊕ *www. fathomfive.com* ✉ *From $210 for boat dives; from $153 for shore dives; $65 for gear rental, if needed.*

Seasport Divers

SCUBA DIVING | Rated highly by readers of *Scuba Diving* magazine, Seasport Divers' 48-foot *Anela Kai* tops the chart for dive-boat luxury, including hot water showers. But owner Marvin Otsuji didn't stop with that. A second boat—the 32-foot catamaran *Ahuhea*—is outfitted for diving, but we like it as an all-around charter. The company does brisk business, which means it won't cancel at the last minute because of a lack of reservations. They limit passengers to 12 on the three-tank, 12-hour Niihau trips (available in summer) but may book up to 18 people per boat on South Shore dives. ■ TIP→ **There are slightly more challenging trips in the morning; mellower dive sites are in the afternoon. Night dives are offered, too.** The company runs a good-size dive shop

for purchases and rentals, as well as a classroom for certification. ✉ *2827 Poipu Rd., Poipu* ⊕ *Look for yellow submarine in parking lot* ☎ *808/742–9303* ⊕ *www. seasportdivers.com* ✉ *From $165 for certified divers; $125 1-tank shore dive, plus $40 gear charge.*

Snorkeling

Generally speaking, the calmest water and best snorkeling can be found on Kauai's North Shore in summer and South Shore in winter. The East Side, known as the windward side, has year-round, prevalent northeast trade winds that make snorkeling unpredictable, although there are some good pockets. The best snorkeling on the West Side is accessible only by boat.

A word on feeding fish: don't. As Captain Ted with Holo Holo Charters says, fish have survived and populated reefs for much longer than we have been donning goggles and staring at them. They will continue to do so without our intervention. Besides, fish food messes up the reef and—one thing always leads to another—can eliminate a once-pristine reef environment.

As for gear, if you're snorkeling with one of the Napali boat-tour outfitters, they'll provide it; however, depending on the company, it might not be the latest or greatest. If you have your own, bring it. On the other hand, if you're going out with Z-Tourz, the gear is top-notch. If you need to rent or want to buy, hit one of the "snorkel-and-surf" shops, such as Snorkel Bob's in Koloa and Kapaa, Nuku-moi Surf Co. in Poipu, or Seasport Divers in Poipu. ■ TIP→ **If you wear glasses, you can rent prescription masks at some rental shops—just don't expect them to match your prescription exactly.**

Continued on page 208

SNORKELING IN HAWAII

Molokini Crater

The waters surrounding the Hawaiian Islands are filled with life—from giant manta rays cruising off the Big Island's Kona Coast to humpback whales giving birth in the waters around Maui. Dip your head beneath the surface to experience a spectacularly colorful world: pairs of milletseed butterflyfish dart back and forth, redlipped parrotfish snack on coral algae, and spotted eagle rays flap past like silent spaceships. Sea turtles bask at the surface while tiny wrasses give them the equivalent of a shave and a haircut. The water quality is typically outstanding; many sites afford 30-foot-plus visibility. On snorkel cruises, you can often stare from the boat rail right down to the bottom.

Certainly few destinations are as accommodating to every level of snorkeler as Hawaii. Beginners can tromp in from sandy beaches while more advanced divers descend to shipwrecks, reefs, craters, and sea arches just offshore. Because of Hawaii's extreme isolation, the island chain has fewer fish species than Fiji or the Caribbean—but many of the fish that live here exist nowhere else. The Hawaiian waters are home to the highest percentage of endemic fish in the world.

The key to enjoying the underwater world is slowing down. Look carefully. Listen. You might hear the strange crackling sound of shrimp tunneling through coral, or you may hear whales singing to one another during winter. A shy octopus may drift along the ocean's floor beneath you. If you're hooked, pick up a waterproof fishkey from Long's Drugs. You can brag later that you've looked the Hawaiian turkeyfish in the eye.

Picasso Triggerfish

Milletseed Butterflyfish*

Yellow Tang

Moorish Idol

Hawaiian Whitespotted Toby*

Saddleback Wrasse*

Redlip Parrotfish

Hawaiian Turkeyfish*

Zebra Moray Eel

Stocky Hawkfish

Green Sea Turtle (Honu)

Spotted Eagle Ray

*endemic to Hawaii

POLYNESIA'S FIRST CELESTIAL NAVIGATORS: HONU

Honu is the Hawaiian name for two native sea turtles, the hawksbill and the green sea turtle. Little is known about these dinosaur-age marine reptiles, though snorkelers regularly see them foraging for *limu* (seaweed) and the occasional jellyfish in Hawaiian waters. Most female honu nest in the uninhabited Northwestern Hawaiian Islands, but a few sociable ladies nest on Maui and Big Island beaches. Scientists suspect that they navigate the seas via magnetism—sensing the earth's poles. Amazingly, they will journey up to 800 miles to nest—it's believed that they return to their own birth sites. After about 60 days of incubation, nestlings emerge from the sand at night and find their way back to the sea by the light of the stars.

SNORKELING

Many of Hawaii's reefs are accessible from the shore.

The basics: Sure, you can take a deep breath, hold your nose, squint your eyes, and stick your face in the water in an attempt to view submerged habitats . . . but why not protect your eyes, retain your ability to breathe, and keep your hands free to paddle about when exploring underwater? That's what snorkeling is all about.

Equipment needed: A mask, snorkel (the tube attached to the mask), and fins. In deeper waters (any depth over your head), life jackets are advised.

Steps to success: If you've never snorkeled before, it's natural to feel a bit awkward at first, so don't sweat it. Breathing through a mask and tube, and wearing a pair of fins take getting used to. Like any activity, you build confidence and comfort through practice.

If you're new to snorkeling, begin by submerging your face in shallow water or a swimming pool and breathing calmly through the snorkel while gazing through the mask.

Next you need to learn how to clear water out of your mask and snorkel, an essential skill since splashes can send water into tube openings and masks can leak. Some snorkels have built-in drainage valves, but if a tube clogs, you can force water up and out by exhaling through your mouth. Clearing a mask is similar: lift your head from water while pulling forward on mask to drain. Some masks have built-in purge valves, but those without can be cleared underwater by pressing the top to the forehead and blowing out your nose (charming, isn't it?), allowing air to bubble into the mask, pushing water out the bottom. If it sounds hard, it really isn't. Just try it a few times and you'll soon feel like a pro.

Never touch or stand on coral.

Now your goal is to get friendly with fins—you want them to be snug but not too tight—and learn how to propel yourself with them. Fins won't help you float, but they will give you a leg up, so to speak, on smoothly moving through the water or treading water (even when upright) with less effort.

Flutter stroking is the most efficient underwater kick, and the farther your foot bends forward the more leg power you'll be able to transfer to the water and the farther you'll travel with each stroke. Flutter kicking movements involve alternately separating the legs and then drawing them back together. When your legs separate, the leg surface encounters drag from the water, slowing you down. When your legs are drawn back together, they produce a force pushing you forward. If your kick creates more forward force than it causes drag, you'll move ahead.

Submerge your fins to avoid fatigue rather than having them flailing above the water when you kick, and keep your arms at your side to reduce drag. You are in the water—stretched out, face down, and snorkeling happily away—but that doesn't mean you can't hold your breath and go deeper in the water for a closer look at some fish or whatever catches your attention. Just remember that when you do this, your snorkel will be submerged, too, so you won't be breathing (you'll be holding your breath). You can dive head-first, but going feet-first is easier and less scary for most folks, taking less momentum. Before full immersion, take several long, deep breaths to clear carbon dioxide from your lungs.

If your legs tire, flip onto your back and tread water with inverted fin motions while resting. If your mask fogs, wash condensation from the lens and clear water from your mask.

TIPS FOR SAFE SNORKELING

- Snorkel with a buddy and stay together.

- Plan your entry and exit points prior to getting in the water.

- Swim into the current on entering and then ride the current back to your exit point.

- Carry your flippers into the water and then put them on, as it's difficult to walk in them, and rocks may be slippery.

- Make sure your mask fits properly and is not too loose.

- Pop your head above the water periodically to ensure you aren't drifting too far out, or too close to rocks.

- Think of the water as someone else's home—don't take anything that doesn't belong to you, or leave any trash behind.

- Don't touch any sea creatures; they may sting.

- Wear a T-shirt over your swimsuit to help protect you from being fried by the sun.

- When in doubt, don't go without a snorkeling professional; try a guided tour.

- Don't go in if the ocean seems rough.

Green sea turtle (Honu)

Kauai's calmest water and best snorkeling is on the North Shore in summer and South Shore in winter.

BEST SPOTS

Just because we say these are good places to snorkel doesn't mean the conditions are always right or that the exact moment you arrive, the fish will flock—they are wild, after all.

Boat tours on catamarans and inflatable rafts (Zodiacs) take you to some of the places listed here. Check with the company to see which snorkeling spots might be visited as part of a trip, keeping in mind that captains may have to make changes due to weather condition. Z-Tourz (⊕ *kauaiztours.com*), with its focus on snorkeling, is one good option.

Beach House Beach (Lawai Beach). Don't pack the beach umbrella, beach mats, or cooler for snorkeling at Beach House on the South Shore. Just bring your snorkeling gear. The beach—named after its neighbor The Beach House restaurant—is on the road to Spouting Horn. It's a small slip of sand during low tide and a rocky shoreline during high tide; however, it's right by the road's edge, and its rocky coastline and somewhat rocky

bottom make it great for snorkeling. Enter and exit in the sand channel (not over the rocky reef) that lines up with Lawai Beach Resort's center atrium. Stay within the rocky points anchoring each end of the beach. The current runs east to west. ⊠ *5017 Lawai Rd., makai (ocean) side of Lawai Rd., park on road in front of Lawai Beach Resort, Koloa.*

Kee Beach. Thanks to a permit system that limits the number of visitors, Kee Beach on the North Shore doesn't get as crowded as it used to, and it can be a good snorkeling destination if the water conditions are right. The snorkeling is best early in the morning or later in the afternoon. ■TIP➔ **Snorkeling here in winter can be hazardous. Summer is the best and safest time, although you should never swim beyond the reef.** A parking area allows for 100 vehicles at a time. Get your permit ahead of time at ⊕ *gohaena. com.* ⊠ *At end of Rte. 560, Haena.*

Lydgate Beach Park. This beach park on the East Side is typically the safest place to snorkel on Kauai, though not the most exciting. With its lava-rock wall creating a protected swimming pool, it's a good spot for beginners, young and old. The fish are so tame here it's almost like swimming in a saltwater aquarium. Also here are a lifeguard, a playground for children, plenty of parking, and full-service restrooms with showers. ⊠ *4470 Nalu Rd. Just south of Wailua River, turn makai (toward ocean) off Rte. 56 onto Lehu Dr. and left onto Nalu Rd., Kapaa.*

Niihau. With little river runoff and hardly any boat traffic, the waters off the island of Niihau are some of the clearest in all Hawaii, and that's good for snorkeling and excellent for scuba diving. Like Nualolo Kai, the only way to snorkel here is to sign on with one of the tour boats venturing across a sometimes rough open-ocean channel: Blue Dolphin Charters and Holo Holo Charters.

Nualolo Kai. What was once an ancient Hawaiian fishpond is now home to the best snorkeling along Napali Coast (and perhaps on all of Kauai). The only way to access it is by boat, including kayak. Though many boats stop offshore, only a few Napali snorkeling-tour operators are permitted to come ashore. We recommend Capt. Andy's and Kauai Sea Tours.

Poipu Beach Park. You'll generally find good year-round snorkeling at this South Shore beach, except during summer's south swells (which are not nearly as frequent as winter's north swells). The best snorkeling fronts the Marriott Waiohai Beach Club. Stay inside the crescent created by the sandbar and rocky point, and within sight of the lifeguard tower. The current runs east to west. ⊠ *Hoone Rd. From Poipu Rd., turn right onto Hoone Rd., Koloa.*

Tunnels Beach (Makua). The search for Tunnels (Makua) on the North Shore is as tricky as the snorkeling. Park at Haena Beach Park and walk east—away from Napali Coast—on the beach until you see a sand channel entrance in the water,

almost at the point. Once you get here, the reward is fantastic. The nickname of this beach comes from the many underwater lava tubes, which attract marine life. The shore is mostly beach rock interrupted by three sand channels. You'll want to enter and exit at one of these channels (or risk stepping on a sea urchin or scraping your stomach on the reef). Follow the sand channel to a drop-off; the snorkeling along here is always full of nice surprises. Expect a current running east to west. Snorkeling here in winter can be dangerous and is not recommended; summer is the best and safest time for snorkeling. ⊠ *Haena Beach Park, near end of Rte. 560, across from lava-tube sea caves, after stream crossing, Haena.*

Stand-Up Paddling

This is an increasingly popular sport that even a novice can pick up—*and* have fun doing. Beginners start with a heftier surfboard and a longer-than-normal canoe paddle. And, just as the name implies, stand-up paddlers stand on their surfboards and paddle out from the beach, which requires calm water, especially for beginners. The perfect place to learn is a river or bay (think **Hanalei** or **Kalapaki**) or a calm lagoon (try **Anini**). But this sport isn't just for beginners. Tried-and-true surfers turn to it when the waves are not quite right for their preferred sport because it gives them another reason to be on the water. Stand-up paddlers catch waves earlier and ride them longer than longboard surfers. Professional stand-up paddling competitions have popped up, and surf shops and instructors have adapted to the sport's quick rise in popularity.

EQUIPMENT AND LESSONS
Not all surf instructors teach stand-up paddling, but more and more are, like Titus Kinimaka's Hawaiian School of Surfing (*see the Surfing section*).

Winter brings big surf to Kauai's North Shore. You can see some of the sport's biggest celebrities catching waves at Haena and Hanalei Bay.

Back Door Surf Shop

WATER SPORTS | Along with its sister store across the street—Hanalei Surf Company—Back Door provides just about all the rentals necessary for a fun day at Hanalei Bay, along with clothing and new boards. ✉ *Ching Young Village, 5–5190 Kuhio Hwy., Hanalei* ☎ *808/826–9000* ⊕ *www. hanaleisurf.com/our-sister-stores.*

Hawaiian Surfing Adventures

WATER SPORTS | This Hanalei location has the largest variety of surfboards and stand-up boards and paddles for rent by the hour or day. Check in at the storefront and then head down to the beach, where your gear will be waiting. The 90-minute private and group lessons start on the scenic Hanalei River and then move to Hanalei Bay if the students are ready and conditions are right. This Native Hawaiian–owned company also offers surfboard and kayak rentals and surfing lessons. It is closed Sunday. ✉ *5134 Kuhio Hwy., Hanalei* ☎ *808/482–0749* ⊕ *www.hawaiiansurfingadventures. com* ✉ *Paddleboard rental from $30;* surfboard rentals from $20; group lessons from $65.

Kauai Beach Boys

WATER SPORTS | There's no hauling your gear on your car with this outfitter, which is right on the beach at Kalapaki. The 90-minute classes are offered four times daily. In addition to stand-up paddle lessons, they offer surfing lessons and a chance to paddle a traditional outrigger canoe. ✉ *3610 Rice St., Lihue* ☎ *808/246–6333* ⊕ *www.kauaibeach-boys.com* ✉ *$89 for 90-min surf or SUP lesson.*

Surfing

Good ol' stand-up surfing remains extremely popular on Kauai, especially in winter's high-surf season on the North Shore. If you're new to the sport, we highly recommend taking a lesson. Not only will this ensure you're up and riding waves in no time, but instructors will also provide the right board for your

Questions for a Surf Instructor

Thinking about taking surf lessons? These are a few good questions to ask your potential surf instructor:

■ Are you legally permitted to operate on the beach?

■ What equipment do you provide? (If you're a beginner, you'll want to hear about their soft-top beginner boards. You'll also want to know if they'll provide rash guards and aqua socks.)

■ Who will be my instructor? (It's not always the name on the company logo. Ask about your instructor's qualifications.)

■ How do you select the location? (Ideally, you'll be assured that they pick the location because of its gentle waves, sandy beach bottom, and good year-round conditions.)

■ What if the waves are too big? (Under the best circumstances, they'll select another location or reschedule for another day.)

■ How many students do you take at a time? (Don't book if it's more than four students per instructor. You'll definitely want some personal attention.)

■ Are you CPR- and lifeguard-certified? (It's good to know your instructor will be able to help if you get into trouble.)

experience and size, help you time a wave, and give you a push to get your momentum going. You don't need to be in top physical shape to take a lesson. Because your instructor helps push you into the wave, you won't wear yourself out paddling.

If you're experienced and want to hit the waves on your own, most surf shops rent boards for all levels, from beginners to advanced. ■TIP➜ **Just be aware that surfing on Kauai is often more challenging than elsewhere.**

BEST SPOTS

Perennial-favorite beginning surf spots include **Poipu Beach Park** (the area fronting the Marriott Waiohai Beach Club), **Hanalei Bay** near the pier, and the stream end of **Kalapaki Beach.** More advanced surfers move down the beach in Hanalei to an area fronting a grove of pines known as **Pine Trees,** or paddle out past the pier. When the trade winds die, the north ends of **Wailua** and **Kealia** beaches are teeming with surfers. Breaks off **Poipu** and **Beach House/Lawai Beach**

attract intermediates year-round. During high surf, the break on the cliff side of **Kalihiwai** is for experts only. Advanced riders will head to **Polihale** to face the heavy West Side waves when conditions are right.

EQUIPMENT AND LESSONS

Blue Seas Surfing School / Surf Kauai With Charlie

SURFING | FAMILY | Surfer and instructor Charlie Smith specializes in beginners (especially children), and though he operates primarily at Poipu Beach on the South Shore, lessons are offered elsewhere on the island. His soft-top longboards are very stable, making it easier to stand up, and he provides surf boots and shirts. He specializes in small group or private lessons, so personal interaction is a priority. Private lessons include a video. ✉ *1959 Hoone Rd., Koloa* ☎ *808/634–6979* ⊕ *surfkauaiwithcharlie. com* ⊡ *From $75 for a 90-min small-group lesson; $150 for 90-min private lesson.*

Humpback whales arrive near Kauai in November and stick around until early April. You can see these majestic creatures breach and spout from shore, or take a boat tour.

Hanalei Surf Company

SURFING | You can rent short- and long-boards here and shop for rash guards, wet suits, and some hip surf-inspired apparel. ✉ *Hanalei Center, 5–5161 Kuhio Hwy., Hanalei* ☎ *808/826–9000* ⊕ *www.hanaleisurf.com.*

Nukumoi Surf Co.

SURFING | Owned by the same folks who own Brennecke's restaurant, this shop arranges surfing lessons and provides board (surfing, body, and stand-up paddle), snorkel, and beach-gear rental, as well as casual clothing. Their primary surf spot is the beach fronting the Sheraton. ✉ *2080 Hoone Rd., Koloa* ☎ *808/742–8019* ⊕ *www.nukumoi.com* ✍ *$75 for groups for 90 min; $250 for private sessions.*

Progressive Expressions

SURFING | This full-service shop has a choice of rental boards and a whole lotta shopping for clothes, swimsuits, and casual beach wear. ✉ *5428 Koloa Rd.,* *Koloa* ☎ *808/742–6041* ⊕ *www.progressiveexpressions.com.*

Tamba Surf Company

SURFING | Kauai's homegrown surf shop is your best East Side bet for surfboard, stand-up paddle, and snorkel gear rentals. It also sells new boards and offers surfing lessons. Tamba is a big name in local surf apparel. ✉ *4–1543 Kuhio Hwy., Kapaa* ☎ *808/823–6942* ⊕ *www.tamba.com* ✍ *$75 group lesson.*

Titus Kinimaka's Hawaiian School of Surfing

SURFING | Famed as a pioneer of big-wave surfing, this Hawaiian believes in giving back to his sport. Beginning and intermediate lessons are offered on the half hour eight times a day at Hanalei, with a maximum of three students. If you want to learn to surf from a living legend, this is the man. Advanced surfers can also take an extreme tow-in lesson with a Jet Ski. ■**TIP**➔ **He employs other instructors, so if you want Titus, be sure to ask for him. (And good luck, because if the waves are going off, he'll be surfing,**

What's That Whale Doing?

Although humpbacks spend more than 90% of their lives underwater, they can be very active above water while they're in Hawaii. Here are a few maneuvers you may see:

■ **Blow:** the expulsion of air that looks like a geyser of water.

■ **Spy hop:** the raising of just the whale's head out of the water, as if to take a look around.

■ **Tail slap:** the repetitive slap of the tail, or fluke, on the surface of the water.

■ **Pec slap:** the repetitive slap of one or both fins on the surface of the water.

■ **Fluke up dive:** the waving of the tail above water as the whale slowly rolls underwater to dive.

■ **Breach:** the launching of the whale's entire body out of the water.

not teaching.) Customers are able to use the board for a while after the lesson is complete. ✉ *Quicksilver, 5–5088 Kuhio Hwy., Hanalei* ☎ *808/652–1116* ⊕ *www.hawaiianschoolofsurfing.com* ✎ *$75, 90-min group lesson; $250 Jet Ski surf; $130, 90-min stand-up paddle lesson.*

Tennis

If you're interested in booking some court time on Kauai, there are public tennis courts in Waimea, Kekaha, Hanapepe, Koloa, Kalaheo, Puhi, Lihue, Wailua Homesteads, Wailua Houselots, and Kapaa New Park.

Many hotels and resorts have tennis courts on property; even if you're not staying there, you can often rent court time. Rates start at around $20 per person per hour. On the South Shore, try the **Grand Hyatt Kauai Resort & Spa** (☎ *808/742–1234*) and **Poipu Kai Tennis** (☎ *808/742–8706*). On the North Shore, try **Hanalei Bay Resort** (☎ *808/826–6522*) in Princeville.

For specific directions or more information, call the **County of Kauai Department of Parks & Recreation** (☎ *808/241–4463*).

Whale-Watching

Every winter North Pacific humpback whales swim some 3,000 miles over 30 days, give or take a few, from Alaska to Hawaii. Whales arrive as early as November and sometimes stay through April, though they seem to be most populous in February and March. They come to Hawaii to breed, calve, and nurse their young.

TOURS

Nothing beats the thrill of seeing a whale up close. During the season, any boat on the water is looking for whales; they're hard to avoid, whether the tour is labeled "whale-watching" or not. Consider the whales a benefit to any boating event that may interest you. If whales are definitely your thing, though, you can narrow down your tour-boat decision by asking a few whale-related questions, like whether there's a hydrophone on board, how long the captain has been running tours in Hawaii, and if anyone on the crew is a marine biologist or trained naturalist.

Several boat operators will add two-hour afternoon whale-watching tours during the season that run on the South Shore (not Napali). Operators include Blue Dolphin, Catamaran Kahanu, and Holo Holo Charters (*see the Boat Tours section*). Trying one of these excursions is a good option for those who have no interest in snorkeling or sightseeing along Napali Coast, although keep in mind, the longer you're on the water, the more likely you'll be to see the humpbacks.

One of the more unique ways to (possibly) see some whales is atop a kayak. For such an encounter, try Outfitters Kauai's South Shore kayak trip (*see the Kayaking section*).

A few lookout spots around the island have good land-based viewing: Kilauea Lighthouse on the North Shore, the Kapaa Scenic Overlook just north of Kapaa Town on the East Side, and the cliffs to the east of Keoniloa (Shipwreck) Beach on the South Shore.

Zip Line Tours

Whether you call this popular, relatively new adventure on Kauai "zipping" or "zip-lining," chances are you'll scream like a rock star while trying it. Strap on a harness, clip onto a cable running from one side of a river or valley to the other, and "zip" across. The step off is the scariest part. ■ TIP→ **Pack knee-length shorts or pants, athletic shoes, and courage for this adventure.**

Outfitters Kauai

ZIP-LINING | This outfitter offers four zip line adventures, including the state's longest and biggest lines. Adventures range from a 2-mile zip to a shorter version that has you flying in a head-first position at speeds up to 50 mph. Tandem lines spare you from going it alone. The most popular adventure is the Kipu Zipline Safari Tour, which features an 1,800-foot tandem zip, a paddle on the Wailua River, and a hike. Outfitters Kauai emphasizes safety, and a zipper must be at least seven years old. ✉ *230 Kipu Rd., Poipu* ☎ *808/742–9667, 888/742–9887* ⊕ *www.outfitterskauai.com* ⊜ *From $50.*

Index

218

Photo Credits

Front Cover: Thomas Doering/ GettyImages [Description: Aerial view of Wailua Waterfalls in Hawaii]. Back cover, from left to right: Bennymarty/Dreamstime. Hawaii Tourism Authority (HTA). MNStudio/Dreamstime. **Spine:** Panachai Cherdchucheep/Shutterstock. Interior, from left to right: Steveheap/Dreamstime (1). Danwatt417/Dreamstime (2-3). Sergiyn/Dreamstime (5). **Chapter 1: Experience Kauai:** Mfron/Dreamstime (6-7). Jodielee/Dreamstime (8-9). BorislavaR_iStockphoto (9). Jeff Whyte (9). Tor Johnson/Hawaii Tourism Authority (10). Faina Gurevich_iStockphoto (10). Sara Bowen of Mālama Hulē'ia (10). Anson Chappell/Flickr (10). Trudywsimmons/Dreamstime (11). Bonita Cheshier (Bonniemarie)/Dreamstime (12). MNStudio/Dreamstime (12). Kyrien/Dreamstime (12). Ralf Broskvar/Shutterstock (12). Jeff Whyte/ Shutterstock (13). Nikkigensert/Dreamstime (13). Suzanne Marcoux (Fleurdly)/ Dreamstime (13). Bonniemarie/Dreamstime (13). Izanbar/ Dreamstime (14). MNStudio/ Dreamstime (14). Luau Kalamaku (15). Douglas Peebles Photography / Alamy Stock Photo (16). Tim Saunders (16). Brian G. Oar/Fairways Photography (16). Flyingwolf/Dreamstime (16). Steveheap/Dreamstime (17). Tor Johnson/Hawaii Tourism Authority (22). Ralf Broskvar/ Dreamstime (22). Hawaii Tourism Authority (HTA) (22). Tor Johnson/Hawaii Tourism Authority (23). Julianufer/ Shutterstock (23). Nstanev/iStockphoto (24). Daeja Fallas/Hawaii Tourism Authority (HTA) (24). Matthew Ragen/Dreamstime (24). Bill Florence/Shutterstock (24). Fominayaphoto/Shutterstock (24). Fominayaphoto/Shutterstock (25). Danita Delmont/ Shutterstock (25). MNStudio/ Shutterstock (25). LANature Graphics/ Shutterstock (25). Maximkabb/iStockphoto (25). Marilyn Gould/Dreamstime (26). Douglas Peebles Photography / Alamy Stock Photo (26). Ancha Chiangmai/Shutterstock (26). Pr2is/Dreamstime (26). Vfbjohn/Dreamstime (26). Eddygaleotti/ Dreamstime (27). Koondon/Shutterstock (27). Caner CIFTCI/Dreamstime (27). Elmar Langle/iStockphoto (27). Big Island Visitors Bureau (BIVB) / Kirk Lee Aeder (27). Brent Hofacker/Shutterstock (28). Hawaii Tourism (28). Dana Edmunds (28). Magdanatka/Shutterstock (29). Big Island Visitors Bureau (BIVB) / Kirk Lee Aeder (29). Lost Mountain Studio/Shutterstock (30). Alla Machutt/iStockphoto (30). Hawaii Tourism Authority (HTA) / Brooke Dombroski (30). Temanu/Shutterstock (30). Mongkolchon Akesin/Shutterstock (30). Hawaii Tourism Authority (HTA) / Heather Goodman (31). Olgakr/iStockphoto (31). Hawaii Tourism Authority (HTA) / Dana Edmunds (31). Hawaii Tourism Authority (31). Hawaii Tourism Authority (HTA) / Heather Goodman (31). Cathy Locklear/Dreamstime (35). HVCB_photo01a (36). Thinkstock LLC (37). Linda Ching/ HVCB (39). Sri Maiava Rusden/HVCB (39). Kelly Alexander Photography (40). Kelly Alexander Photography (40). Leis of Hawaii/leisofhawaii. com (40). Leis of Hawaii /leisofhawaii.com (40). Leis of Hawaii/leisofhawaii.com (40). Leis of Hawaii/ leisofhawaii.com (40). Tim Wilson [CC BY 2.0]/ Flickr (41). Dana Edmunds/ Polynesian Cultural Center's Alii Luau (42). Douglas Peebles Photography / Alamy Stock Photo (42). Purcell Team / Alamy Stock Photo (42). Douglas Peebles Photography / Alamy Stock Photo (42). Douglas Peebles Photography / Alamy Stock Photo (42). Oahu Visitors Bureau (43). Hawaii Visitors and Convention Bureau (43). Hawaii Visitors and Convention Bureau (43). Oahu Visitors Bureau (43). Hawaii Visitors and Convention Bureau (43). **Chapter 3: The North Shore:** Kumakuma1216/iStockphoto (67). Nickolay Stanev/ Shutterstock (76-77). Joel Carillet/iStockphoto (79). STLJB/Shutterstock (83). Backyard Productions LLC/iStockphoto (85). Sergiyn/Dreamstime (90-91). Sergiyn/Dreamstime (92-93). Estivillml/iStock (93). Estivillml/iStock (93). Design Pics Inc / Alamy Stock Photo (94-95). Photo Resource Hawaii / Alamy (95). Ventu Photo/Shutterstock (95). IndustryAndTravel/ Shutterstock (96-97). Photo Resource Hawaii / Alamy (98). Alexander Demyanenko/ Shutterstock (98). **Chapter 4: The East Side:** Tommy Song/Dreamstime (99). Juergen Wallstabe/Shutterstock (109). Muhawi001/Flickr (112). Roger Fletcher / Alamy Stock Photo (117). Sara Bowen of Mālama Hulē'ia (122-123). Cphoto/Dreamstime (129). Kauai Visitors Bureau (130). Jack Jeffrey (131). Raisbeckfoto/iStockphoto (133). **Chapter 5: The South Shore:** Everett Atlas/Shutterstock (135). Alexander Demyanenko/Shutterstock (143). Maria Luisa Lopez Estivill/Dreamstime (144). Adam Springer/iStockphoto (149). Tor Johnson/Hawaii Tourism Authority (HTA) (151). **Chapter 6: The West Side:** SVongpra/ Shutterstock (161). SMJoness/iStockphoto (173). MNStudio/Shutterstock (176-177). **Chapter 7: Activities and Tours:** Jim kruger/iStockphoto (179). Tor Johnson/Hawaii Tourism Authority (HTA) (183). Americanspirit/Dreamstime (187). Courtesy of St. Regis Princeville_Golf (191). Galyna Andrushko/Shutterstock (193). Bob Pool/ Shutterstock (198). Ron Dahlquist/HVCB (203). Shane Myers Photography/ Shutterstock (204). Orxy/Shutterstock (206). Gert Vrey/Dreamstime (206). Shane Myers Photography/ Shutterstock (207). YinYang/iStockphoto (208). Jarvis gray/Shutterstock (210). Chase Clausen/Shutterstock (212). About Our Writers: All photos are courtesy of the writers.

*Every effort has been made to trace the copyright holders, and we apologize in advance for any accidental errors. We would be happy to apply the corrections in the following edition of this publication.

Notes

Notes

Notes

Fodor's KAUAI

Publisher: Stephen Horowitz, *General Manager*

Editorial: Douglas Stallings, *Editorial Director*; Jill Fergus, Amanda Sadlowski, *Senior Editors*; Kayla Becker, Alexis Kelly, *Editors*; Angelique Kennedy-Chavannes, *Assistant Editor*

Design: Tina Malaney, *Director of Design and Production*; Jessica Gonzalez, *Graphic Designer*; Erin Caceres, *Graphic Design Associate*

Production: Jennifer DePrima, *Editorial Production Manager*; Elyse Rozelle, *Senior Production Editor*; Monica White, *Production Editor*

Maps: Rebecca Baer, *Senior Map Editor*; Mark Stroud and Henry Colomb (Moon Street Cartography), David Lindroth, *Cartographers*

Photography: Viviane Teles, *Senior Photo Editor*; Namrata Aggarwal, Payal Gupta, Ashok Kumar, *Photo Editors*; Eddie Aldrete, *Photo Production Intern*

Business and Operations: Chuck Hoover, *Chief Marketing Officer*; Robert Ames, *Group General Manager*; Devin Duckworth, *Director of Print Publishing*

Public Relations and Marketing: Joe Ewaskiw, *Senior Director of Communications and Public Relations*

Fodors.com: Jeremy Tarr, *Editorial Director*; Rachael Levitt, *Managing Editor*

Technology: Jon Atkinson, *Director of Technology*; Rudresh Teotia, *Lead Developer*

Writers: Joan Conrow, Cheryl Crabtree, Mary F. Williamson

Editor: Linda Cabasin

Production Editor: Monica White

9th Edition

ISBN 978-1-64097-523-1

ISSN 1934-550X

All details in this book are based on information supplied to us at press time. Always confirm information when it matters, especially if you're making a detour to visit a specific place. Fodor's expressly disclaims any liability, loss, or risk, personal or otherwise, that is incurred as a consequence of the use of any of the contents of this book.

SPECIAL SALES
This book is available at special discounts for bulk purchases for sales promotions or premiums. For more information, e-mail SpecialMarkets@fodors.com.

PRINTED IN CANADA

10 9 8 7 6 5 4 3 2

About Our Writers

Joan Conrow is a longtime journalist and editor who has written extensively about Hawaii politics, culture, environment, travel, and lifestyles for many regional and national publications. Joan lived on Kauai for nearly 30 years before relocating to the high desert of New Mexico. She helped write the original Fodor's guide to Kauai, and she updated the East Side and Activities and Tours chapters of this edition.

Cheryl Crabtree first visited Hawaii as a kindergartner, a trip that sparked a lifelong passion for the Islands and led to frequent visits. She spends months at a time in residence on Oahu, and for this edition of *Fodor's Kauai,* she updated the North Shore chapter. Cheryl has contributed to *Fodor's California* for nearly two decades and is a regular updater for *Fodor's National Parks of the West* and *Fodor's Oahu.* She also contributes to numerous regional and national publications.

Mary F. Williamson grew up in Honolulu and lives on Kauai, where her husband's family moved in the late 1800s. A former nonprofit director, she now organizes bicycle races and helps small businesses and organizations with public communication and events. She updated the Experience Kauai, Travel Smart, South Shore, and West Side chapters of this guide.